MGB

GUIDE TO PURCHASE & D.I.Y. RESTORATION

LINDSAY PORTER

To adviser, mentor and very good friend, Paul Skilleter, who started me off on the whole thing.

Other Haynes Publishing Group titles of interest to MG enthusiasts:

MGB Owner's Workshop Manual (111)
MGA Owner's Workshop Manual (475)
MG Midget Owner's Workshop Manual (265)
MG Midget – Guide to Purchase & D.I.Y. Restoration by Lindsay Porter (F336) – in preparation.
MGB Super Profile by Lindsay Porter (F305)
The MG Story by Anders Clausager (F324)
MG-Foulis Mini Marque History by Peter Filby (F229)
MG: The A, B & C by Chris Harvey (P069)
MG Past and Present (New Edition) by Rivers Fletcher (F425)

All of the above should be available from good bookshops. In case of difficulty please write to the publisher.

ISBN 0 85429 303 5

A FOULIS Motoring Book

First published 1982, reprinted 1983 (twice) 1984, 1985 & 1986

Published by:
Haynes Publishing Group
Sparkford, Near Yeovil, Somerset
BA22 7JJ, England

Haynes Publications Inc.
861 Lawrence Drive, Newbury Park,
California 91320, USA

Editor: Rod Grainger
Page layout: Tim Rose
Printed, in England, by: J.H. Haynes & Co. Ltd

Contents

Foreword by Roche Bentley

The history of the MGB is well documented in this book and I particularly liked the references to the adolescence period. The MGB saw many major and minor changes in its long life and Lindsay details these well. The tips on buying are really comprehensive and I would be stuck if asked for something to add. The detailed descriptions of how to complete restoration work and major repair are really well described and Lindsay's policy of conferring with experts like John Hill, Peter Laidler and Pearl McGlen works to great advantage.

The MGB will never die, the Club, the members and enthusiasts will see to that. The suppliers will ensure that parts are available for many years to come and if present owners and would-be owners read Lindsay's book and take the advice to heart, then the condition of our cars must only improve.

Being asked to write the foreword for this new book on MGs is indeed an honour, as I honestly believe that this extremely well researched, and easily readable, volume will be the last technical book on MGBs to be published. The reason: Lindsay Porter has said it all here in this book. Any future compilation of facts on MGBs must be considered as a "repeat".

Within the MG Owners' Club I meet literally hundreds of MGB owners each year and speak or write to many more. I am always saddened by the numbers of enthusiasts who rush out and buy the first MGB they see and who are misled by claims made by less than honest sellers. MGBs are snapped up because they are "Collectors' Items", which indeed they are, but if enthusiastic would-be MGB owners would just stop, think and then read this book, then many tears and pounds would be saved . . .

Using this book

The layout of this book has been designed to be both attractive and easy to follow during practical work on your car. However, to obtain maximum benefit from the book, it is important to note the following points:

1) Apart from the introductory pages, this book is split into two parts: chapters 1 to 7 dealing with history, buying and practical procedures; appendices 1 to 8 providing supplementary information. Each chapter/ appendix may be sub-divided into sections and even sub-sections. Section headings are in italic type between horizontal lines and sub-section headings are similar, but without horizontal lines.

2) Photograph captions are an integral part of the text (except those in chapters 1 and 2) — therefore the photographs and their captions are arranged to "read" in exactly the same way as the normal text. In other words they run down each column and the columns run from left to right of the page.

Each photograph caption carries an alpha-numerical identity, relating it to a specific section. The letters before the caption number are simply the initial letters of key words in the relevant section heading, whilst the caption number shows the position of the particular photograph in the section's picture sequence. Thus photograph/ caption "DR22" is the 22nd photograph in the section headed "Door Repairs".

3) Figures — illustrations which are not photographs — are numbered consecutively throughout the book. Figure captions do not form any part of the text. Therefore Figure 5 is simply the 5th figure in the book.

4) All references to the left or right of the vehicle are from the point of view of somebody standing behind the car looking forwards.

5) Because this book majors upon restoration, regular maintenance procedures and normal mechanical repairs of all the car's components, are beyond its scope. It is therefore strongly recommended that the Haynes *MGB Owner's Workshop Manual* should be used as a companion volume.

6) We know it's a boring subject, especially when you really want to get on with a job — but your safety, through the use of correct workshop procedures, must ALWAYS be your foremost consideration. It is essential that you read, and UNDERSTAND, appendix 1 before undertaking any of the practical tasks detailed in this book.

7) Whilst great care is taken to ensure that the information in this book is as accurate as possible, the author, editor or publisher cannot accept any liability for loss, damage or injury caused by errors in, or omissions from, the information given.

Introduction & Acknowledgements

With MGB production finished for good and even Abingdon razed to the ground, some say that there can never be another *real* M.G. sports car. Whether they are right or not, it is indisputable that there will never be another new MGB. Or will there . . .? Let's say you took an MGB, one that has seen better days, took the wings off, repaired the body and rebuilt interior and mechanics. You'd make it *as good* as new! And really, that's what this book's all about; it's a guide covering every stage in the purchase and restoration of an MGB so that if the work is carried out properly, you could end up with the next best thing to a brand new car. You'll be maintaining one of the inevitably dwindling numbers of the last of the real sports cars; the last Abingdon MGB. The fine traditions embodied in every one of them can, now, only be upheld by the restorer — which is why there is a chapter on the history and the heritage that lies behind the cars — and it is hoped that every owner, whether carrying out a minor repair or a full-blown rebuild, will remember to include something of the proud spirit of Abingdon in his tool kit.

There are so many to thank for their help in the preparation of this book but there is no question as to where to start. Without the help of my wife, Shan, the book would never have been. Her talents as typist, sub-editor, critic and especially as researcher *sans-pareille* have been greatly in evidence throughout the months of preparation and as a consequence there is a lot of "her" woven through its pages.

My good friend Paul Skilleter is to be thanked for having given a great measure of help and inspiration while Nigel Rogers, friend and neighbour in the best Herefordshire tradition has been invaluable in his preparation of my own MGB during its restoration for many of the shots used in this book. Chris Reynolds and Graeme Barson of Autotech Ltd. supplied bodywork services and advice of the finest quality and Colin Barnes of Lifesure helped with advice on MGB insurance.

Pearl and Derek McGlen provided the very best advice to be had anywhere on the MGC, (and a number of pictures, too) and Peter Laidler was similarly helpful with V8 material. Steve Glochowsky, President of the American MGB Association, supplied American pictures and much data on U.S. cars and Ken Smith of the A.M.G.B.A. U.K. Chapter was also most helpful in this respect.

Prompt, helpful darkroom work of the highest quality was supplied by Alan Wood, while cartoonist Mick Martin was a real "find" from the days when I edited *Practical Classics* Magazine's Club News pages. Peter Franklin, ex-Abingdon Personnel Manager gave an insight (literally!) into the last days at Abingdon and Roy Brocklehurst (Syd Enever's successor there) kindly gave his forthright "on-the-record" views on the demise of the MGB.

Many other owners and DIY enthusiasts have given of their

advice and time and to all of them I am most grateful.

From the practical point of view, two men have contributed hugely to the content of this book. John Hill of The MGB Centre, Redditch, England, expended a vast number of man-hours in setting-up material from his unparalleled stocks for bodywork restoration and mechanical repair shots in spite of extending premises in the middle of the book's preparation, was as helpful as could be. Jon Miller, Steve Langdell, Graham Warbick, Dave Cartwright and the rest of the MGB Centre staff were unfailingly friendly and most helpful.

In the United States, John H. Twist of University Motors, Michigan, spent many a Winter's evening preparing his notes and photographs and it quickly became obvious that there could be no one more knowledgeable about the mechanics and electrical systems of the MGB than he: it is a priviledge to share his knowledge here.

Perhaps the best thing to have come out of this book for its author at least, is that every one of the people mentioned here has become more than a source of expert information and more of a personal friend than could ever have been imagined. My grateful thanks are due, and gladly given, to them all!

Lindsay Porter

1 Heritage

In The Beginning . . .

When the last MGB rolled from the sudden emptiness of Abingdon's redundant production line on 22nd October 1980, it ended an era of sports car motoring which could be said to have begun there some eighteen years and four months earlier when the first production MGB was built but which, in truth, had its roots at least as far back as the early 1920s.

In 1910 William Richard Morris opened a retail garage known as The Morris Garage in some old stables which he owned, in Longwall Street, Oxford. At about the same time, however, he began to build cars at nearby Cowley under the auspices of a company which later, in 1919, became known as Morris Motors Ltd.

This latter activity so fascinated the volatile twenty-three-year-old Morris that he became more and more involved in motor-car production until the point came where he had to entrust the expanding and successful "The Morris Garages" (as they had become) to a general manager.

In 1921, Cecil Kimber, a man whose name has since become of revered importance to M.G. enthusiasts was appointed as Sales Manager to The Morris Garages. He was enterprising and immediately successful — so much so that when the General Manager took his own life in 1922, Kimber, then 34 years of age, was asked to fill the vacancy.

Kimber's obvious drive and immediacy of action set in motion a chain of events which are beyond the scope of this essentially restoration orientated book to unravel, but which led to the metamorphosis from which M.G. emerged as manufacturers of motor cars in their own right. As in all the best stories, this one is surrounded with mystery, myth and controversy, but the "facts" which underpin the tale seem to be that:

— Kimber arranged to build rebodied versions of the Morris Oxford with a tourer body known as "Chummy", lowered suspension and up-market appointments. It was never sold as an "M.G.".

— In 1923, production was transferred from Longwall Street to Alfred Lane, Oxford.

— Also in 1923, Kimber's own Chummy was modified and entered in the Land's End Trial. He won one of the many gold-medal awards, but preferred an optional pair of cufflinks!

— In late 1923 or '24, six Cowley chassis were fitted with bodies made by Raworth. Some consider these to be the first M.G.s but they do not seem to have been referred to as M.G.s at the time.

— The M.G. emblem was seen, enclosed in an Octagon, for the first time in an advertisement in May 1924.

— From 1st September 1924, the "M.G. Super Sports" was offered with three body variations based once again on the honest but uninspiring Morris Oxford, in addition to the continuation of a range of closed bodies on the same chassis.

— Through 1924 and 1925 a hybrid sports car using a Hotchkiss engine, one-off chassis modifications and a body by Carbodies was built at Longwall Street. It was entered by Kimber into the 1925 Land's End Trial and he again qualified for a gold medal. This car was subsequently "adopted" as the first M.G. by the Nuffield Group's publicity department (in spite of evidence to the contrary) and christened "Old Number One".

Production of Cowly-based M.G.s continued at an increasing pace over the next few years and, in 1928, The M.G. Car Company was registered in its own right. In the same year the Company introduced, at their first independent Motor Show stand, both the large, fast and prestigious 18/80 Six and the Morris Minor based M-type Midget with quite startling performance for its day and its size. The Midget was based on Morris' new "baby" car, the overhead camshaft Morris Minor, whose engine had been acquired as part of the Nuffield Group's takeover of Wolseley. They in turn, had developed the diminutive but powerful engine unit from a Hispano-Suiza aero-engine design and, in fact, when used in the Minor family saloon, the engine was a detuned version of that fitted to the M.G.

The first M.G. Midget was the most significant car to have been produced by the Company, at least in terms of the marque's evolution, and was highly successful with over 3,200 being made. Its significance lies in the fact that it was truly a recognisable Sports-Car, being sporting in performance and not merely "Sporting" in appearance as had been the case with most previous offerings. Moreover, that performance was achieved with the use of proprietary, largely unspecialised components mildly rearranged in such a way that their achievement as a whole exceeded the sum of their parts. This theme is important in that it was to be seen running throughout all successful M.G. production for the next half-century.

M-type Midgets were produced until 1932 amongst a splendid profusion of other Midgets and six-cylinder Magnas, none of which matched the M-type for sales but some, such as the C-type, chalked up satisfactory track successes.

In 1932, upon the demise of the M-type, a new Midget known as the J-type first saw the light of day. Although with basically the same mechanical layout as its predecessor and consequently a similar performance appeal, the J-type, perhaps more than any small M.G. before it, contrived to combine a great degree of visual appeal with speed borne of efficiency and lightness. From this point on, the profusion of growths was pruned back a little with the effect of strengthening and more readily defining future development. A succession of six-cylinder cars in both open and closed forms were developed, culminating in the WA whose production was ended in 1939 by the onset of the Second World War while the Midget line, that with which we are most concerned here, evolved by 1936 into the legendary TA Midget.

Just one year after M.G.'s Nuffield masters enforced their departure from the motor sport scene, a larger-engined, larger-bodied Midget appeared known at the time as the T-type. Gone was the stretched version of the original M type "Wolseley" engine and in its place was found another implant from the same firm. The Wolseley 10 engine of 1292cc was tuned and fitted; mated to a synchromesh gearbox (except for the earlier cars) and made to power a car of softer suspension but better roadholding than its predecessors. Hydraulic brakes replaced the Kimber-favoured cable-operated variety. These "modernisations" outraged purists of the time in much the same way that motoring generations later, the MGB was to upset the motoring "masochists" of the Sixties.

The Autocar of 1936 praised the new car's roadholding abilities in saying, "General handling is good, for although the springing is a shade softer, and hydraulic shock absorbers are now fitted all round instead of at the back only, the Midget can be put into a fast curve confidently and be swung around an acute turn with a most satisfactory feeling of security." The road test went on to describe the innovation of "a green tinted lamp [which] is illuminated as long as the cars speed remains below 30 m.p.h." But reservations were cast and the article added archly that "It is understood that the necessary modification has already been incorporated."

The TB Midget hardly had a production run at all before war erased all attempts at creating motor cars, but it did herald the introduction of an engine with reduced stroke compared to that of the TA, which was subsequently fitted to the post war TC. This car was a widened version of the TB and began another thread which was to run unbroken through the remainder of M.G. history, for, in 1947, for the first time, more TCs were sold abroad than in Britain . . .

MGB Parentage

The story so far has attempted to give a context to the circumstances in which the MGB can be regarded as a classic sports car; that of a heritage which is second to none in its singlemindedness of purpose and supreme in its success in building simply exciting sports cars. From late 1949, with the introduction of the M.G. TD, specific components which were eventually to be incorporated into the MGB began to be fitted to the M.G. cars of the day.

Though the TD was later said by *The Autocar* to have "lost pretty well all the endearing starkness of its predecessors", it was probably this very "loss" that enabled it to be the first M.G. to become at all well-known in America, for while it retained the trusty 1250cc engine, it benefitted from a new box-section frame upswept over the rear axle, a

wider body and independent front suspension. This suspension set up had been designed by none other than Alec Issigonis (later Sir Alec, designer of two of the most significant landmarks in British motoring — the Morris Minor and the Mini) and was destined for use in a new Series E Morris 8-based M.G. saloon. (Which, in the event was not introduced until 1947 as the rather hybrid M.G. YA.)

The suspension, however, was used two years later in the TD where its efficiency gave both increased comfort and improved roadholding. In effect the system comprised a kingpin about which the steering operated, suspended by a pair of "wishbones" — one at top and bottom — the bottom one of which bore upwards against a coil spring while the top, acting as the top face of the moving parallelogram, was also the link to a hydraulic shock absorber. Steering was by rack and pinion.

For a while the TD was a runaway sales success but as the design began to age and competition from such cars as the Triumph TR2 increased, so it became increasingly obvious that a replacement was necessary.

In the early Fifties, three events took place which had a bearing, either direct or indirect, upon the evolutionary process with which we are concerned. First, a special bodyshell was prepared at Abingdon and mounted upon an M.G. TD chassis in order that a private entrant could enter Le Mans in 1951. This bodyshell, designed by Abingdon's Chief Designer, Syd Enever, is so very like that of the MGA to come that no shred of controversy can exist as to *that* car's bodily origins.

Second, at the start of 1952, M.G. already a part of the Nuffield Group, became a component within the British Motor Corporation when the Nuffield and Austin giants merged to become the world's fourth largest automobile producer, after the U.S.A.'s "Big Three", the significance of which would soon be felt at Abingdon.

And third, in 1953, the M.G.

Magnette was announced to replace the YA/YB series of pre-war-designed cars. That this last is significant can be no more than interesting speculation but it must be noted that the magnette, derived as it was from Gerald Palmer's Wolseley design, was the first unitary-bodied car to be built at Abingdon and was still under production there when Abingdon's own design team was beginning to crystallise its first thoughts on the MGB and could well have been at the back of the designers' minds when they decided upon unitary construction for the MGB.

The other two developments were significant in more empirical ways, however. The 1951 Le Mans body had been developed by 1952 to the point where Syd Enever and John Thornley (by now M.G.'s General Manager) could offer the B.M.C. management a genuine TD replacement. Unfortunately for M.G. a decision had already been taken to produce an Austin-Healey, the "100" model, leaving no resources available for the new M.G. As a result of a fall in TD sales a stop-gap model called, unsurprisingly, the TF was introduced with "modernised", more rounded bodywork but a sales curve which showed that an increasingly discriminating public were not to be fobbed-off. As a desperate throw the TF was given the Magnette's 1466cc engine which it was felt by many, should have been fitted in the first place. This increased power but not sales especially and crucially in the United States where the TF was regarded as no more than a slap in the face by those expecting more from a new model of M.G. The development of EX 175 was sanctioned at last by the management.

If the new car, to be called the MGA, took on the body and chassis of the 1952 prototype, its engine and drive train were radically different in a way which adds another important piece to the jigsaw puzzle of our story. BMC were embarking upon a policy which, in conjunction with many other political and economic factors

in British life, was to have a devastating effect upon the variety of motor cars and components on offer. The term used was — and still is — that of rationalisation and its effect was to ensure that fifties cars as disparate as the A40 range, the Morris Oxfords, the M.G. Magnette, many commercial vehicles and then the MGA were all fitted with basically the same engine and gearbox. The engine, known as the B-series, had three main bearings, twin carburettors (for the MGA) and, it must be confessed, sat happily within the MGA's chassis rails and went rather well. The gearbox was originally designed for column-change use but had been converted to stick-shift and in the MGA was fitted with an extension which meant that a short gear lever fell nicely to the driver's hand.

The rear axle was of the "banjo" type (this referring to no more than the rounded shape of the central part of its one-piece casting) and was a three-quarter-floating hypoid-bevel unit, also commonised with much of the BMC range.

This move away from the Midget tradition was probably wise in view of the bad feeling engendered by the TF and reactions to this fresh start were excellent. In terms of production figures, the Abingdon workforce did themselves proud. In 1956, the figure exceeded thirteen thousand and in 1957, twenty thousand. In that year alone, more cars were produced than had been made in all the years before the war and thanks for that were mainly due to the instant appeal generated by the MGA in the United States.

The Autocar test achieved a "best" of 99 m.p.h. from the car, found the acceleration "very good" and that, "Long winding hillside roads are a joy to traverse". It is perhaps significant, though, that the car was criticised for "raining in" and dampening the driver's right leg — a situation that would have been considered part and parcel of sports car ownership a few years previously but not it seems, in 1955.

The swooping curves of the

MGAs production figures were more or less sustained by a policy of development which led to the introduction of improved interior appointments, the fitting of front disc brakes and the uprating of the engine to 1588cc, whose unique capacity could not be tolerated for long by BMC and finally became 1622cc in common with other cars fitted with the B-series engine at the same time.

The MGA Twin-Cam, which appeared in 1958, was something of an enigma — it *might* have taken Abingdon in a direction which could have greatly influenced the MGB still to come but in the event, it did not.

Although excitingly equipped with a race-orientated twin-overhead-camshaft engine (which left no room under the bonnet for the sensible positioning of such components as the distributor — there were access hatches behind both front wheels!) and disc brakes all round, when measured against the reliable, everyday use to which the "standard" MGA could be put, the Twin-Cam was something of a failure. An interesting footnote to Twin-Cam production is that it would seem that customers were able to order a Twin-Cam (with disc brakes, special wheels and all) but with a standard engine throughout its production run. However, when Twin-Cam production ended, the last week or so was taken up entirely with the construction of these now-rare cars which were known, but never catalogued, as the "MGA De-luxe".

The 1588cc Twin-Cam engine, although perhaps briefly considered was never reliable enough for use in the MGB and instead, in the short-term it bequeathed its engine capacity to the MGA.

First Born

Like all good things, the MGA had to come to an end. In 1962 the radically different MGB was introduced and in a letter of that year sent to *Road & Track* magazine Mr. Tony Birt, Advertising Manager of Hambro Automotive Corporation, M.G.'s U.S. distributor claimed that, "everything is new [of the MGB] but the octagon". In view of the marque's history, it is instructive to look back and see just how much of the MGB was indeed brand new. The body was without a shred of doubt all-new. The tail bore a strong resemblance to the Abingdon-produced Austin-Healey Sprite Mk II/M.G. Midget Mk I and the front wing door line, door handles and rear bumper could be seen to have strong antecedents in Abingdon's late Fifties design project, EX 205/1, but the MGB's sensational profile and dramatic front-end sculpting were all its own. The radiator grille brilliantly combined the appeal of the traditional M.G. radiator shell with a modern, aggressive touch. In short, the MGB's styling, without being in the least brash or blatant was, and is, a masterpiece of design suggesting all the effortless speed that it was in fact capable of producing.

What is more, the MGB's new body was not only aesthetically brilliant, it was technically superb too. The new car was three inches shorter in both wheelbase and overall length than the MGA and two inches wider and within that framework included greatly increased cockpit space, wind-up windows, more leg room and far more luggage space. While both cars shared an identical volume at 262 cubic feet, the MGB provided a lot more car for its size and yet without any increase in weight over its predecessor. The answer, of course, lay in the adoption of unitary construction such as that which had already been used on the Magnette and the Sprite/Midget. However, while the Sprite's lighter structure had been relatively easy to build and was suitable for a smaller scale production run, that of the MGB was complex and demanded the use of sophisticated and expensive tooling, requiring a lengthy production run to pay for the high initial setting-up costs — a requirement that must have been met three times over!

The car's designer Syd Enever had been accused of erring, if anything, on the side of caution and excessive size in his design of the MGA's chassis and he was clearly determined that the MGB would be no less sturdy. In practice, he was so successful that the MGB is only significantly weakened by quite advanced corrosion. Front twisting loads are transmitted along vestigal front chassis rails and complex inner-wing structures, back into a quite massive double bulkhead, between which is a plenum chamber carrying air for the heater. Even the radio speaker support is a structural member helping to tie-in part of the bulkhead to the strong gearbox tunnel. Sills — vital on an open car — are three-section members, containing an enclosed vertical membrane sandwiched top and bottom between the other two and the rear parcel shelf-cum-battery box adds to the car's lateral stiffness at the rear. Also new was the car's interior with improved — though still leather — seats, well trimmed doors and a new dashboard layout, albeit with several familiar looking instruments.

But what of the MGB's mechanical arrangements? The engine was larger than that of the MGA by 11%, an increase necessitated by a frontal area which was 2% greater and a drag coefficient which was worse by a more significant amount. Therefore to push the same weight of car through increased wind resistance would have resulted in a slower car if the same size engine had been used. The MGB's 1798cc engine was still a "B"-series unit but it had come a long way from its MGA days and even further, through 1622, 1588 and 1489cc from the days when it had been used in 1947 in 1200cc form in the Austin Devon. This final engine stretch had necessitated the elimination of the water jacket between the central cylinders and between the central exhaust ports in the head but the technique, known as "siamesing" was far from new, having been

instrumental in successfully powering three million Model A Fords and has given absolutely no problems to half a million MGBs either. The first MGB engine's bottom-end was similar to that of the 1622cc engine with 3 main bearings and, apart from the weakness which time was to expose in this area, the latest engine was a great success and a great improvement giving 95bhp (86bhp — MGA 1600 Mk II) and 110lb ft of torque (97lb ft).

The gearbox was essentially the same as that of the MGA, although with improved synchromesh and the banjo rear axle was unaltered save for a slightly lower ratio to compensate for the difference in gearing caused by a 1" reduction in road wheel size to 14". Front suspension with its oldest antecedents of all was virtually unchanged and as successfully effective as ever while steering was marginally lower geared.

Put to the Test

While it is clear that many of the MGB's mechanical components were far from new, Tony Birt's letter was in essence true because the car *as a whole* was quite unique. Motoring magazines on both sides of the Atlantic and both sides of the world were quick to pass judgement on the car, among the first being *Autocar* who reported on it in September 1962. They were impressed in their usual sober way and felt that it was "a forward step in that the car is faster than the previous model, and yet more docile and comfortable. Moreover, from any angle it looks good . . . and it should be as big a success in home markets as it will surely be abroad".

Motor were a month later in getting to grips with the 'B. They too liked the car in most respects, commenting that, "there is, in fact almost every modern saloon car amenity, except for a back seat and courtesy switches to operate the map-reading lamp when a door is opened," but in common with most owners, they did not like the hood. "Raising and lowering the hood was, however, a slow process," they said, "at least for anyone not well-drilled in the procedure, suggesting its suitability for California's reliable climate rather than for Britain's erratic weather and hood frame joints close to passengers' heads looked potentially dangerous."

Road & Track confined themselves to a technical exploration of the MGB's qualities not at that time having one available for road test, it seems, and in Australia it took a year before *Wheels* got its hands on a 'B in August 1963. They found a problem which has often plagued owners since, causing annoyance even when no positive damage has occurred — "Developing 94bhp at 5500rpm the engine has an 8.75 to 1 compression ratio which does not agree with local fuel mixtures. We encountered running-on problems almost every time the engine was closed down, but there was never a trace of pinging." Also, perceptively, *Wheels* noted that, "Pedal placement is not particularly satisfactory for the sporting driver since it is not possible to heel-and-toe when braking and changing down simultaneously," and then, "Some confusion can occur when operating the electrical switches at night." Presumably being in New South Wales they had no necessity to be confused by the amazing illogicality of the heater controls, too! Although no euology this, the magazine liked all the points praised elsewhere such as comfort, space, roadholding and speed.

Car & Driver's test, reported in the last month of 1964, made one keep looking at the photographs to ensure that they were talking about the MGB at all. "There are a number of fullsized domestic cars that will get through a fast, rough corner with less bother than the MGB . . . The operation [of the folding soft-top] can hardly be described as difficult . . . cockpit ventilation . . . is virtually nonexistent", but their prophetic powers were faultless when they concluded, "Detroit pressures, in the form of all-synchro transmission, whopping horsepower and proper handling for relatively meager amounts of money — and of course the potent new Sunbeam Tiger — may ultimately force M.G. into developing a more powerful engine, a new suspension and an improved transmission." With the sad and singular exception of the latter, they could not have been more correct . . .

Car & Driver's test car was still fitted with a 3 main bearing engine but in fact, in October 1964, an engine with a redesigned bottom end and 5 main bearings was fitted. This modification was made because, in spite of an oil-cooler having been fitted as standard to export cars and as an option to British cars, 3 main bearing cars had been slightly prone to crank-whip under the extremes of use for which the car was, of course, designed. As a consequence, engines which were hard pressed had a life as low as 60,000 miles or so and, if used after the evidence of bottom-end rumble had presented itself, could destroy their rear oil scroll which was a fixture in the rear of the crank/block assembly, which invariably and expensively — although it rarely happened — meant a scrap engine. To be fair to BMC, the engine was modified before any customers complaints could have been received and as soon as possible after the problem was perceived. Moreover, 3 main bearing engines which have completed over 120,000 miles without a crank regrind and are still showing good oil pressure are not unheard of. It was just that the 5 main bearing engine was as solid and unburstable as the car's body, and was virtually impossible to wear out at much less than 100,000 miles unless the most drastic neglect had taken place. To add a belt to the braces, an oil cooler was fitted as standard in Britain from the same time.

At around this stage, BMC were working on prototypes, in conjunction with Healeys, for a

large engined addition to the MG range. The first fruits were not to be borne until 1967.

In the meantime, the MGB proper was to gain an addition to the family which would make a lasting impact. In October 1965, the MGB GT was announced which was a virtually unchanged Roadster up to the waistline — except for the front wings which no longer had cut-outs through which the Tourer's windscreen supports could pass — but which was fitted with a permanent roof and a large, estate car-like, rear door which transformed the uses to which the MGB could be put. The soft overall outlines of the 'B were topped with a relatively angular superstructure which had a close affinity to BMC's 1100 of the time and which looked very much as though it had been designed to go there in the first place. And when one considers the 1959 prototyp EX 205, it no doubt had, in concept at least. The MGB GT was officially described as 2 + 2 for a long time, but in reality the '' + 2'' had to be a very small pair indeed to squeeze themselves onto the padded perch provided behind the front seats. However, the car's load carrying capacity was greatly increased, visibility was improved through the deeper screen and because the rear glass was far less prone to ''misting'' in damp weather than the Roadster's rear screen, all in all, the car provided a far more comfortable method of travelling on a typical English day, which stands a one in three chance of being a rainy day.

Performance-wise, the weight penalty incurred brought some surprising results. The Roadsters stiffness was already good for an open car, but the GT's was even better and allied with a better weight-distribution and the anti-roll bar, which was fitted as standard to all cars two months after the GT's launch, the GT cornered marginally better than the Roadster — but it must be emphasised that the difference *was* marginal. Naturally acceleration was slightly down, but top-speed was maintained because of the better aerodynamics

involved. The GT also incorporated a modification which was not to be applied to the Roadster until some eighteen months later, in April 1967; that of a Salisbury tube-type rear axle.

Also in 1967 two of *Car & Driver's* predictions came true almost simultaneously. Firstly, the MGB was fitted with a new sturdier 4-synchromesh gearbox and was also offered with an automatic option which was very much liked by *Autocar*, but the new MGB variant from which these stemmed was the real star of the show. Unfortunately for the new car, appropriately named the MGC, it was more a first-night flop than a true star. Fitted with a redevelopment of the old Austin-Healey 3000 engine which had proved too heavy and too tall for the standard MGB and which thus enforced a redesign of the car's under-the-skin front end, the MGC should have still been a winner in terms of the sheer performance that many enthusiasts, particularly those in the U.S.A. were looking for, but instead it was a relative failure. Undoubtedly, the car lacked the raw acceleration that had been expected from its redesigned engine; undoubtedly it understeered due to the excessive weight up front, but not disasterously. One motoring journalist of the day put much of the 'C's failure down to another factor: ''BMC were in a terribly demoralised state at the time of the MGC's launch and this was shown in what virtually amounted to contempt for the motoring press, which naturally responded, if not consciously, with a sort of 'well blow you' attitude.''

Standard MGBs, as well as receiving the widely welcomed new gearbox were also fitted with reversing lights as standard, a negative earth alternator which improved the charging rate immensely — a vital factor to a car where voltage drop from the twin-battery connections can cause starting problems in damp weather unless batteries are in tip-top condition — and American cars were fitted with a ''wall-of-padding'' safety orientated dashboard, energy

absorbing steering column and dual circuit brakes. In addition the first emission control equipment was fitted to U.S. cars forming the thin end of a very fat wedge!

In many ways this was the golden era of the original-style of MGB motoring, one which lasted until October 1969. Cars were still fitted with a choice between a second- and third-rate soft top but the car appeared very much as it had in its original, unsullied form. The dashboard was changed slightly so that the light switch became easier to find, the seats reclined (when opted for) after pulling a lever instead of taking a spanner to a pair of nuts and bolts on the seat backs, and the car's electrics were improved. The gearboxes on offer were first class, the leather on the seats really *was* leather, emission equipment was not too intrusive and all was well with the world of the MGB. Except sales!

Adolescence

After the bumper year of 1966, when GT sales took-off, sales had fallen back gradually until in 1967 and 1968 Roadster sales were at their lowest since launch. In 1969 the year of the launch of the first facelifted MGB, sales rose again quite dramatically and continued to surge forward in 1970. The ''new'' MGB (for little but a few significant details were changed) had a typical adolescents lack of respect for convention and to the horror of those purists who become enraged to the very point of writing a letter to *Motorsport* the traditional M.G. grille was dropped. In its place was a recessed black grille with a chrome surround and in keeping with the new image, Rostyle (mag-style) wheels were fitted in place of the standard M.G. pattern disc wheels. Over-riders were finished with black rubber inserts and the traditional leather seats were supplanted by those of a black vinyl covered variety, but recliners were

now the standard offering and most testers found the new seats more supportive than the old. Front wings were fitted with blue B.L. badges which were generally disliked and it was with some delight that an American customer reported that his badges — of the glued-on variety — had had the decency to drop off during shipment!

The difference in production figures between the post-October 1967 period, when real technical improvements were made to the car and the post-October 1969 period when changes were purely aesthetic is, perhaps an apt comment in itself upon the priorities of the buying public at the time.

The unorthodox 'B was given useful detail improvements in September 1970 and again in October 1971 when a new fascia with face-level air vents was fitted.

In October 1972, the appeal of the 'B reverted very much to an as-you-were stance with the reappearance of the traditional radiator more in keeping with M.G. tradition than its predecessor's had been but apart from a few internal trim changes, very little seemed different. Perhaps that is why sales were on a downward trend between 1972 and 1975.

The U.S. magazine *Popular Imported Cars* reported in their 1973 road test on the new model that while weight and price had risen, "not everything has gone up. At 78.5, horsepower is down 12.5 compared to that developed by the original 'B." The reasons for a lack of interest in developing the car around this time can be found not at Abingdon but elsewhere. A combined effort between Triumph and the Austin engineers at Longbridge produced, by the early Seventies, an experimental car known as "The Bullet" which was to enter production in 1975 as the Triumph TR7. It is probable that by 1972, The Bullet was being considered as a direct MGB replacement so that an expensive MGB update would have been ruled out. In the event that prediction was partly true because only one month after the introduction of the TR7,

which was then available only in closed form, the MGB GT was withdrawn from the American market after only a handful of raised ride height "rubber bumper" 'Bs had been shipped. There was a story in circulation at the time that the GT was withdrawn because it was too heavy! The story went that when a car was certified for exhaust emission, it had to be driven on a rolling road with a built in inertia setting to match the weight of the car. Therefore the heavier the car, the higher the setting and the harder the car had to work. At this higher work load, it was said, the Roadster just passed muster while the GT failed to make it and there were thus no "Federalised" single carb GT released in the U.S.A. The one month gap between the demise of the American market GT and the introduction of the far from successful TR7 cannot be seen by many as pure coincidence, however!

Far more sensational than the pot-pouri TR7 and yet even more of a failure in numerical terms, was the MGB V8. In the mid-60s, the Rover company, later to become part of the same B.L. group as M.G., acquired the rights to a Buick V8 engine which no longer had a place in Buick's range. It was first used by Rover in 1967 but was then bought from Rover in small numbers and put to sensationally good effect in a new, long-bonneted, 130mph Morgan called the Plus 8. Also in 1969, Rover offered the engine as an option in their new saloon and in 1970 they introduced a kind of cross between the Jeep-style Land Rover and a medium-sized up-market saloon called the Range Rover. This all-terrain vehicle was equipped with a detuned, but still powerful, version of the ex-Buick engine, giving 137bhp against the standard unit's output of 150 or so.

In 1970 an independent engineer by the name of Ken Costello began experimenting by fitting an MGB with the Rover V8 unit. Weighing in at around 320lb the aluminium engine was barely heavier than the standard cast-iron MGB unit and the car was a

tremendous success, except that the exceptional power of the engine was such that gearboxes, rear-axles and rear springs were often up to or beyond their tolerances. In 1971 and 1972 and with a "Thank-you" to Costello for doing much of the development work that was so quiet that nobody heard it, B.L. developed their own, "official" MGB V8. It was introduced in 1973 in GT form only, to take advantage of the GT's inherently stiffer body shell and fitted with the lower powered Range Rover engine. In 1975, the V8 was caught up in the standard MGB revisions (which was hardly surprising since their body shells and much else besides were absolutely identical) and was then offered with rubber bumpers. In spite of its tremendous performance and fuel consumption that was scarcely worse than that of the four-cylinder cars, the MGB V8 sold to only 2591 customers in its four years of production for reasons which one can only guess at. One of the principal reasons was undoubtedly that the V8 was never offered in the United States, partly because the hassle of developing the car for emission control regulations was never thought worthwhile.

However, the V8's cult-status in Britain and almost mythical standing in the U.S.A. are hardly borne out by road tests of the time. *Autocar* summed up the car by saying, "Good performance with remarkable economy . . . Smooth fuss-free engine with good torque but little engine noise. Perennial MGB faults. Too expensive." And this latter point was probably the most convincing reason of all for the lack of sales. In 1974, it was possible to buy a 3-litre Ford Capri with almost equal performance, four genuine seats and greater comfort *plus* a Mini for shopping for the cost of a V8!

Both the MGB and the V8 shared bulkhead and flitch panel pressings, these modifications being virtually the only structural ones necessary to enable the V8 engine to slot into the existing bodyshell. In September 1974 modifications of a more visually

startling and technically demanding nature were carried out to all cars, to the undoubted near-apoplexy of those who had been upset in 1969.

The Final Facelift

The huge, black urethane covered bumpers fitted to all MGBs from the 1975 model-year on made a dramatic difference to the car's appearance and camouflaged a couple of hundredweight of supporting steelwork and a raised ride height. Roy Brocklehurst, Syd Enever's successor later claimed that these modifications involved the factory in, ''the equivalent of a major model facelift with a hell of a lot more engineering integrity behind it.'' The modifications not only made a difference to the car's appearance but, lacking the anti-roll bar at the rear which was to be fitted from mid-1976 and yet with the newly increased body height and extra crash-resistant weight, the car rolled rather badly. *Autocar's* sober 1975 assessment of the car concluded that, ''The 1½'' increase in ride height . . . seriously increases roll and makes the car roll-oversteer too readily, and it is therefore somewhat twitchy even under public road conditions.'' However, the English owner's compensation that, ''the car is usefully faster in both acceleration and maximum speed'', reaching a maximum in one direction of 109mph, was not shared by owners in the States. There, emission control regulations meant that the 'Bs breathing arrangements were dramatically altered making it asthmatic and downright sluggish. A single 1¾'' Zenith carb meant that the American cars would never use the last quarter of their 120mph speedometers and could be out accelerated by M.G. Midgets and Triumph Spitfires. In California the situation was even worse with the compulsory fitting of a catalytic (cataclysmic?) converter adding a further twist to the garotte on performance.

In fairness to B.L., these quite devastating changes to the character of the car were not entirely of their own choosing. From 1968-on Abingdon had found itself caught in a rising torrent of enforced, legislative changes to engine, interior and bodywork, largely emanating from the United States in which to survive involved working harder and harder at carrying out modifications which nominally increased the safety of their cars but which, in practice, often meant that cars *primary* safety attributes were diminished. A first class example of this was the increase in ride height to enable the MGB top comply with American laws regarding bumper and headlight height. The modified car certainly met the letter of the law but could a car which took longer to brake because of increased weight, which took longer to overtake, at least partly for the same reason and which, worst of all, lost a significant amount of its cornering ability be considered inherently safer? There has even been controversy over whether raised bumpers actually caused greater injuries in the event of collision with pedestrians. Is a pedestrian safer being thrown up and onto the bonnet from impact with a low bumper line rather than being pushed down and under the vehicle from a high bumper? What ever the strengths of the arguments here, it seems probable though ironic that such legislative pressure actually increased the production span of the MGB in the short term; 40 development engineers working full time from 1968-on just to keep the car legally on the road left insufficient effort to spare for the development of a replacement.

During the early months of the ''Rubber Bumper'' reign, British Leyland decided to celebrate the 50th Anniversary of M.G. by issuing a limited number of MGB GTs. Seven hundred and fifty cars were built and were standard in virtually every respect except that they were fitted with every option then available such as overdrive, tinted glass and head restraints but in addition gold-painted V8 wheels

and tyres were fitted, and the bodywork was painted in British Racing Green with a gold stripe.

Just one more version of MGB was to evolve and this was little different from that which had gone before. In 1976, in addition to the fitting of the rear anti-roll bar already mentioned, the car was given a small range of alterations which took the car in the only direction which was by now the only one logical to it — that of increased comfort, away from the out and out sportiness which had been its goal for so long. Seats were covered in ''deckchair'' striped fabric, V8-style instruments were employed incorporating an electric clock, carpets were to be found on the floor and lower geared steering complemented the use of a smaller steering wheel. To all intents and purposes, this was it; the final MGB which saw the name of MGB of the Abingdon works and the successor to Morris Garages through to the final month of production, in October 1980.

However, during that month only, the once-proud Abingdon workforce set about producing a small last testament to all that M.G. had stood for. The last one thousand cars to roll from the production line were known as the ''Limited Edition'' model and were painted in Pewter (Roadster) or Gold (GT) and were offered with distinctive alloy wheels or wires as alternatives. It was the end, in spite of efforts to save the MGB, and in spite of earlier, much earlier proposals for a replacement. Why? Clearly the general world recession and the trans-Atlantic credit cutting duette which Britain and America were playing together up to and during the time of the car's demise had the effect of making it more expensive for people to buy cars generally, but the views of Roy Brocklehurst, one time Chief Designer at Abingdon were given in early 1981 by which time Roy was a leading British Leyland executive.

He said that the ever faster moving treadmill of U.S. safety and emission regulations was a positive disincentive to sell any car there and

that an ever more complex spider's web of product liability suites were being brought about by litigation-happy individuals in which every defence, even the majority of successfully defended cases, produced another strand in the web of case histories in which the manufacturer was almost bound to find himself trapped at some time in the future.

As far as an MGB successor was concerned, B.L. had to invest where they could see the greater returns accruing. "In a sense you could say that it was a choice between a successor for the MGB and putting Metro (B.L.'s highly successful new Mini) back several years. Given that the costs for the development of any new volume car are astronomical — on top of which the engineering effort needed just to keep a car "afloat" on the U.S. market, which any sports car needs, means that the financial targets necessary to realise a satisfactory return on that astronomical investment are forever receding in front of you."

Finally, he made the most telling point of all and one which the British people — British Leyland's "shareholders", would no doubt agree, "We have to keep reminding ourselves that we are not in business to make cars but to make money."

Making money was certainly *not* something that the MGB was doing at the end. The last two years of production showed a rapid drop in production and an even faster drop in sales — so much so that in the Spring of 1981 six months after production had ended there were enough cars still in American showrooms for a whole year's sales while in England, John Hill of the MGB Centre found himself still able to order an MGB Roadster to the colour and specification he wanted in August of that same year.

However, if the demise of the MGB can be seen as inevitable, the closure and subsequent disposal of the factory at Abingdon, Oxfordshire which was the site of the first M.G. production in its own right and where the last car to be produced was the last MGB, can only be described as rather hard faced on the part of the B.L. management. The story is best summarised by Roche Bentley, Secretary of the M.G. Owners' Club, writing in the June 1981 edition of the Club magazine, *Enjoying M.G.* Under the heading of "Final Death of Abingdon", Roche wrote, "A few weeks ago B.L. held an auction of memorabilia and office effects at the M.G. factory at Abingdon. I personally did not attend and frankly I was disgusted at the whole affair. I consider that B.L. should have distributed the items worth having to the now redundant M.G. workforce in the form of a free lottery. Thus the men could have obtained souvenir hand tools, plaques and things like firemen's helmets fairly and at no cost and the important, valuable items such as the original M.G. flag and Cecil Kimber's desk could either have been given to Cecil Kimber's family or donated to B.L. Heritage Limited. The remaining items such as racking and old typewriters and chairs could have been sold to a local trader. But to have hundreds of people picking through the last remains of fifty years of Abingdon was, to my mind, morbid and sick. I will never forgive B.L. for the way in which they announced the closure of Abingdon and the redundancy of the 1100 workforce via the media on the day following the M.G. Abingdon celebrations and I think that their latest method of disposing of the last relics was heartless.

"By the way, not many people realise that the failed sale of the M.G. factory did not come about at a reported £30,000,000 and that a few months ago B.L. sold the complete factory and all the surrounding space for a bargain £5,000,000 to an insurance company. I'm sure that the Aston Martin consortium and M.G. Owners' Club could have raised that price from public subscription to maintain M.G. in a workable form."

How sad and how unnecessary that a great name in motoring should end its days among such controvercy with Roche Bentley's feelings being echoed by most enthusiasts who attended the final sale — and what infertile ground in which to plant the seeds for the Metro M.G.

The Aston Martin plan to save Abingdon had failed. A few minor concerns and also the M.G. Owner's Club tried marketing new MGBs in lowered, chrome bumper form or with V8 engines but none made an impact. Now, only restorers can "Save The MGB", and that is what this book is about . . .

"You're right Mr. C, they won't copy you this time!"

H1. Mr. A. Stafford's Concours winning MG TF. This was the first car to use the Issigonis design front suspension eventually to be used by the MGB.

H2. 100,000 MGAs were built but this one is the rarest of all; the De-Luxe MGA was built around the Twin-Cam bodyshell/running gear but with a standard OHV engine.

H3. "FFE 140E" represents one of the earliest MGB GTs. In both open and closed forms the car has a simple, appealing visual image never surpassed by later styling changes.

H4.   One of the McGlen's family of MGCs, this one ("Puggy the Poltergeist") in standard trim. The beefier look comes from the larger, 15 inch wheels and bonnet bulges (Photo: Pearl McGlen).

H5.   The last few MGCs were bought by University Motors Ltd. in London. Most were given cosmetic treatment such as the painted "teardrop" on the bonnet and attractive bonnet badge shown here but others were mechanically modified and VERY potent.

H6.   The 1969 MGB was fitted with the first grille WITHOUT historic M.G. links ever used on an M.G. Other trim changes were made but the spectacular bumper extension shown here is a typical American "extra". Note the obligatory treble wiper system. (Photo: S. Glochowsky).

H7. The temptation to fit Rover's superb ex-Buick lightweight V8 proved too great and Ken Costello went into small-scale production, beating Abingdon to it. Note the huge GRP bonnet bulge, not found to be necessary on the Costello Mk II.

H8. When B.L.s own V8 appeared it was surprisingly "anonymous". Wheels similar to those on the later "Jubilee" were fitted, the car had a raised ride-height and a badge on the back near side only — the only part seen by other drivers!

H9. The last of the chrome-bumper 'Bs had a grille which, at least, had recognisable roots. American 'Bs were becoming really slow! (Photo: S. Glochowsky)

H10.   The last of all of the chrome-bumper 'Bs had number plate lights moved from over-riders to the bumper itself.

H11.   MGB Jubilee's were built with trim changes more distinctive than that of the V8 — British Racing Green with a gold stripe and gold-finished V8-type wheels.

H12.   The last of the "standard" MGBs was much like any other rubber bumper car but within its skin were a huge range of detail alterations — see relevant Appendix for details.

H13.   Last few cars were known as ''Limited Edition'' and were given special colour schemes and detail specification changes including a front spoiler and alloy wheels seen on no other MGBs.

H14.   Abingdon's workers honoured the last car to come off the production line with an impromptu, unofficial wake. Personnel Manager Peter Laidler took this snap-shot of the L.H.D. U.S.-spec. car, surrounded by some of those who helped create it. Their obvious sense of pride is somewhat ironic under the circumstances . . .

H15.   The ex-Buick V8 engine transformed the MGBs performance figures but made a negligible effect upon sales. It was badly overpriced.

② Buying

Buying a 'B is easy! Buying the *right one*, however, takes a little patience, a little knowledge and — often — no little time. Even a car such as the MGB with its justified reputation for reliability and longevity is prone to faults and weaknesses due to the ravages of corrosion, wear and, all too often, downright neglect. On the other hand, the car's ever growing popularity means that unscrupulous sellers are presented with an ideal opportunity to gloss over weaknesses in a problem car and pass it off as a good example of the marque. This chapter aims to provide the prospective purchaser with a sequence of checks on a car under consideration which should be virtually foolproof in ensuring that a car is as good — or only as bad — as it seems. It should also provide the owner who is in the process of deciding whether to rebuild his or her car with the information necessary to make an estimate of the total amount of work — and thus expenditure — required.

Take Your Pick

First of all, the prospective owner has to make a decision on which model of 'B to buy. Although the 1962 version of the car was derided as being "soft" by MGA enthusiasts (it often still is, in fact!), the owner of a 1980 car would instantly *know* that he had stepped back in time if driving positions were swapped with the owner of an early model. Some idea of the changes that took place is given in Chapter One while the Appendices detail the technical and numerical background to the developments. On the whole, changes were made by stealth rather than obviously and dramatically.

It is possible however, to place the MGB's evolution into era, although the manufacturer's own model changes do not necessarily reflect these. The first covers the early, 3 main bearing-engined cars with simple, uncluttered appearance and few refinements — even the heater was an optional extra! Because of the difficulty in obtaining spares for these cars (and exchange engines have not been available for many years) they really come more into the "Collectors" category than any other MGB. In practice most remaining early cars have been "modernised" with "wrong" engines, axles and gearboxes, doors and door fittings and even seats so an original one in good condition would be well worth having.

5 main bearing-engines, available from October 1964, are much longer lived units, the earlier 3 bearing units being subject to crank "whipping" and relatively rapid wear, although carefully cared for examples are capable of quite prodigious mileages without the slightest bother. Although the improved "tube-type" rear axle was fitted to Tourers from April 1967, the next true era begins in October 1967 (2nd Series MGB) when a greatly improved and all-synchro box was fitted with an under rated and little bought automatic option.

Tidy looking reversing lights were standard, battery charging was improved by the substitution of an alternator for the old-fashioned dynamo and a sensible array of safety and emission control modifications were made, although to U.S. cars only. A British or American 'B of this era, which carried through to October 1969, especially if fitted with reclining seats, wire wheels and overdrive, is probably the most desirable "pure" MGB of all. Unspoiled by so called "styling" or corporate badges, unfettered by well meaning but often counter-productive safety regulations, still with leather upholstery, this MGB above all is clean, efficient and real fun to own.

From October 1969, 3rd Series MGBs (or 5th Series if you illogically include MGAs in the serial run, as did the manufacturers) were presented with exhaust emission controls and a "sharper", more modern appearance. British models "go" just as well as their predecessors. It simply becomes a matter of taste as to whether a black grille is preferred to chrome and vinyl seats to leather. Although there were trim changes made, this era carries on to late 1974, when purists were knocked reeling by Abingdon's answer to the problems posed by U.S. safey legislators.

"Black-bumper" MGBs were not only given a face-lift, but a body lift, too, causing handling to deteriorate badly. These cars were much heavier than their predecessors, weighing in at over the ton! Further emission control "refinements" caused a further cutback in power to American cars which then gave a miserable 65bhp (D.I.N.). However, many U.S. enthusiasts have since "de-Federalised" their cars. "Black-bumper" 'Bs until August 1976 must, surely, be the MGBs to avoid, because after that date anti-roll bars were added which put back most of the lost cornering ability and also detail modifications were made taking the car to its by then-logical and well equipped conclusion.

Final note must be made of the Abingdon "Specials". In 1975 750

MGB GTs were built to commemorate B.L.'s own version of M.G.'s 50th Anniversary. Unfortunate in that they included the worst mechanical features of the cars of the time, these MGB GT Jubilee model cars were different in little but trim from their standard counterparts except for the V8-style road wheels and 175-section tyres. The Limited Edition MGBs were rather different in that they were, genuinely, the last 1,000 MGBs ever made. The last Tourer and the last GT were kept by B.L. themselves while the remaining 579 GTs and 419 Tourers were sold — and sold within a very short time of their announcement. These cars had trim changes such as body stripes, and were distinctively painted and badged. Without a shred of doubt these are going to remain the most valuable and prestigious of MGBs, a sad but proud testament to a great workforce and a great car.

Where to Look

Half-a-million MGBs were built. In rough terms, one third stayed at home, one third went to grace California while the rest of the world (but mostly the rest of the U.S.A.) had to share the remainder of the cars.

Consequently, British and Californian owners will find a reasonable number of MGBs advertised in the local press while everyone else has to look that bit harder. The two most important clubs for 'B owners (AMGBA in the States and MGOC in the U.K.) carry a "Cars for Sale" column in their magazines, the British club's magazine being published monthly and always offering a very wide range of MGBs.

In the more highly MGB populated areas, the everyday car auctions sometimes have MGBs on offer but time and the opportunity to check the car over can be severely limited. Very low mileage cars or those with an interesting

history are sometimes offered by the "quality" auction houses such as Sothebys — but be prepared to pay! Another approach and one which has been used with great success by the author, is to find the most popular medium for selling MGBs in your area, be it the local press or the club magazine, or even the publications of a neighbouring area, and place a series of advertisements stating "MGB Wanted" with some details of what is required. Unfortunately some newspapers — those in Paris being an example — refuse to accept such advertisements, but the technique is quite common and highly successful in the U.K.

John Twist of University Motors, Michigan, U.S.A. writes, "In the U.S. the best way of finding an M.G. is through the local newspaper want ads. Other means include: bulletin boards in foreign car shops and parts outlets; various club publications; several of the major collector magazines such as: *Hemmings Motor News; Cars and Parts; Road & Track* — these are monthly publications offering For Sale and Wanted columns. In addition there are two M.G. magazines now in print — *M.G. Magazine* which is obtainable from 2, Spencer Place, Scarsdale, NY 10583 and *Abingdon Classics,* from PO Box 233, Mulberry, Florida 33860.

"When a potential purchaser of an M.G. enters University Motors and wants an impression of the M.G. he wants to purchase we first look in the files (we have a cross-reference for chassis numbers) and can give an idea of any previous work performed on it. Other shops may be able to carry out this paperwork inspection, too. It's important that if the seller says that the MGB has recently been "tuned" or "rebuilt" (or some other such term meaning twenty different things) that the buyer call the shop where the work was performed and ask about the extent of the work completed and their impression of the car."

'B-ing Sure

Checking over a prospective purchase not only can but *should* be very time consuming if the ''right'' car is to be bought rather than a glossed-over heap of trouble. What follows is an elimination sequence in three separate parts, each one taking longer and being more thorough than the last, this approach having the virtue of saving the purchaser both time and embarrassment. It is always easier to withdraw at an early stage than after an hour spent checking the car over, with the aid of the owner's comments and mugs of coffee! Thus, Stage A aims to eliminate the obvious ''nails'' without having to probe too deeply, Stage B takes matters somewhat further for cars that pass the first stage while Stage C is the ''dirty hands'' stage, the one you don't get into on a snowy February evening unless you are *really* serious.

Tool Box

Old, warm clothes (if the ground is cold). An old mat or a board if the ground is wet. A bright torch. A pair of ramps. A screwdriver or other probe. Copies of the following pages and a notepad. Pencil. A bottle, trolley or scissors jack. Axle stands.

Safety

Safety should be carefully considered and any necessary steps taken. In particular, do not rely on a handbrake holding a car on a slope or ramps. NEVER crawl under a car supported by a jack only.

''Something not quite right with that stripe . . .''

Using the checklist

The checklist is designed to show step-by-step instructions for virtually all the checks to be made on a car offered for sale. After each check, the fault indicated is shown in brackets. *e.g.,* the instruction:

''Look along wings, door bottoms, wheel arches and sills from front and rear of car'' is followed by the fault, shown in brackets, as (Ripples indicate filler presence/crash damage. £££). The pound Sterling signs require some explanation. They are intended to give a guide to the cost of rectifying the fault if it exists. £ indicates that the cost is likely to be less than the cost of a new tyre, £££ stands for the cost of a new set of tyres, or more, while ££ means that the cost is likely to be between the two. The cost guide relates to the cost of the component/s only, other than in the case of bodywork — allow more if you have the work done for you.

When examining a car you are advised to take this book (or copies of the relevant buying checklists) and a notebook with you. As each item is checked a record can be kept in the notebook. You may wish to record a running cost total for necessary repairs as faults are discovered — this could be a useful bargaining tool at the end of your examination.

It is strongly recommended that the repair and restoration sections of this book and also Haynes MGB Workshop Manual are examined so that the checker is fully familiar with every component being examined.

Stage A — First Impressions

1. Is the car ''square'' to the ground and are bonnet, bumper, grille, door to hinge-pillar gaps even and level? (Closed-up door gaps and rippled front wings usually indicate poorly repaired crash damage. £££ +)
2. Look along wings, door bottoms, wheel arches and sills from the front and rear of the car. (Ripples indicate filler presence. £££)
3. Check quality of chromework, especially bumpers. (Dents, dings and rust. ££)
4. Turn on all lights, indicators and reversing lights and check that they work. (Sidelights/marker lights rust in their sockets. ££. Rear licence/number plate lamps earthing/grounding problems plus other specific component problems)
5. ''Bounce'' each corner of the car. (Worn shock absorbers allow the corners to feel springy and bounce up and down. Each damper — £)
6. Check visually for rust — gain an overall impression at this stage. (From cosmetic, to dire! £ to £££ + — see following sections)
7. Check for damage in rubber bumpers if fitted. (Rips and other damage. ££)
8. Examine general condition of interior at-a-glance. (Rips, dirt, parts missing. ££ or £££)
9. If car advertised as ''unrestored'' check rear wing/panel seam, which will be visible in unrestored cars (Genuine cars may be worth much more. £££)
10. Check fit of curved part of rear chrome bumpers. (Accident damage. Possibly £££)
11. Check hood for: fit around windows, rips and clarity of screen. (Hood replacement. £££)
12. Quality of paintwork. Does it shine when *dry*? Are there scratches beneath the shine? Is it chipped? (Neglect or poor-quality, cover-job respray. £££)
13. Does the seller/his surroundings *look* like those of an enthusiast? (Maintenance. £££)

Stage B — Clean Hands!

If a car doesn't match up to requirements after Stage A, don't be tempted — reject it! There are

always more cars to be seen. Stage B decreases the risk of making a mistake without even getting your hands too dirty!

Check hard for body corrosion in all the places shown below. Use a magnet to ensure that no filler is present − magnets will only ''stick'' to steel. Work carefully and methodically.

Bodywork-Checklist

1. Front apron, beneath grille. (Accident damage, corrosion, cheap repair. ££)
2. Front wing Headlamp area. (Corrosion. Filler. £££, if severe)
3. Lower front wing-continuation of sill line. (Corrosion. Filler. Damage. £££, if severe because hidden corrosion indicated).
4. Vertical line a few inches back from front wheel arch. (Corrosion. Filler. £££)
5. Sills. (Corrosion. Filler. Damage. £££ to replace)
6. Door bottoms. (Corrosion. Filler. ££ or £££)
7. Door skins below window/ ¼ light vertical dividing strip. (Splits. Filler gives only a temporary repair. ££)
8. Measure door fit along their rear, vertical edges. (Open at bottom, closed at top means sagging bodywork − virtually terminal. £££+)
9. Rear wheel arch. (Corrosion. Filler. £££)
10. Open door. Lift up and down and note ''looseness''. (Hinge wear. £. Corroded door. £££)
11. Check the area along the length of the chrome strip. (Corrosion around trim clips. Unless severe, usually cosmetic. £)
12. Check the bottom corners of the windscreen glass − GTs only. (Corrosion. £££)
13. Check the base of the tail lights − GTs especially but Roadsters prone too. (Corrosion. £££)
14. Look for cracking at the left side of the boot/trunk lid of later cars where the suppoort connects to it. (Fatigued steel requires welding, possibly plating and boot/trunk lid respray. ££ or £££)

Interior

1. Examine seat and backrest. (Worn, thin or split covers. Leather £££, Cloth/Plastic ££)
2. Tip seat forward. Check for damage. (Scuffing and tears. Leather £££, Cloth/Plastic ££)
3. Check dash. (Cracks, tears or scratches. ''Wrong'' instruments. £ to £££)
4. Check condition and cleanliness of hood/headlining. (From £ if dirty to £££ for replacement)
5. Examine steering wheel/ gearknob. (Correct parts fitted? £/££)
6. Test inertia reel seat belts, if fitted. (Should hold when tugged sharply. £)
7. Check door trim and door/window handles. (Wear and scuffing at bottoms, buckling of hardboard backing, broken handles. £ to ££, if parts available)
8. Ensure that the seats fold forward, that the ''paddle'' allows different backrest positions (where fitted) and that they slide and lock. (Failure to slide easily, expecially on the drivers side, is often an indication that the floor is weak. £££)
9. Wind both windows up and down − there should be no restriction. (Usually lack of lubrication. £)

Mechanical

Ask owner to start engine. Let it idle − thorough warming-up takes quite a while on the road − this will help. (Does he/she let it idle on choke? Harmful practice!)
1. Pull and push steering wheel and attempt to lift and lower at right angles to steering column. (Clonking indicates: wear in column bush, loose column connections. £. Wear in steering column U/J. £)
2. Pull bonnet release. Is it stiff? (Seized mechanism or cable. £)
3. Open bonnet. Check for non-standard air cleaners, rocker cover, etc. (If originality is important. £-££)
4. Is oil cooler in place? n.b. Not standard on very early, U.K. cars. (Sometimes removed when leaking. Replacement £. Potential engine

damage in hot climates £££)
5. Check engine/engine bay for general cleanliness and presence of oil. (Leaking gasket/lack of detail care. Probably £)
6. Listen to engine Tappets should be audible. Bottom-end rumble, timing-chain tinkle − non-adjustable − should not. (Worn engine. Timing chain and sprockets ££. Worn crank. £££)
7. Is paint peeling around clutch/brake cylinders? (Carelessly spilt fluid strips paint. £, plus time)

STOP ENGINE AND LEAVE FOR A FEW MINUTES

8. Remove radiator cap SLOWLY with rag and beware of spurting, scalding water. Inspect coolant level and its general cleanliness. (Orange indicates rust and a long time since it has been changed. n.b. For 1977-80 models the coolant in the overflow tank is not a good indicator of the actual cooling system. Remove the cap at the top of the thermostat with a spark plug socket, bearing in mind safety. Check for oil on top of water. Remove dipstick. Check for water droplets in oil. (Head gasket problems. Probably £££)
9. Remove engine oil filler cap. Look for yellow or brown slimy sludge or foaming. (Severe bore/valve guide wear. £££)
Look for white foaming or ''goo'' inside cap. (Faulty ELC − Evaporative Loss Control system. £)
10. Car out of gear. Handbrake off. Push car backwards and forwards for a few yards. (Creaking wire wheels indicate need for rebuild or replacement. ££ each)
11. Inspect the fins of the radiator. (Newer MGBs have greater problems with oxidation than older cars. Exchange radiator. ££)
12. Examine engine mountings for signs of previous removal. The motor mounts should have fine thread bolts, nuts on the underside, lockwashers on all nuts. The top starter bolt − 1968 and newer − should carry the gearbox wiring loom and/or the engine-to-gearbox bolt just to the top of the starter should carry the loom on its rear side − under the bolt head.

(Previous engine removal is not necessarily bad but it will be interesting to known why!)

13. Jack both front wheels off the ground together. Turn steering wheel from lock-to-lock. (Roughness indicates wear in steering rack. Replacement or overhaul. ££-£££)

Road Test

If you, the tester are driving ensure adequate insurance cover. Otherwise simulate the following tests with the owner driving.

1. Start up. Is starter noisey on engagement? (Worn starter dog. £)
2. Is it difficult to engage first gear? *n.b.* Expect a long, heavy clutch pedal. (Worn clutch and/or worn selector mechanism. £££)

Drive for three or four miles to become familiar with the car and to warm engine.

3. Drive at 30mph. Brake gently to a halt. A: Does car "pull" to one side? B: Do brakes rub or grind? (A: Worn pads or shoes. £. Seized callipers. ££. B: Worn pads or shoes. £, but more if discs or drums ruined.)
4. Drive at 30mph in 3rd gear. Apply then release accelerator four or five times. Listen for transmission "clonk". (Worn universal joint. £. Worn differential. £££. Worn halfshaft/driveshaft. ££. Worn wirewheel splines. ££)
5. Drive at 40mph. Lift off accelerator. Listen for differential whine. (Worn differential. £££, if severe or unbearably noisy.)
6. Accelerate hard in 2nd gear to 40mph then lift off. Listen for engine knocking. (Worn engine bearings. £££), also —
7. — does gearbox jump out of gear? (Worn internal selector mechanism. £)
8. Drive as in 6./7. above but lift off in third gear. Does gearbox jump out of gear? (Worn internal selector mechanism. £)
9. Drive at 50mph in 4th gear. Change into 3rd gear. Does gearbox "crunch"? (Worn synchromesh. £. Faulty/worn clutch. ££)
10. Drive at 30mph in 3rd gear.

Change into 2nd gear. Does gearbox "crunch"? (Worn synchromesh. £. Faulty/worn clutch. ££)
11. Do front wheels flutter or shake at 40mph? (Wheels out of balance. £. Worn front suspension. ££)
12. Check that road conditions are suitable. With ratchet knob depressed pull the handbrake on whilst travelling at 20mph or so. Don't risk a skid! (Car pulls to one side — faulty handbrake on that side. — See 20 below. If the starter motor engages (yes, really!) on 1976-80 cars, a diode, located behind the glovebox is faulty. £) *n.b.* in severe winter conditions, various parts of the handbrake mechanism can freeze simulating other mechanical problems.
13. When cornering does the steering wheel attempt to return to the "straight-ahead" position when loosed? (If not probably indicates tight kingpins. (Renewal. ££)
14. In second gear at about 30mph accelerate hard, then decelerate hard, don't brake. (If car veers to left or right, the rear axle is loose or the springs are faulty. New axle U-bolts. £. New rear springs. ££)
15. At low speed brake and listen for front-end clonks. (Loose wire wheels. Retightening is free! But worn splines on wheels and hubs. £££. Or, the distance tube at the base of the kingpin is too long or worn. ££)
16. When stationary, operate the brake pedal. Apply light pressure in repeated strokes. (If the pedal slowly works its way to the floor — even over a minute, the master cylinder is faulty. This problem more common to dual circuit systems. ££)
17. Operate the red brake warning light or ensure that it illuminates when the key is turned to the "Start" position (1975-80), then push on the brake pedal as hard as possible. (If the light illuminates the rear brakes probably leak. Replacement wheel cylinder. £. Sometimes only adjustment is required)
18. Accelerate from about 1000rpm in top gear, full throttle. (Pinking/spark knock probably indicates maladjusted timing. Can

cause piston damage over a long period. ££ or £££)
19. 1975 cars on. Accelerate to 5,500rpm then change up to second. ("Popping" through the exhaust indicates faulty emission controls — U.S. cars — or over-rich carburettor setting)
20. At highway speeds (55mph maximum in USA) climb a slight hill with a very light throttle. (Hesitation, coughing, snapping or spitting indicates over-lean carburettor setting. Can cause valve damage over a long period. ££)
21. Does overdrive flick in and out promptly in 3rd and 4th? *n.b.* Early vacuum-operated overdrive switches only switch "out" with throttle depressed. 1977-80 cars only have overdrive on 4th. (Slowness indicates worn solenoid switch. £. Possibly more severe overdrive wear. £££)
22. Stop car. Apply parking brake firmly. Engage 2nd gear. Gently let out clutch — but depress again *as soon as car shows any signs of distress.* (If car pulls away, worn rear brakes. £. Oil in brake drum. ££. If car remains stationary but engine continues to run — worn clutch. ££+)
23. Switch off engine. Does it "run on" or "diesel". *n.b.* Quite common with all 'Bs before 1973. (Revs less than 800 on tickover. Probably carbon build-up in cylinder head. £ + time. Revs more than 800 on tickover, probably idling adjustment requires slowing down. 1973-on models with anti run-on valve — the ELC system is faulty. £-££)

N.b. "Running-on" or "dieseling" sometimes unavoidable in U.S. (especially pre-'73 MGBs) as gasoline of high enough octane is no longer available.

Boot/Trunk Inspection

1. Is the spare tyre inflated and with a good tread? (Replacement. £ — obviously!)
2. Does the jack work? (Replacement. £, or lubrication)
3. Is there a hammer for wire wheels — all wire wheeled cars — and a spanner — 1968-80 wire wheeled cars? (Replacement. £)

4. Is there a key for the boot/trunk lock? (Replacement key if right number can be found, or even replacement lock. £)

5. Does the boot (trunk) light illuminate – if fitted? (Switch, bulb or wiring fault. £)

Stage C – Dirty Hands

This is the level at which the car – by now being seriously considered – is given the sort of checks that make as sure as possible that there are no serious hidden faults which could still make the purchaser change his or her mind. It might also throw up a few minor faults to use as bargaining points with the seller!

While Stage A took only a minute or so and Stage B took quite a while longer, Stage C involves a lot more time, inconvenience and effort, but if you want to be sure, it's the most vital stage of all.

Safety: Ensure that wheels are chocked when using jacks or ramps. NEVER go under a car supported only by a jack.

1. Jack rear wheels off ground, one at a time. Grasp wheel, twist sharply back and forth – listen for "clonks". If wire wheels fitted, do wheels move relative to brake drum? (Worn splines on hubs/wheels. £££)

2. Jack up front wheel at wishbone, partially compressing front suspension. Spin wheel and listen for roughness in wheel bearings. (Imminent wheel bearing failure. £)

3. Grip roadwheel top and bottom – ensure car weight cannot fall onto hand – and rock in the vertical plane. (Play indicates: wear in wire wheel splines. £££. Wear in wheel bearing. £. Wear in kingpin. ££)

4. From beneath car, examine rear of rear brake drums and insides of wheels for oil contamination. (Failed oil seal/blocked differential breather. £)

5. Lift carpets, check floor for rusting, particularly adjacent to inner sills in footwell. (Significant corrosion. Possibly £££)

6. Feel inside front inner wings for corrosion at tops of wedge-shaped box sections. (Severe corrosion. £££)

7. Remove mud, if present, from around rear spring hangers. Probe for presence of corrosion with screwdriver. (Significant corrosion. £££)

8. Examine and probe around inside of rear wheel arches and area inside boot/trunk in line with rear wheels. (Corrosion. £££)

9. Sniff around fuel tank from beneath and look for evidence of fuel staining, especially from front of tank and from around the sender unit. (Tanks corrode from above, from outside. Replacement ££ in UK-£££ in U.S.)

10. Probe around jacking point, crossmember and under-sill area with a screwdriver. Check visually for distorted jack tube and support. (Severe corrosion. £££)

11. Examine insides of front apron, particularly at ends. (Corrosion. ££)

12. Examine insides of rear apron, particularly at ends. (Corrosion. ££)

13. Inspect the engine for oil leaks. *n.b.* There will almost invariably be some!
Check: Front seal on timing chain cover. (Not common but usually caused by blocked Evaporative Loss Control system.)
Check: Rear seal, leaked oil usually comes through gearbox bellhousing drain hole. (Sometimes gearbox oil leak to blame. £. Otherwise rear oil seal on 5 main bearing engines. £. Or, badly worn oil scroll on 3 main bearing engines caused by severe crank whip. Scrap engine or heavy rebuild costs from professional engineers. £££)
Check: Side covers – tappet inspection plates – on left side of engine. (Very common on single-carburettor, U.S. models. The heat is so high at the catalytic converter that the gaskets fail. £)
Check: Around the oil filter. (Spin-on cannisters can come loose as can bolt-mounted type. Badly fitted rubber seal on bolt-mounted type. £)

14. Examine the front of the rear axle for oil leakage and oil thrown onto the body. (Slight leakage not uncommon. Heavy leakage

suggests a faulty seal, clogged vent or overfilled differential casing. £)

15. Grasp each shock absorber linkage in turn and shake them. (Worn bushes, linkages or shock-absorbers. £ each).

16. Look for evidence of grease on grease points. (Lack of servicing. £ to £££)

17. Condition of exhaust system and exhaust mountings. (Replacement exhaust ££ or £££ in U.S.)

18. Check brake discs for deep scoring. (Replacement or reground discs. ££)

19. Check, visually, condition of battery/batteries – from above – and battery mountings – from below. (New battery/batteries. £-££. Corroded mountings. ££)

20. From under the bonnet, grasp the throttle shaft – twin carb models only – and attempt to shake it at each end. (Excessive movement results in an uncontrollable idle and vacuum leaks. Exchange or replacement carbs. ££)

21. Determine the free play of the clutch pedal. (If more than 1 inch or so, the clevis pin in the pedal/master cylinder pushrod is worn. £)
N.b. Springs should be attached to both pedals. Move the pedals from side to side. (More than slight movement indicates worn pedal bushes or the bolt holding the pedals is loose. £)

22. Check the steering wheel for excessive free play by attempting to rotate it *lightly* with the car stationary and the front wheels on the ground. More than 1" at the circumference of the wheel is excessive. If freeplay exists, grasp the steering universal joint (under the rear air cleaner on left-hand drive cars) and feel for looseness in joint while someone else twists steering wheel back and forth. (Replacement universal joint. £. But often caused by worn front shock absorbers, in which case. ££. 1968-80 cars – U.S. – but later cars in U.K. with collapsible steering systems – fault lies in play between the two portions of the inner column. ££)

Notes for American Purchasers *from John Twist of University Motors, Michigan.*

Ensure that there is a title plate on the MGB (front right inner fender 1963-1969) and on the top of the dash (can be seen from outside the car) and on the door sill from 1970-80. These numbers **MUST** correspond with the numbers given on the title — and all but 1980 models begin with GHN or GHD. (We've seen some MG 1100 titles passed along with MGBs!) Don't pay for and receive the MGB without getting the title. The title is your protection that the car is legally yours!

There is little protection for you if the car has been stolen — you can always call the local police and have a title check made to see if the car is "hot".

Most states require, prior to licensing, that a "safety check" be made by the local police if the car comes from out of state. The common items checked are: lights, brakes, Vehicle Identification Number, wipers, washers — and in some states the exhaust and other items have to be inspected. It's foolish to show up for the inspection knowing that a certain item is not working — call first to find out what is required.

The banks, savings and loans and credit unions will lend money on MGBs but only to the amount shown in the "Blue Book" or National Automotive Dealers Association (N.A.D.A.) monthly report. These listings only go back ten years or less and the loan values are often well below that the purchaser may believe is proper for the car — but that is the way it is! There are only a few exceptions — but you can attempt to "beat the system" by having several appraisals of the car done by dealers or reputable shops, affording the bank a better idea of what they are loaning the money for.

Whatever faults are found remember that all faults are repairable. If you want the car, use the cost of repair for leverage when conducting the final price with the owner. Any MGB will require some repair and maintenance immediately after purchase — plan on at least the amount indicated by the £££ symbols used here for a complete lube and tune. [*Author's note — probably only ££ in the U.K.*]

Whatever the budget is, don't spend it all on the car leaving yourself shy of the money needed to do the repairs. Remember M.G.'s motto — Safety Fast! — and make sure you can afford to run your MGB safely as well as fast!

Buying an MGC
by Pearl McGlen

To begin with, a glance down the classified columns of most motoring magazines and, indeed, Club publications such as the excellent *Enjoying MG* of the MG Owners Club will show a very wide divergence in the prices being asked for MGCs. This difference can, in some cases, amount to an astonishing £1,000 plus for what appear — on the surface at any rate — to be almost identical cars in what sound like identical condition! Be very careful — all too often a car will be advertised as having undergone a total "rebuild" when it would probably be truer to say "new door skins, an oil change and a quick blow over in cellulose"! Take my word for it, a totally rebuilt MGC, if the work was done properly, has cost a great deal of money and there is no way that you are going to buy such a car for the ridiculously low prices sometimes temptingly quoted in advertisements.

To begin with, the MGC is a horse of quite a different colour to the well known and recognised MGB. Outwardly they may appear very similar, inwardly there are few similarities at all with the exception of the actual interior trim and the body from the bulkhead back.

The MGC has, however, become something of a legend in its extreme longevity. There are still C's about at the time of writing, with well over 100,000 miles on their clocks (some can even boast twice that figure!) and in the main these cars are still solid, reliable and suffer from few of the ills that would beset a less robust car of similar vintage and mileage.

MGCs suffer very few problems in the engine and gearbox department. They are not generally prone to overheating, excessive oil consumption, gearbox or axle problems. The engines, when properly maintained, are good for at least 100,000 miles and many go a lot further without recourse to any rebuilding. The gearboxes too are excellent and, probably because the C is something of a "lazy" car are not beset by the sort of problems you would expect from a V8 for instance which develops a great deal more torque and thus puts much more strain on the gearbox which, like the back axle rarely gives much trouble in these cars.

Probably the C's most problematic mechanical area lies in the front suspension, *i.e.* the kingpin/torsion bar system which is quite unique and is not shared with any other MG. However, make no mistake about it, there is nothing weak about this suspension set up. In fact it is very strong indeed, the problems which do arise only occur because of lack of maintenance. If the kingpins are not regularly greased they wear and the result is, at best, extreme wheel wobble at speed and, at worst, dangerous steering and front wheel tracking completely out of alignment which, if not already failed by the MOT (in Britain), could cause a serious accident. Brand new kingpins are no longer available for the MGC but it is possible to have your own reconditioned, provided of course that they have not been allowed to get to the stage where they have actually seized up. Mind you in Britain no MOT testing station should ever allow a car to get to this point as it is not something which occurs overnight.

When you go to view an MGC bear in mind that a good, clean,

original car is far preferable to one which has been "messed about". By this I mean a car which has had lots of undesirable non-standard equipment put on it. Beware of the C which has had fibreglass, flared wings fitted and non-standard large wheels and tyres. Often the engine has also been "souped up", not always by experts, and the resultant car can be worth a great deal *less* than a nice original example, even if the latter does not look so potent!

At the same time you have to bear in mind that there *were* a handful of MGC's which were expertly tuned and modified, some from new, such as University Motors' Specials and Downton tuned cars. These particular MGC's *provided that they are really genuine,* are very desirable and collectable indeed, but *BEWARE!* Far too many people have tried to jump on the bandwagon of success enjoyed by Downton and University Motors cars, and there are a lot of "hybrids" around with rather dubious ancestry!

Chassis numbers can play an important part in assessing whether a claimed UM Special is genuine or not as it is fairly safe to say that there were no UM Specials prior to 1970 and it would be a very rare car indeed which was a genuine UM and had a chassis number any lower than 7,000 + . Genuine UM cars usually had their suspension modified, normally to Koni shock absorbers all round, which was sufficient to improve the cars' handling quite considerably but some "improvements" carried out were merely cosmetic.

Apart from those UM Specials which were Downton modified (producing more torque and greater horsepower whilst still retaining excellent flexibility and economy) Downton also converted several privately owned MGCs and these were done over a period of years from early 1968 to as late as early 1975. The majority of these cars have invoices from Downton Engineering to back up the work which was carried out on them, but occasionally the paperwork can go astray and then it is important (if the

car you are viewing is claimed to be a Downton) to check that the cylinder head is suitably engraved with the Downton head number and various tuning information. The owner should be able to point this out to you, if not, be suspicious that the car is not genuine. It is quite possible that the car in question *has* been tuned, but by someone else, and − surprising though it may sound − very few, if any other tuning firms have had the same astonishing success with the MGC as did Downton Engineering under the auspices of Dan Richmond. Most tuners can make the MGC go a great deal faster as it is a very rewarding subject to tune, but almost without exception they produce a less flexible, rougher running machine with an unquenchable thirst and an owner probably wishing he or she had left well alone!

Always try and get the most desirable optional extras on your car if you can, *i.e.* wire wheels, overdrive, sunroof − if it is a GT − and, if you also are lucky enough to have the choice, go for one of the later models which can be distinguished readily enough by the all-black, later type reclining seats which took over from the non-reclining, coloured piping variety. These cars are usually denoted by a G or H registration in Britain. The later cars also had their axle ratios raised numerically which decreased them in practise thus giving a car which is more rapid through the gears although not quite so long-legged and economical as the earlier, high ratio-axled cars.

One of the most vital parts of the MGC body is the bonnet. No other Abingdon MG has such a distinctive bonnet with its large power bulge and smaller, distinctive "tear drop" necessary to give clearance to the carburettors. By far the majority of these bonnets were produced in aluminium which is good news, but there were a few made in pressed steel and today, although it is impossible to buy a brand new alloy bonnet it is possible to buy a new steel one. These are extremely expensive however and it

is therefore desirable to try and purchase a car which has a good bonnet free from dents and damage. Alloy bonnets are notoriously "soft" and dent easily but on the credit side they do not rust although some corrosion can occur along the line of the stainless steel strip which decorates the front of the large power bulge, caused by an electrolytic reaction between the steel nuts which hold the strip in place and the alloy itself. It is well worth removing this strip and replacing and well-greasing the tiny nuts and bolts in order to prevent this corrosion from progressing too far.

Another important point is that, to preserve the highest possible value, a car should be kept in its original paint livery. A list of the actual colours used for the MGC is available in the appendix of this book and the only deviations from the list should be on genuine University Motors Specials many of which were resprayed in a different colour to suit either the whims of their new purchasers or University Motors themselves. Some of these were rather bizarre, bright orange and two tone yellow and blue being two examples and no one could be blamed for wishing to revert to the cars original paint scheme if they purchased such a car! Fortunately, quite a few UMs were left in their original colours and simply had extras added to them.

A heated rear screen is a useful extra to have. This was not fitted as standard equipment to the CGT and it is an added bonus in originality to have the genuine rear heated screen and not one of the later type as fitted to MGBs.

Although wire wheels are always more attractive and possibly may add a few pounds to the price/value of a car, steel wheels can and do look very smart with their huge moon-like chrome discs and have the added bonus that they do not go out of balance as easily as wires, are much stronger and easier to keep clean and rustfree.

Overdrive is obviously a very desirable extra in these days of high fuel costs and, on a lengthy journey,

can be of great benefit. However, if your car is not going to be used regularly for long distances it will still be found to be quite economical without the benefit of overdrive and one added bonus will be that it is one thing less to go wrong!

It must also be mentioned that the big, straight six engine as fitted to the MGC was also fitted in one other car only and that was the Austin 3-Litre limousine. However, there were essential differences, such as a slightly lower compression ratio, different thermostat housing, milder cam and the oil dipstick situated on the opposite side of the engine. The engine numbers are also slightly different and therefore it is not too difficult to spot an MGC which has an Austin-3-Litre engine fitted. Having said this, much of the Austin engine can be used as a straight replacement for that of the MGC. In practice though the 'C engine is so long lived and disinclined to give trouble that there is little demand for replacements whether from the Austin 3-Litre or elsewhere!

Oil pressure when hot should be approximately 15lbs on tickover and at least 50lbs running, while a good engine will often read 70lbs plus when running. In any case this engine is very easy indeed to work on being easily accessible and very straight forward. Probably its greatest disadvantage is its sheer weight which calls for special equipment should you need to remove it.

Condition of the interior of the MGC you wish to buy is also important unless you want to dig deep into your pocket for the cost of re-upholstering the Connelly leather seats, etc! Often these leather seats will still be in excellent condition after many years but the stitching will have perished allowing the seat seams to split, (often only the driver's seat which gets the hardest wear). If this is the case then all that is required is to get a sadler to re-stitch the seams.

In my view, the MGC is one of the greatest "characters" ever built at Abingdon. It's a gentle giant which is getting rarer as each year passes — if you want to travel by 'C check the bodywork as for the MGB and the specific mechanical areas I mention here. Most mechanical repairs rate £££ in this buying guide's parlance.

University Motors Specials: How To Spot One

A total of 141 cars were bought in by the London, England, firm of University Motors at the end of production and all of these *should* have chassis numbers from 7000 onwards. Of this total only 23 cars were Roadsters.

Although it is impossible to be accurate, as no records exist, it is believed from reliable sources that only an approximate total of 21 MGCs were actually modified by University Motors and made into official "Specials". The remaining cars were simply sold as standard 'Cs. Of the 21 genuine Specials, only a handful had the very special "Slatted" black grille which replaced the standard item. This was often linked with a matt black bonnet bulge, vinyl roof and sun roof. Badges varied; some were supplied with a distinctive and attractive heavy, round, chromed badge in the UM colours of red/white and blue whilst others had a smaller, rectangular badge attached to the wings. One or two had their headlights replaced with square versions (and subsequent reshaping of the wings) some were resprayed in different colour schemes, one or two were two-tone, and the majority of the actual "Specials" also had the powerful Downton-tuned engines, the most popular seeming to have been the Stage 2 (No 43 conversion) which retained the twin carbs, but one or two even rarer models had the very powerful Stage 3 (No 45 conversion) fitted with the triple carb set up.

All UMs appear to have had Koni shock absorbers fitted all round, all had Motolita steering wheels and a certain amount of chroming in the engine bay. Some have flared wheel arches and larger (wider) wheels and tyres but it is hard to establish whether these were fitted by UM or at a later date. Many had special alloy wheels fitted, especially those with steel wheels, and Cosmic wheels were apparently popular although there are again one or two very rare cars with the magnificent J.A. Pearce Magnesium knock-off wheels fitted.

All genuine UMs with Downton conversions would obviously carry identifying cylinder head numbers.

Replacement parts for Downton tuned cars are still readily available from firms such as Maniflow (the staff are ex-Downton). Peter Wood at Westwood Portway Group, and the MGB Centre at Redditch but they *are* expensive.

Buying an MGB GT V8
by Peter Laidler

When I go to buy, for myself or another, I take a long hard look at the seller. Whether you agree or not, I believe that if the seller and his garage look like a tip, then there is every chance that the car is going to be one as well. Additionally, let us make no bones about it, the MGB GT V8 is an expensive car to maintain even if you do do it all yourself and even more so if it is maintained by a garage. So, if the seller looks as though he can't even afford a Mini, then it's certain that he can't afford to run the V8 and it will have been poorly maintained and neglected.

The next thing is to ask yourself, "What do I think of it at first glance?" *i.e.* first impression . . . Looking further, do not be fooled by the car that has about 20,000 miles on the clock and looks like a real old dog. Accept the fact that the youngest V8's were built in 1977 although the great majority are older than that and anything with less than 50,000 miles on the clock is a rare bird and should be treated with suspicion. There *are* such cars but in the main they are now quite well known within the regular V8 club circles.

Now let's have the figures. There were only 2,591 genuine MG built production V8s, all were GTs and have chassis numbers on a plate near the oil filter starting at GD2D1 numbers 101 to 1,956 for a chrome bumper car and from 2,101 to 2,903 for the rubber bumper car but excluding numbers 2,633 to 2,699 inclusive. There are the Costello versions and more recently the superbly built and finished Abington Classic Sports Car versions.

The Bodywork

This aspect is well documented elsewhere. What applies to the 'B also applies to the V8 as apart from minor bulkhead and nose alterations they are virtually identical to the 'B.

The Interior

The V8 only came out with 4 colours of interior trim, except for the very last two which had black and silver striped trim. These colours were black, navy blue, ochre, a bright yellow colour and autumn leaf, a mid-brown colour. I understand that Ochre and Autumn Leaf are now completely "not available" and that Navy Blue is difficult to get. Black upholstery is being made by the popular seat trim suppliers. Accept that if the seat and door trims are damaged then some of them are now "not available". The seat covers can be carefully removed from the frames and washed in warm soapy water, as can any dirty trim pads (see "Upholstery" section of this book).

The Engine

The V8 engine is in the main a clean engine and therefore beware of one that is covered in oil. While the engine is running slowly, listen for any tapping noises coming from the rocker covers or from within the centre of the engine, deep within the inlet manifold. Any tapping or rattling is sure to be the hydraulic cam followers. There are 16 of these and they last about 50,000 miles, in my experience, along with the

rocker shafts. These should really be replaced in sets. It is not difficult to do but the cost of parts is more than £££ in the book's price-check symbols.

The water pump is also subject to failure and this can be felt by rocking the nose. It sounds like a dull rumble when it is worn. Take the car for a drive and when it is thoroughly warmed up check the oil pressure. It is rare for a V8's oil pressure to climb over 40lbs per square inch, and when idling and warm sometimes only just flickers around the 10lb mark. What is important though is that the pressure should be constant. If during a good hard run the pressure stays at, say, 30lbs, then I would say that it is good enough *so long as it is a CONSTANT 30lbs.* The V8's is not a high pressure system but a high volume system (which is also the reason why the oil level should be carefully maintained). The question of losing oil is another subject, and any V8 with oil thrown all over the engine is suspect. The Thames Valley Police V8s were sold with about 150,000 miles on the clocks and they were not using any oil thus oil consumption on a sound V8 should therefore be negligible, but it should be regularly changed (say, every 3,000 miles along with the filter). In my opinion dirty and thick oil carbons-up the cam followers and rocker shafts and ruins them — I have seen it all too often! All of the major components for the V8 engine should be readily available for many years to come. With such a gem of an engine on their hands I doubt whether Leyland will drop it from their inventory.

The Running Gear

This is to all intents and purposes identical to the 1800 'B. There are differences in the suspension spring settings but these are about all. The brakes are similar but with wider discs and callipers to match and both are readily available. The kingpins and bushes are identical, the rear axle is similar, but beware of one that has anything more than the slightest clunk as the complete

axles and the special crownwheel and pinion are now "no longer available".

The gearbox has always been the biggest drawback of this car. The cruel fact of life is that the gearbox is at the limit of its torque capacity in the V8 and the special laygear that gives the V8 its remarkable, and some say perfect gear ratios is not conducive to sheer strength. For those who practice traffic light racing the laygear and first gear simply tear themselves apart (£ and ££ respectively in this buying guide's price-check symbols). The annoying part about this problem is that "it just happens" — there is no warning except perhaps the quietest clicking noise and then bang! It's gone! All the parts that make the V8 gearbox special are available at time of writing exept for the main casing.

The Exhaust Manifolds

Much has been said about these items in the past. If they are split at the 'Y' junction then it is certain that they have been bolted up too tightly. They are available from Leyland and the latest batch are of an apparently higher quality than the earlier type. If they are cracked, then negotiate a suitable reduction from your dealer if you can, as they are now priced in the £££ range. The old ones *can* be cast welded but for the work to be done properly it is a job for a coded welder with correct cast rods. Most enthusiasts now have export Range Rover gaskets between the manifold and the heads to eliminate metal to metal contact.

The Wheels

These are now "no longer available" and very scarce indeed. Made by Dunlop, they went NLA from Leyland about two years ago. By now the chrome might be in poor condition on neglected cars. The only people Dunlop are said to suggest to strip, polish, re-chrome and assemble are Motor Wheel Repair Service at Shepherds Bush, London. Obtain a couple of spares while the going is good!

Summing-Up

In general, there are V8s of all types from poor to mint. A poor example will take many hundreds of pounds to bring up to good condition and perhaps thousands to bring up to mint condition. There is no hard and fast rule as to prices; you simply get what you pay for. I know some people think that any old V8 in poor condition is worth a fortune but the truth of the matter is that a poor example is not worth much more than the price of a poor 1800 'B. After all, to bring the body up to scratch costs the same but the remainder, the engine and gearbox costs a small fortune. [*Author's note — There are however, far fewer V8s and their sheer scarcity is bound to mean that prices of all V8s will rise faster than those of equivalent 1800 'Bs.*]

There are some parts that are now "No Longer Available" from Leyland but these are in the main the parts that other manufacturers have brought up in order to make their own V8s. These parts don't wear out and are confined to the special inlet manifold and adaptor, oil pump base and a few other things. The good news of course is that these same car builders have solved their own problems by having these parts made and that they are usually for sale and available to the V8 owner.

Having decided to buy a V8, I would always use the criterion my father used. He said that it is always better to buy just better and just more expensive than you want to. That way you always feel that you have done well for yourself. How true! Remember that the V8 is an expensive car to maintain but not to run. I think it prudent to comment that most of the people that I know who are intent on keeping the car "forever", have got a small second car as well. With so few V8's having been made it's far better to wear out your Mini first!

When you have got yourself a V8 here is a list of publications without which it will be virtually impossible to properly run the car: Workshop Manual (AKD 3259 from British Leyland), Workshop Manual Supplement (AKD 8468 from MG Owners Club), The Parts List MGB V8 (AKM 0039 from MG Owners Club), User Handbook MGB V8 (AKD 8423 from MG Owners Club).

Buying — In Conclusion

Having examined a car in this sort of depth, it is likely that the prospective MGB/C/V8 owner will be confronted with an almost frightening array of faults. Although the price check symbols will help in determining the most expensive faults, the following notes will help to provide some sort of perspective to those faults now all too clearly on view.

Body rot and underbody corrosion are far and away the two worst enemies of the MGB range. Although the car is sturdily constructed any rot found should be viewed on the iceberg principle; for every spot of corrosion evident on the outside, things will certainly be ten times worse on the inside and that includes the critical, vertical membrane invisibly contained within the sill sections. The chapter on sill replacement will give some idea just how vitally important the sill areas are, containing as they do, most of the car's longitudinal strength, particularly in the case of the Tourer.

Upholstery is also expensive to repair (with the exception of D.I.Y. seat recovering kits from John Hill) and many dashboard and door trim panels will soon be irreplaceable while leather seats have always been very expensive to repair or replace. Good soft tops are expensive and cheap replacements not worth considering. Most mechanical parts are readily available and will continue to be as long as there are people like John Hill around who, in association with B.L. Heritage, is prepared to remanufacture parts as they become obsolete. The exceptions to this rule, however, are some of the early cars' components and those fitted to 'Cs and V8s. In the main, then, the most tolerable MGB faults are those to be found within its mechanical areas.

However, the prospective owner who is determined to own a first class example of the marque can find him or herself in a real dilemma. Is it best to buy a rough but complete example and restore it to known standards or would an "original, low-mileage" example be preferable? In practice both alternatives have their disadvantages. A complete body restoration can cost a great deal of money if the work is carried out by a top-class firm making the commerical restoration of all but a few cars an uneconomic proposition — but then of course that is where this book comes in! The *only* way to be sure of getting rid of rust is to restore the bodywork and the only way to make economic sense out of the project is to do it — or to do much of it — yourself.

Popular myth has it that little used cars are the best buys but, unless it has languished in California's sunny climes, the older car with absolutely no rust inside its inner panels is so rare as to be almost non-existent. Even the lowest mileage examples are found to have some inner corrosion — invariably to the amazement of their owners if they are unfortunate enough to require crash damage repair.

Whichever option the enthusiast finally decides upon, there can be no doubt about which car should be avoided like the plague and which can be detected using the procedures shown in this chapter. This is the average — to high priced MGB, with glossy paint and chrome spinners shining seductively in the Spring sunshine, effectively blinding the would-be purchaser to the artificially smooth, plastic filled body and the endless expense and heartache to come.

Choose well to start off with — and enjoy years of motoring in one of the last of the simple enjoyable sports cars.

MGB Insurance

Many prospective owners are put off from buying an MGB because of the danger of high insurance premiums. However, premiums from some companies are higher than others and there is a reason for this. Some motor insurers specialise in providing the lowest cost policies on the lowest risk cars and to them any sports car is anathema, their dislike being expressed in the form of prohibitively high quotations. No insurer will ever admit to being in this category and so it pays to shop around for quotes.

On the other hand, it is logical that those brokers recommended by the M.G. Owners' Club will be able to place insurance with companies that look favourably on the MGB (but young drivers or those with a bad crash-damage or drink/driving records will always be highly expensive to place). Of the M.G.O.C. recommended insurance brokers, the author has had direct experience of Lifesure Ltd., of 34, New Street, St. Neots, Huntingdon, Cambs. PE19 1NQ. They have proved friendly, helpful and thorough in every way and of course, are able to provide motor insurance for other vehicles, too. One very valuable type of cover offered by Lifesure and by the M.G.O.C.'s other recommended brokers is known as "Agreed Value" cover and it is especially suitable for the owner of the restored or low mileage vehicle.

Michael Payne of Lifesure explains, "Agreed Value" is a way of ensuring that a particular vehicle's value is recognised and

B1. *Whether buying for rebuild or just to use, a car with original equipment is a definite "plus". Replacement of small but, to the purist, vital parts can often be infuriatingly difficult. This photo shows an early MGB engine compartment.*

accepted, in effect "agreed" by the vehicle's Insurer. Normally the Insurer will require a written valuation from an approved valuer who has either seen the vehicle or been provided with a complete history of it. An "Agreed Value" safeguards the owner of the vehicle by ensuring that, should a total loss claim occur, the set figure agreed at the inception of the insurance is paid by the Insurer as opposed to the "Market Value" of the vehicle which is normally taken from Motor Trade Guides and does not take into account the pedigree and attention that is often lavished upon collectors cars. This form of insurance is no longer restricted to vintage and veteran cars. Many modern vehicles, such as MGs as well as other marques which have been discontinued by the manufacturers, but are in such an excellent condition as to set them apart from the ordinary car, benefit from it.

By no means all the Insurers will provide this form of protection, indeed many refuse to become involved with it, although in many cases it should be a vital factor in the insurance of the car.

A typical wording from an Insurer regarding "Agreed Value" is set out below although the wording

B2. *MGC engine compartment.* ▷

does vary from various Insurers providing the facility.

"In the event of the motor car (including accessories and spare parts) being lost or totally destroyed and, in the event of the Insurers being liable to pay for the loss, the sum payable is agreed at £......** subject otherwise to the terms, exceptions and conditions of this Policy."

**Value determined by written valuation prepared by a qualified Motor Engineer."

It cannot be over-emphasised that if the owner of an above-average MGB wishes to protect the value of his car and not be in the position of having to accept the often derisory amounts offered by insurance companies on a "take-it-or-leave-it" basis in the event of a write-off, Agreed Value cover is essential.

B3. Early GT interior. Note the white piping on the leather seats.

B6. U.S. dashboard 1977-80 (Picture: S. Glochowsky).

B9. This is a severe case but the buyer should feel inside the wing of the car under consideration and take a careful look through the adjacent holes in the inner flitch panels, under the bonnet.

B4. Early 1969 Tourer interior. Replacement leather is very expensive.

B7. Post 1975 saw a single carburettor and other strangulations fitted to U.S. cars. Some owners have reverted to twin S.U.s (Picture: S. Glochowsky).

B10. Doors and sills can rot badly – including the lower wings in line with the sills . . .

B5. Later models had face-level vents and a centre console plus more comfortable seats.

B8. Latest engines in U.K. had increased space in an engine bay designed to accept the V8. Electric fan was standard.

B11. . . . and this shows what it was like with the outer sill removed. Inner members are ALWAYS worse than expected.

B12. MGCs are little more difficult than MGBs to restore but engines are much heavier (Photo: Pearl McGlen).

B16. Note the seam between the filler cap and reversing light. This is usually filled in during restoration and is thus a clue as to whether an excellent, early car is really "unrestored and original".

B18. Even severe corrosion can be camouflaged with plastic filler. This wing base looked quite presentable until "attacked". The magnet test is crucial here — see text.

B13. MGC front suspension parts are unique to that car and in very short supply so check carefully. Here the telescopic damper has been removed. (Photo: Pearl McGlen).

B17. Wings frequently rot around the headlamp surround, behind the sidelight and at the ends of the apron, behind the bumper. (Picture: S. Glochowsky)

B19. B.L. badges on a pre-October '69 car probably mean that it has been fitted with later wings. Another rot spot, incidentally, is a vertical line to the right of this picture. The mud-shield behind it should also be checked carefully, especially at its base.

B14. Rear bumper alignment provides a clue to any past accident damage. (Photo: S. Glochowsky)

B15. The beading between front wings and the top bulkhead panel can deteriorate.

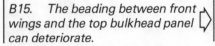

B20. Other favourite rot-spots are: 1 – Inner sills, check underneath carpets and/or rubber mats. 2 – Jacking points and under-sill areas, and 3 – rear spring hangers. Probe the latter two with a screwdriver.

B23. Most "desirable" options, value-wise, are overdrive, wire wheels and reclining seats (on earlier cars). These non-standard chrome plated wire wheels require constant attention if they are to look their best.

B25. In England, any form of "customising" is likely to lower the value of an MGB in the eyes of most enthusiasts but in the U.S. work was often carried out by the dealer as in the case of this 1978 Roadster which was Pinstriped before it was put in the showroom. (Picture: S. Glochowsky).

B24. Engine mountings on "V8-bodyshell" cars (with forward mounted, electrically cooled radiators) are prone to breakage. Check carefully.

B26. Poor vinyl or cloth seat covers can be replaced with one of John Hill's kits in the U.K., but leather can be VERY expensive to repair properly.

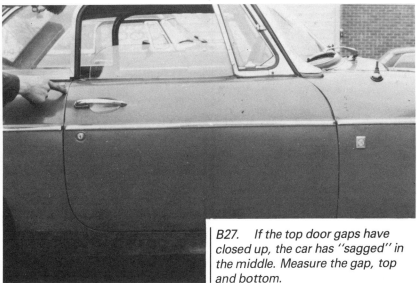

B27. If the top door gaps have closed up, the car has "sagged" in the middle. Measure the gap, top and bottom.

B28.   Roadster hood rear ''windows'' become clouded in time. Light clouding can be removed by polishing with metal polish but it usually means a new — expensive — soft-top. If the rest of it is in sound condition the ''window'' can be cut out and a new one stitched in by a high-class upholsterer at a fraction of the cost of a new hood.

B29.   Soft-top rips are unsightly and can never be patched satisfactorily and are thus an expensive fault.

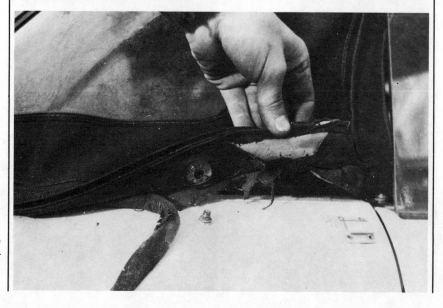

B30.   Soft-top fabric can rot where it clips down to the bodywork. Lift it up and take a look. You could be in for a surprise!

3 Bodywork

In many ways, this section of the book is the most potentially useful one to the restorer. At the time of writing MGB bodywork restoration has been covered in no other book and yet it is the most crucial area of the car. Poor bodywork reduces the life, safety and value of the MGB while restored bodywork (in conjunction with a suspension rebuild) puts back the joyously taut handling which the car possessed when new.

Those enthusiasts without welding equipment have several courses still open to them (quite apart from the obvious and most expensive one of leaving it to the highly expensive — and completely uninvolved — professional). It is possible to hire electric arc welding equipment in most large towns, although this type of welding equipment is usually found to be too fierce for outer body panels even by the most experienced hands. For "chassis" work, for tack-welding inner wings or door skins, however, arc welding is fine. In the U.K. most Technical Colleges and Evening Institutes run evening classes where beginners can learn the rudiments of arc or gas welding.

Incidentally, brazing can also be carried out with an arc welder with the addition of the appropriate accessory.

Gas welding is far more versatile than arc welding, at least as far as thin-gauge metal is concerned, but gas bottles are harder and more expensive to obtain and are far less safe to store and use. In the U.K. British Oxygen sell a very expensive pair of mini-bottles called a "Portapack" while there are signs of independent concerns coming along with cheaper gas-welding alternatives — look out for the ads in magazines such as *Exchange and Mart*.

The third alternative open to the home restorer is to carry out everything except the actual welding. This is not as difficult as it seems, as well as saving the enormous labour charges incurred for stripping, cutting-out old metal, fitting new parts accurately and finishing off. It is also likely that an experienced welder will produce safer, stronger welds than the home restorer. In addition, the cost is not likely to be greater since no welding equipment needs to be bought or hired. On the other hand, there is the problem of transportation to and from the welder's premises — and doing it *all* yourself is undoubtedly highly satisfying if the job is done well!

If this third alternative is chosen, the guidelines shown in this chapter are followed right up to the point where the repair sections are held in place with self-tapping screws or steel pop-rivets (aluminium ones are useless — they melt before the weld can be started) and then the welding alone is carried out by the professionals.

Tool Box

At the start of every section, a "Tool Box" section appears, listing most of the tools and equipment needed to enable you to carry out the work. No list of "essential" workshop tools is presented here

but simply the advice that it is safer and cheaper in the long-run to always buy (or hire) the best tools available.

Safety

At the start of every section is a "Safety" note. Naturally, safety is the responsibility of each individual restorer and no responsibility for the effectiveness or otherwise of advice given here nor for any omissions can be accepted by the author — "Safety" notes are intended to include useful tips and no more. Some more useful information on workshop practice and general safety measures is given as an appendix — you are strongly advised to read this appendix before starting any of the tasks detailed in this book.

Roadster Screen Removal

One of the ways in which Roadster front wings differ from their GT counterparts is in the slot in the wing-top through which the Roadster's screen frame's supporting legs are slotted. Unfortunately the presence of these legs means that before a Roadster's front wings can be removed, the screen has to be taken off. And before the screen is taken out it is usually considered advisable (though by no means essential) that the dashboard is removed.

Dashboard removal is covered in the "interior" section — although it must be emphasised that the screen *can* be removed with the dashboard in position and the glove-compartment box removed, though it is an awful fiddle!

Tool Box

AF socket or ring and open-ended spanners. Rag and white spirit to remove old mastic (sealer). Tube of mastic.

Safety

If the screen is broken, cover the cockpit with an old sheet to catch the glass splinters should the glass fragment. Wear thick gloves.

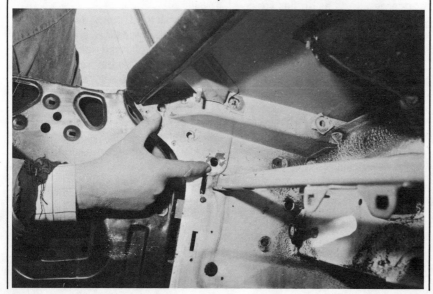

RSR1.   These two bolt holes are the ones through which the only two bolts which secure the screen on either side of the body pass. Note their position relative to the dashboard — in line with the dashboard top roll which remains in place when the fascia is removed.

RSR2.   The two chrome bolts which hold the central screen tie rod have next to be removed. It will be found necessary to slacken them and then to lift the screen before they can be completely undone and removed. Similarly, when refitting make sure that they are located and screwed part of the way down before the screen legs are bolted into place. Lift the screen up and forwards and away — note the "dog-leg" shape of the support legs. Cover the screen with a cloth and store it somewhere safe.

Front Wing Removal

Removal of Roadster and GT front wings is basically similar except that the Roadster's screen is attached by supporting legs which protrude downwards through holes in the wing tops; consequently, the Roadster's screen has to be removed before the wing can be taken from the car. See the previous section for details. Ensure that sidelamps and headlamp wires and those connected to the side-markers on U.S. cars are disconnected and free before commencing.

Tool Box

A range of AF socket, ring and open-ended spanners. Releasing fluid. Welding torch or blowlamp — to help release seized nuts. Impact screwdriver. Hacksaw.

Safety

Basic workshop procedure — see Appendix.

FWR1. The bottom of the front wings are held in place by three crosshead screws. They invariably become "welded" in place with rust by the time that the front wing needs to be removed. Try heating each screw and applying releasing fluid and also try to loosen them (after cleaning out the head) with an impact screwdriver. If all else fails, cut, drill or grind the screw head off.

FWR2. Behind the facia panel, the wing tops are held by three bolts. Removal is not easy — re-alignment when the wing is being replaced is even harder but essential in order to prevent a gap between the wing top and the bulkhead top panel.

FWR4. Two bolts hold the fronts of the wing to the inner panels.

FWR6. There is something very noble about leaving the easier bolts until last! A line of bolts runs down the channel in which the bonnet edges close. Ensure that the locknuts which hold the radiator steady and the bonnet release are removed first.

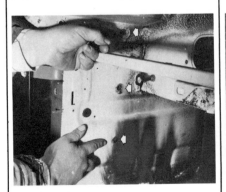

FWR3. Three more easily accessible bolts are situated behind the footwell trim panels.

FWR5. Three more bolts hold the front wing to the front apron. Again, they tend to rust solid. Undo them if they will come undone; otherwise cut, drill or grind them off.

FWR7. Taking care not to damage the surrounding bodywork and especially the leading edge of the door, lift the wing free.

N.b. When refitting a wing, fit all the bolts loosely before tightening any of them up.

Front Inner Wing Repair

Tool Box

All necessary repair sections; welding equipment; tin snips; Monodex-type cutter; hacksaw; bolster chisel and hammer; industrial gloves.

Safety

The usual safety precautions should be taken when welding and when cutting ultra-sharp sheet metal. Move anything flammable from around the area being welded and remember to protect fuel lines from flames and heat.

Many restorers find the front inner wings a real ''Shock! Horror!'' area when rebuilding their MGBs. They budget in time and money for a straightforward front wing renewal, only to find that the rust bug has been nibbling away where he likes it most — in the dank, dark, unseen crevices.

FIW2. ALL rot MUST be cut out. Here the top flange had also deteriorated. The vertical plate holding the fuse box has been separated by drilling out the spot welds and then being carefully chiseled free and bent out of the way. At this stage, all trim, wiring and other flammables have to be moved out of the way.

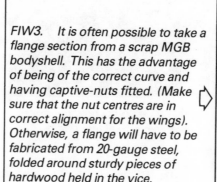

FIW3. It is often possible to take a flange section from a scrap MGB bodyshell. This has the advantage of being of the correct curve and having captive-nuts fitted. (Make sure that the nut centres are in correct alignment for the wings). Otherwise, a flange will have to be fabricated from 20-gauge steel, folded around sturdy pieces of hardwood held in the vice.

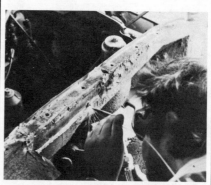

FIW4. The inner-wing repair panels available for the MGB are quite comprehensive with the exception of the flange area mentioned and the rear ''box'' which can be very simply repaired with a section fabricated from 20-gauge steel sheet. Note the ''mini-mud shield'', rubber and bifurcated rivets for fixing into place, which helps to prevent the future ingress of mud.

FIW1. The wedge-shaped box, above the front wheel is a prime target for corrosion. It forms a shallow ledge which becomes layered-over in road dirt and salt water, deteriorating very quickly. Feel inside the wing when any holes will be apparent. (Often the top plate feels whole but through rusting is as brittle as a thin sheet of ice, giving way beneath light pressure). Unfortunately this car has also rotted further back, in an area concealed by the mud shield inside the wing. Check from inside the engine bay although steering rack and master cylinders make it difficult.

FIW5.   Hold the repair panel(s) in place with self-tapping screws before welding them in.

FIW6.   Then paint and underseal them to seal out the elements that caused the problems in the first place.

FIW7.   The same area of the MGC is very similar except that the wedge-shaped box section is not available as a repair section. It would be relatively simple to fabricate, however. (Photo: Pearl McGlen)

The MGBs inner wings are more important than those of most cars as they play an important part in transmitting torsional loadings into the car's massive double-bulkhead — which makes it all the more important that they are protected thoroughly against further corrosion and that the whole area is hosed down periodically, not forgetting to remove the vertical mud shields to ensure that no mud is becoming trapped behind them.

41

Rear (Outer) Wing Repair

Tool Box

Monodex-type cutter or other non-distorting panel cutter; Mini-angle grinder (available from tool-hire firms); Thin or electrician's bolster chisel; Medium-heavy ball pein hammer; Tin snips; Electric drill; Self-tapping screws or pop-rivet equipment.

Safety

Beware cut edges in sheet metal, especially thin slivers of metal — wear heavy industrial gloves. Always wear gloves and goggles when using an angle grinder. Always remove the fuel tank when welding around the rear of the car. Watch out for welding "splatter" when working beneath the car or inside the rear wheel arches. Note the usual safety points regarding working on a car raised off the ground.

B.L.'s replacement rear wings are unnecessarily generous in size being built around production line requirements rather than the needs of the home restorer. They *can be* fitted of course but since at least 50% of their area covers places where MGBs never seem to rot, they would probably be best left alone. They include a significant part of the boot (Roadsters) or rear-door (GT) channel, the reversing light area (which is why unrestored cars have that seam a little way in from the reversing lights — the temptation to flush them over with filler should be avoided!) and even part of the Roadsters rear panel to which the hood is attached.

RW1.   In practice, MGB wings invariably rot out in a line around the wheel arch, where inner and outer wings meet and also in a line with the outer sills. If the bottom of the wing has corroded, be prepared for the inner sill to have done so, too.

RW2.   Several sizes of rear wing repair panel are available, so that any of the normal rot-areas can be cut out and replaced. Note that none go higher than the chrome trim moulding. The reason is that no corrosion ever seems to get any higher. The trim strip and moulding behind it give an excellent place in which to totally conceal the fact that repair panels have been fitted. (In areas of the world where repair panels are unavailable but full wings can be bought, it might be sensible to cut out your own repair section if the rest of the wing is really sound and so save an awful lot of work).

RW3.   Strip the rear wing down. Remove the rear lights . . .

RW4.   . . . and the rear bumper which comes off after disconnecting the rear license plate lights wiring, in the boot. The nuts are often very stiff and are best removed with some clever footwork.

RW7.   Use an angle grinder to grind off as much metal as possible from the corners around door pillar, wheel arch, beneath the rear of the boot and up the corner of the rear light housing. Where the metal has not quite parted it will be found to cut very easily with a sharp chisel but DO wear heavy gloves.

RW9.   The unwanted steel peels back like a snake shedding its skin. Remember the venom in those sharp edges! Some chiselling will be necessary where the grinder could not be used or where it has not ground right through the metal.

RW5.   After removing the rear bumper (it pulls straight backwards) take off reversing lights, side-markers (U.S.) and chrome trim. It is ABSOLUTELY VITAL to take out the fuel tank.

RW8.   After grinding horizontal corners, the vertical "prow" at the end of the rear lamp's "hull" is best cut through with a hacksaw.

RW10.   The cut-out section is shown here with, above and below it, the two repair sections which have been chosen for this particular job. They overlap in the centre and have to be carefully trimmed to butt joint up against each other.

RW6.   Cut a horizontal line, using a Monodex cutter or a power jigsaw (but NOT a chisel — the panel must not be distorted) from front to back of the old wing, level with the bottom of where the chrome strip went. Note that the strip clips have been removed by drilling off their pop-rivet heads.

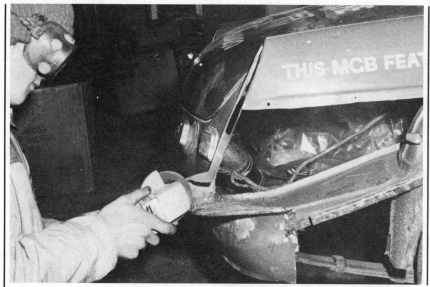

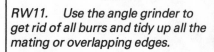

RW11.   Use the angle grinder to get rid of all burrs and tidy up all the mating or overlapping edges.

RW12.   With the outer wing completely removed and showing all its ''undies'', the car is now ready to have its wing replaced, except that on this car the sill requires attention first. The inner wing is also looking disreputable but should be replaced after the outer wing, thus ensuring the correct outer bodywork alignment.

RW13.   The boot tray fits here, but should also be replaced after the outer wing has been at least tacked into place.

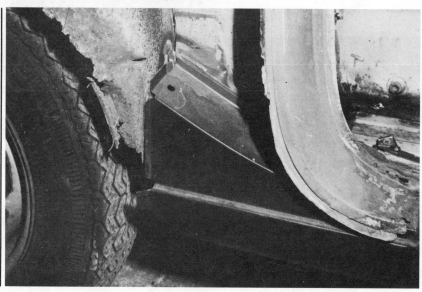

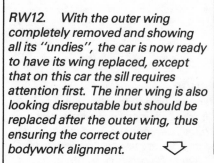

RW14.   With new factory sills fitted, mounting flanges for subsequent inner wing fitting can clearly be seen.

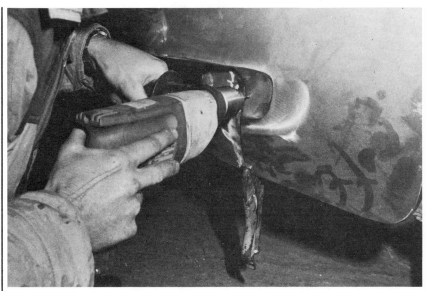

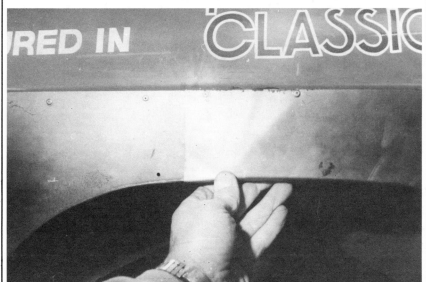

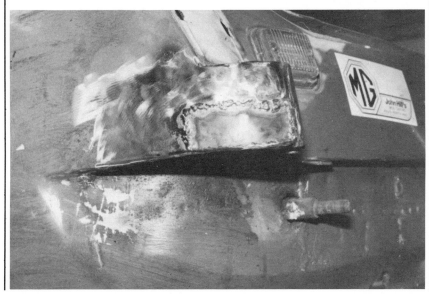

RW15.   The replacement panel is offered up, clamped into place, then drilled . . .

RW16.   . . . for pop-riveting into place. Go to as much trouble as is necessary to ensure a good fit at this stage while adjustment is still possible.

RW17.   The repair panels are pop-riveted into place, tightly butt-jointed at the centre. It only remains to weld the panels into place, perhaps brazing the centre joint for ease of smooth finishing.

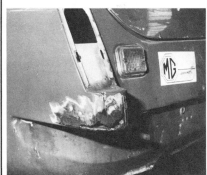

RW18.   If the "hull" beneath the rear lights has rotted out — a frequent occurrence, particularly on GTs, the rotten metal should be cut away . . .

RW19.   . . . and a patch of 20 gauge steel welded or brazed in. Finish off by angle grinding the joints before flushing over with filler.

Rear Inner-Wing Repair

Tool Box

See: Rear Wing Repair

Safety

See: Rear Wing Repair

The MGB's rear inner wings should only be removed and replaced after the outer wing panels and the boot "tray" have been restored. Otherwise the correct line of the rear wings will not be evident and it is to this that the inner panels have to be tailored.

RIW3.   A really bad inner wing, such as this one, is almost paper thin, but its edges are just as sharp as a razor. Wear really thick industrial gloves of the type shown.

RIW4.   From inside the boot, the line of the cut can be quite clearly seen. It is here being tidied-up by being linished with a mini-angle grinder, from beneath.

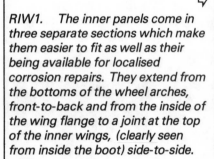

RIW1.   The inner panels come in three separate sections which make them easier to fit as well as their being available for localised corrosion repairs. They extend from the bottoms of the wheel arches, front-to-back and from the inside of the wing flange to a joint at the top of the inner wings, (clearly seen from inside the boot) side-to-side.

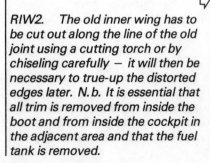

RIW2.   The old inner wing has to be cut out along the line of the old joint using a cutting torch or by chiseling carefully — it will then be necessary to true-up the distorted edges later. N.b. It is essential that all trim is removed from inside the boot and from inside the cockpit in the adjacent area and that the fuel tank is removed.

RIW5.   First piece to be offered up should be the front section, holding it in place with clamps . . .

RIW8.   Welding in a confined space is never fun. Make sure that the equipment is in good condition and correctly set-up to reduce the incidence of spitting or blowing-back. Anyone who has ever swallowed a spark will also keep their mouth closed!

RIW6.   . . . followed by the centre and finally the rear sections. It may be necessary to tailor the sections slightly to fit, using a pair of hand shears, but this is not usually necessary.

RIW9.   View from inside the wing, looking forward shows: the screws removed; the vertical seam welds between existing and new panels; front and centre panels welded together, at the top; the repair panel tack-welded to the outer wing at regular intervals.

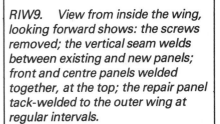

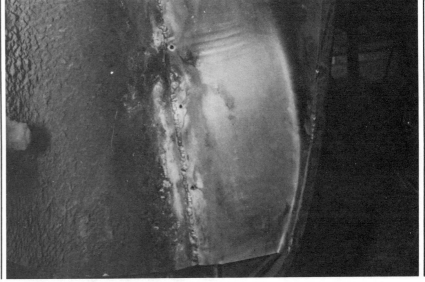

RIW7.   From inside the boot the rear repair section can be seen with self-tapping screws spouting upwards. The line of broken seam welds can clearly be seen showing up the inch or more of overlap between new and existing panels.

RIW10. Because of the double-curvature involved, repair patches could be difficult to make. Follow the tip of Autotech Ltd. and cut patches from another new inner-wing section. Most bodyshops have unwanted left-overs lying around which they will sell for a song — try them. If the inner part of the inner wing has corroded, it will be necessary to fabricate patches like those on a pair of jeans, where necessary.

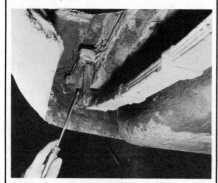

RIW11. Whilst in the vicinity, probe the rear shackle area thoroughly for corrosion.

RIW12. A repair section can be welded on after removal of the rear spring shackle (see "Rear End Overhaul"), the bumper bracket, all corroded metal and — of course — the fuel tank.

Sill Repair

As everyone knows, the MGB was, if anything, *over* designed and offers massive strength for a car without a chassis. Consequently although it *does* rust badly if not protected against the ravages of the elements, it takes an awful lot of rust to make an MGB unsafe. There is, however, one area that is more critical than most and which, moreover, tends to show up as being rusty only when its safety has passed the point of no return and that is the sills area.

The MGB's sills are constructed in the form of a square-sided box section (the box-shaped part covered over by the rubber or carpet at each side of the floor) while the flat part under the door (the kick-plate area) and the curved body panel that is so much prone to stone chipping is little more than a cover. Consequently, it is never enough to replace only the outer part of the sill unless the sill has collision damage and is otherwise sound inside. What is more, whenever rust shows through the outer sill, or through the bottoms of the front or rear wings adjacent to the sills, you can *guarantee* that the crucial load bearing inner sills will be corroded.

Fortunately, all repair sections are available to restore MGB sills to as-good-as-new, including the jacking point which is all too often seen pressed upwards into a weakened sill structure.

Do remember, on a level surface, to support the car's bodyshell at the points where the car's roadwheels impart their thrust into the car's bodyshell, to reduce

"Of course, with the doors off you can see it wants a bit of welding."

the risk of distortion and remember also that quite apart from the finished job having to be sound (and if in doubt, get a pro to do the final welding at each stage) it will be judged by most people on its appearance. Check carefully at each stage that everything fits properly and be prepared to spend a great deal of trouble getting the sill lined up correctly with the door aperture. Only take apart one side of the car at a time to retain as much rigidity as possible but also to give a reference as to how things ought to look — it's surprising just how much can be forgotten once the job is taken apart!

Be prepared to end up doing more work than you originally bargained for. Not only is the car *always* more rusty after it has been taken apart than the world's worst pessimist would ever have suspected but if the sills are bad why shouldn't the front and rear inner wings, front floor — and more — be equally afflicted? And it will be no good expecting to be able to ignore rot in adjacent areas. No one has yet perfected a technique for welding steel successfully to fresh air! However, if all this sounds *too* pessimistic, you can have the consolation that all your effort will result in a car which is as sound as Sid Enever, the designer, intended it and undoubtedly sounder than the "original, un-rebuilt" MGB down the road — because you will *know* what the insides are like!

Tool Box

At least a 2½ lb hammer (a heavy hammer used lightly gives more control than a light hammer used wildly.) A sharp cold chisel, preferably of the "bolster" pattern. A number of self-grip wrenches. Pop-rivets or self-tapping screws and appropriately sized drill bits. Welding equipment and angle grinder (both of which can be hired). Tin snips and/or Monodex cutter. Metal primer. Repair sections as needed.

Safety

Never work under a car that is supported by jacks or piles of bricks. Always use proper axle stands and ensure that the supports do not wobble before going underneath. Always wear really strong industrial gloves when working with sheet metal and wear goggles of an approved type when sanding, grinding or chiseling. Ensure that all tools are in good condition and follow the usual welding safety rules against "flash" from arc welding and fire risks including the provision of a good quality fire extinguisher.

SR3. Roadsters especially but even GTs sag badly when the sills are "gone". A sure check is to measure the door gaps, top and bottom. Sagging sills close the gap at the top and open it at the bottom.

SR6. Lift the mats before ordering parts and check the floor and inner sills in case extra parts are needed. Take out all mats and seats before commencing work.

SR1. This sill looks bad enough, but what about the inside? The front wing and front part of the sill appear sound but note how the jacking point is nestling cosily into the sill above it. Ripe for replacement!

SR4. Don't be tempted by "cover" sills other than as replacement for sound, damaged sills. Note how the "factory" sill behind the axle stand extends behind both wings while the "cover" sill is little more than cosmetic.

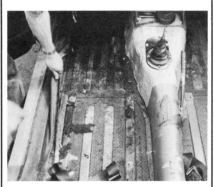

SR7. Peel off the rubber or carpet from the inner sills but take care not to rip it if it is to be used again.

SR2. The full horror story! As is so often the case, the rust worm had eaten its way out, leaving the inside in a terrible state. If the middle of the sill has sagged, jack it up carefully in the centre with a plank of wood between jack and floor. Check carefully against door line.

SR5. Section through a "cover" sill "repair" cut out of a scrap car by John Hill. The shot shows the basic structure of the sills but also the uselessness of the flimsy cover sill.

SR8. With an old wood chisel scrape out the flammable sound proofing adjacent to the sills from beneath the floor ribs. Also remove the footwell trim panel, seatbelt and any wiring or tubing which may have been routed in the area. Have a fire extinguisher handy, just in case . . . Welding fires can be very difficult to put out.

SR9. These are the basic repair sections to be used for a thorough job.

SR10. Bearing in mind that the sills extend behind the rear wings and that rear wings are welded on, the lowest part of the rear wing will have to be cut away — it's usually as rotten as the sill itself anyway. Place the rear wing repair panel to be fitted over the existing panel and scribe clearly around it.

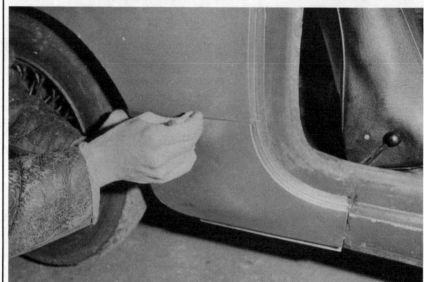

SR11. Hacksaw across the line of the top of the repair section. (Once through, an old hacksaw blade in a padsaw handle is quicker to finish off).

SR12.   Grind off the front corners — wear heavy gloves before pulling away the old rear wing section, which will be the same shape as the repair section.

SR15.   As the front wing section is removed, the reason for much of the corrosion is revealed — years of accumulated salt-laden, water-soaked mud!

SR18.   Close the door and cut through the curved part of the sill, just behind the front wing, with a bolster chisel.

SR13.   At the front end, the front wing can be removed complete, if preferred, as Derek McGlen chose to do on his MGC. (Photo: Pearl McGlen).

SR16.   Back to the rear and a seam can be seen between the top of the sill (kickplate area) and the bottom of the rear door pillar. Cut along it with a hacksaw.

SR19.   After parting the remainder of the sill from the front door pillar, it can be folded forwards and down and cut along its bottom edge (n.b. John Hill's mechanic, Dave, hates wearing gloves. You should protect yourself against cuts, which can be severe, and disease, by wearing them!)

SR14.   Or a front wing panel can be scribed around and the bottom section cut away with tin-snips or a Monodex cutter.

SR17.   Then chisel along the length of the top of the sill from door pillar to door pillar, right next to the top flange.

SR20.   Dress carefully around the flanges at the base of the front door pillar. They must be left on as important sill attachment points.

SR21. Drill out the spot welds where the three sill members were welded together at the top flange before parting what remains with a thin bolster chisel hammered in, vertically from above.

SR22. A part sill — floor repair section is being offered up here because corrosion was not severe in that area on this car.

SR23. John Hill is seen welding a full-length sill floor section to this vehicle, tack welding it at first and checking it scrupulously for alignment before welding it in more thoroughly.

SR24. This sill-floor repair section wraps right around the front inner wing and was held in place with a self-tapping screw before being welded.

SR25. Tacking and positioning complete, John is welding up with approximately 1 ½ inch runs with 1 ½ inch gaps between them giving results somewhat stronger than the original spot welds. This view is of the insides of the long box sections seen in the footwells. If they require repairing it will invariably be in this area. Patch local areas where corrosion occurs and examine the floor adjacent to this area, too.

SR26.   The first stage is now complete. Before closing off, paint with a good metal primer or anti-rust paint. Some of it will burn off, of course, but whatever protection remains will be welcome in years to come.

SR27.   The vertical membrane should also be painted on its inner surface while possible.

SR28.   This section invariably requires some tailoring — around the door pillar, for instance — before fitting properly. Take the time and trouble to fit it properly before holding it in place with clamps, screws or pop-rivets.

SR29.   Ideally, the top flange should be spot-welded and indeed, such welders are available on hire in most areas. In practice, seam welding with gas or arc welder will be more than adequate, provided that the front faces are cleaned up "flush" using the angle grinder, to enable the outer sill to fit closely.

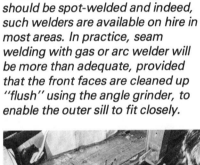

SR30.   Offer the complete sill up and secure with screws or pop-rivets. Be prepared to take endless trouble to ensure that the sill is a good fit, and especially that it lines up with the door before attaching it permanently.

SR31.   Once the position has been determined and the sill is stitched into place, the same system of broken seam welds is used to secure it. Note how the door pillar flanges are fitted to the top of the sill to their mutual strength and benefit. This forepart of the sill will be covered by the front wing. Give it a few extra coats of paint before covering it up.

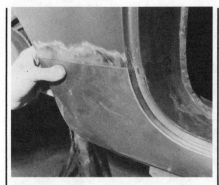

SR32. The covered rear section, too, would benefit from extra protection. Cover it over with the appropriate rear wing repair section. After welding the top joint, grind it down and flush it over with plastic filler or lead loading.

When undertaking a full restoration, sill replacement should be the first job to be carried out. After it is done the owner has the confidence of knowing that the twin backbone of the car has been restored making it stable, secure and ready for anything! But don't forget to inject it with preservative — unless you want to do the job all over again in a few years time!

Door Strip

Before a door can be re-skinned or when a new door shell is to be fitted, the old door has to be stripped of all trim and fittings. (New B.L. doors are supplied bare of any fittings whatever, incidentally).

Tool Box

Crosshead screwdriver. Impact screwdriver and suitable hammer. Small straight point screwdrivers. Long nose and engineers' pliers.

Safety

No real problems — apart from pinched fingers! Wrap door glass in a large cloth and store in a safe place.

DS1. Start by removing the trim rail at the top of the door (2 crosshead screws at each end), then remove the single screw which holds the window winder in place.

DS2. Unscrew the two crosshead screws holding the door pull in place (lift the fold-down handle on earlier models).

DS3. Door catch bezels "break" in the middle — they clip apart then slide out.

DS4. Remove door speakers if fitted.

DS5. The door trim clips forwards and off. Take care, if the trim is an old one, to lever near to the spring clips.

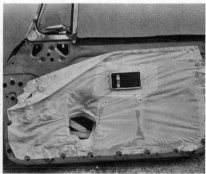

DS6. The protective plastic sheet should be carefully removed and re-used later if not damaged.

DS7. Open wide. This won't hurt!

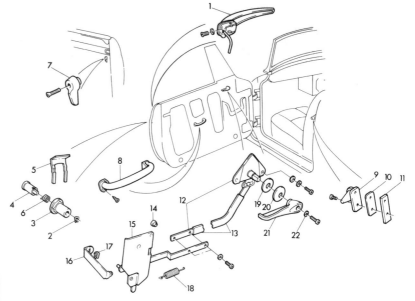

DS8. Carefully screwdriver off the spring clip which holds the latch release rod in place . . .

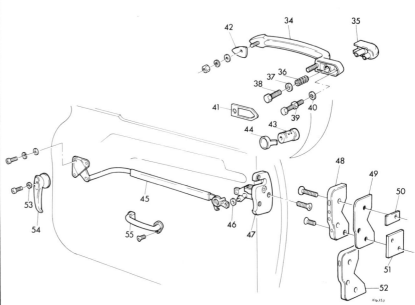

DS9. . . . and the one which holds the locking lever.

Figure 1. *Earlier (GHN3/GHD3) cars used one of two simpler locking systems which were more straightforward to remove and replace. Their components are shown here. Items 1 to 22 apply to earlier sports-tourer only, with pull-out exterior door handles.*

1 Outer door handle	9 Striker	
2 Spring clip	10 Packing	
3 Lock housing	11 Tapping Plate	
4 Lock barrel	12 Remote control	
5 Lock retaining	lock	
clip	13 Anti-rattle sleeve	
6 Self-centring	14 Outside door	
spring	handle buffer	
7 Inner locking knob	15 Lock	
8 Door pull	16 Operating link	

17 Spring clip	44 Retaining clip
18 Tension spring	45 Remote control
19 Fibre washer	link
20 Finisher	46 Anti-rattle washer
21 Inner door handle	47 Lock
22 Spring washer	48 Striker
34 Outer door handle	49 Shim – 0.003 in or
35 Pushbutton	0.006 in (0.08 mm
36 Spring	or 0.16 mm)
37 Shakeproof washer	50 Tapping plate
38 Set screw	(upper)
39 Set screw with	51 Tapping plate
locknut	(lower)
40 Shakeproof washer	52 Striker lock
41 Fibre washer	53 Spring washer
42 Fibre washer	54 Inner door handle
43 Lock barrel	55 Door pull

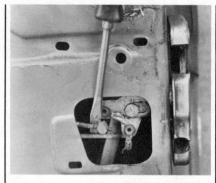

DS10.   Pull them forwards and out of location with the latch.

DS11.   Take out the screws holding the latch unit in place.

DS12.   Remove the latch unit.

DS13.   Remove the four screws holding the latch pull in place . . .

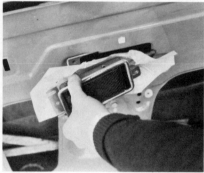

DS14.   . . . and remove it.

DS15.   Take out the window runner top screw.

DS16.   Unbolt the bottom of the runner, either inside the door . . .

DS17.   . . . or from outside, removing the bracket as well. Leave the runner loose, inside the door.

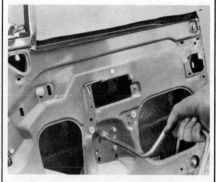

DS18.   Remove the window regulator extension screws.

DS19.   Remove the regulator securing screws. Slide the rollers out of the bottom of the channel fixed to the bottom of the window glass.

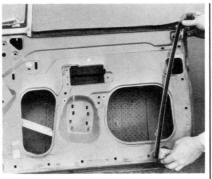

DS21.   Lift the rear glass channel out of the door.

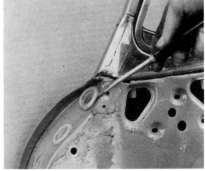

DS23.   Lever the front grommets out of their holes in the front of the door.

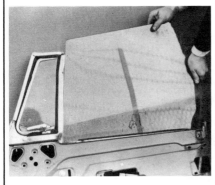

DS20.   Lift the glass up and out of the door.

DS22.   "Persuade" the regulator assembly out of the holes in the door.

DS24.   Remove the two nuts which hold the quarterlight from beneath and the one which holds it from the front of the door.

DS25.   Undo the two nuts which hold the front window channel (an extension of the quarterlight).

DS26.   Lift the quarterlight assembly out of the door.

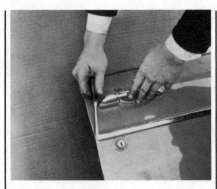

DS27. The chrome trim clips forwards and off (be very careful not to distort it), the door push is held by two nuts — two screw threads protrude from the handle, backwards through the door skin — and the lock is held by a spring clip which slides into a groove in the lock, tight against the inside of the door skin.

DS28. Voila! The now denuded door skin is ready for whatever work is to be carried out.

Door Repairs

MGB doors are prone to giving trouble in two different areas and although both problems can be prevented by careful maintenance, repairing either of them is a largish job. The first and apparently smallest problem is that of door splits which appear in the upper panel of most Roadsters sooner or later, just below the quarterlight. These splits, or stress-cracks are caused by the construction of the doors which incorporate frameless windows supported vertically only by the rear of the quarterlight frame. When the door is shut the pressure of the quarterlight against the screen pillar sealing rubber and the glass itself against a hardtop, when fitted, is fed into the most vulnerable point of the doorskin, the quarterlight frame. The only cars which stand a chance of avoiding this problem are those whose door striker plates are set in such a way that when the door pull button is depressed, the door does *not* spring out against the force of the sealing rubber. In practice this means that the door tends to protrude very slightly along its trailing edge instead of shutting flush but that is the lesser of two evils.

Door splits can be repaired simply be welding along the line of the fault but this is no more than a short-term remedy. The weld itself will never break but the heat-treatment unavoidably given to the surrounding area makes the metal prone to splitting again within a relatively short time, in a line parallel to that of the original split. The only answer is to "let-in" a piece of steel sheet rather like a patch on a pair of jeans, the only difference being that when the patch is fitted, it is used as a template which is placed over the split area of the door panel. It is scribed around, the split section is carefully and accurately cut out and the new piece tack-welded into its place before being filled or leaded over prior to refinishing.

On the other hand, if the door base is also rusted, it would be far easier to simply reskin the door. MGB doors are highly prone to rusting out along their bases due to the ingress of water in spite of the sealing strip along their window aperture. John Hill's door skins and door base repair sections enable the vast majority of doors to be repaired, saving the owner a good deal of money, but some doors are just too far gone and have to be replaced. If the latter is the case, follow the instructions for stripping and refitting a door and for bodywork finishing.

If tackled early enough, severe corrosion is a preventable problem. Doors should be annually injected in all their vulnerable internal sections with a rust preventative such as Waxoyl — a small chore which can save a lot of problems — not forgetting to clean out drain holes in door bottoms, too.

Tool Box

A.F. socket spanners. Pliers. Medium and large points of crosshead screwdrivers. Angle grinder with flexible pad (can be hired from tool-hire stores). Hammer. Hacksaw. Impact screwdriver or wrench. Wooden-topped bench or large sheet of timber on the floor. Welding equipment. Tin snips.

Safety

Clear protective goggles. Protective gloves. Follow usual safety procedures when either electric or gas welding. Remember that cut edges or slivers of steel sheet can be razor sharp.

DR1. With a crosshead screwdriver, remove door handle, window winder handle, door pull, door trim and padded waist rail. Place smaller parts in a labelled plastic bag. Remove plastic liner (where fitted) from behind door trim panel by peeling it away from the door. Keep for later use.

DR2. Remove quarterlight by unscrewing, with a crosshead screwdriver, the two screws securing the quarterlight frame at the base of the door.

DR6. Here John Hill has chosen to leave the quarterlight in place until after the door has been removed. Undo the three crosshead screws holding each hinge to the door using a large point screwdriver. They are usually stubborn and John uses a wrench to gain more purchase on his screwdriver.

Figure 2. Early Roadster door interior.

1 Ventilator securing nuts
2 Regulator securing bolts
3 Regulator arm stop
4 Door lock remote control securing screws
5 Regulator extension securing set screws
6 Front door glass mounting bracket securing screws
7 Rear door glass mounting bracket securing screws
8 Door glass channel securing screws

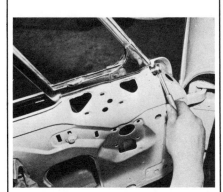

DR3. Undo the two nuts situated beneath the quarterlight through the apertures shown.

DR5. The glass can now be tilted and lifted high out of the door. Wrap it in a cloth and store it safely.

DR4. Remove the plastic grommet and undo the nut securing the quarterlight found there. Undo the four bolts holding the winder mechanism in place (Fig 2, item 2) and the four bolts holding the winder mechanism extension (Fig 2, item 5), slide the steel wheel found on the end of the regulator arm out of its runner on the bottom of the window glass. Lift the glass by hand and remove the winder mechanism. (Let it lie in the bottom of the door, if working alone, and remove it later.) Disconnect the rear channel (Fig 2, items 7 & 8).

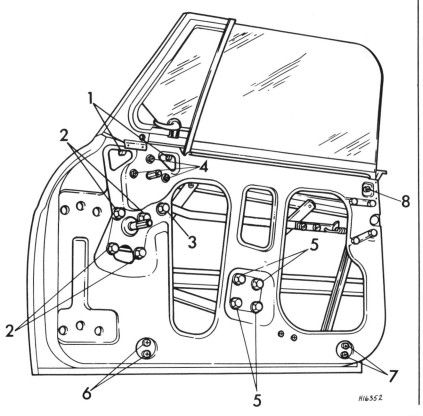

H16352

DR7. Another alternative is to use an impact screwdriver which, when struck with a hammer, imparts a twisting force upon the stubborn screw which is virtually irresistable. Ensure that the screw head is clean before use.

N.b. The hinges are best left fitted to the door pillars. In addition to the four visible screws holding them in place, they are each also secured by a large nut only accessible by someone with very long arms from inside the wings after the mudshields have been removed!

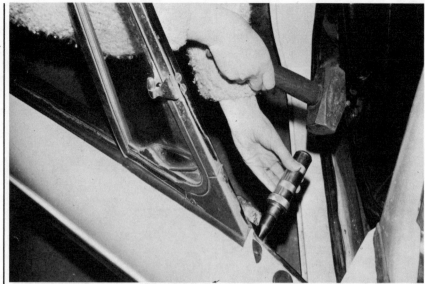

DR8. The door is drawn off the hinge straps by pulling it outwards and away from the hinge pillar.

DR10. Continue up each side and then, wearing heavy gloves, strip off the redundant flange.

DR12(A). Quite often the bottom of the door is sound. If not, mark out the rusted area so that it can be cut away.

DR9. The door skin is held to the body of the door by a simple fold rather like an elongated version of the flap on an envelope. This runs down both sides and across the bottom of the door. Using a mini angle grinder (or a sharp file and plenty of elbow grease!) grind the edge of the fold.

DR11. The only place where the door skin is welded is across the quarterlight fixing area. Simply cut straight through the middle with a hacksaw.

DR12(B). Door base repair sections come complete with curved end pieces welded in place.

DR13. A strong oxidising flame on a welding torch will make a surprisingly neat cut, especially if cleaned up later with the angle grinder. Otherwise use a Monodex-type cutter or power jigsaw with metal cutting blade. A cold chisel would probably distort the door frame.

DR14. This is the door skin and base repair panel as offered by John Hill. The base panel includes both bottom corners but if a little more of the door has rotted, it can be built up from flat sheet steel.

DR16. It is important to ensure an accurate fit. The panel should be lightly tack welded and tapped back into position as it distorts before being fully welded up.

DR18. The door skin is placed upon the floor, flanges upwards . . .

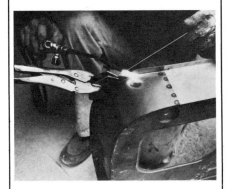

DR15. The repair panel is firmly clamped into place (or held with pop-rivets or self-tapping screws) and welded onto the existing door mainframe.

DR17. The opportunity should now be taken to paint the inside of the main frame (after removing any existing surface rust) and the inside of the new door skin, too.

DR19. . . . the door frame is placed on top and the whole assembly placed upon a wooden board. The upright flange should be tapped inwards a few degrees all the way round.

DR20.   The fold should be continued a little at a time going around the whole length of the flange time and again. If the folding process is not done as evenly as possible the metal will stretch with a real risk of kinking taking place.

DR23.   The repaired door can now be refitted to the car. Hinge screws should not be fully tightened until the door gear has been fitted so that correct door and quarterlight alignment can be ensured.

DR24.   MGB doors rust from the inside-out. Even doors as badly rusted as this one in the foreground can be brought back to the condition of the one fitted to the 'B behind it.

DR21.   To achieve a really tidy looking fold free of hammer marks, finish off with a piece of wood, as shown. Note how the door has been tipped during the whole process in such a way that the part being hammered has always been in contact with the board beneath it.

Having repaired the door it would be advisable to seal out as much water as possible by fitting a new window sealing strip.

The new door skin will have to be drilled to match the holes in the new strip which is simply pop-rivetted into place. See the section on "Finishing and Painting" for information on how to refit chrome trim and how to re-paint the door. It would be advisable to paint the door before refitting it if its rebuild is not part of a total restoration.

While fitting a new door skin is not incredibly complex or expensive it is, of course, fairly time consuming. You can avoid ever having to do it again by religiously following the advice on anti-corrosion treatment given elsewhere in this book.

DR25.   Door splits cannot be repaired with filler! All that happens is that the filler is pushed straight back out again within a day or two. Fitting a door mirror which bolts through the panel can help to cut down the risk of splitting — those which are fitted with self-tapping screws won't help, though.

DR22.   The skin only requires welding at the position of the quarterlight mountings. Note how even this small area has been clamped to avoid distortion. If the door frame has been accidentally distorted, or if the folding has not made the door quite rigid enough there is no reason why the replacement skin should not be tack welded in three or four places inside the folds.

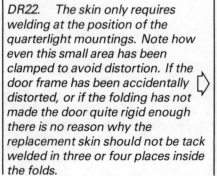

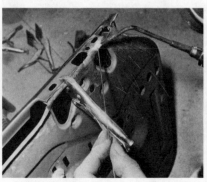

Windscreen Glass Replacement (Roadster)

Tool Box

Once the frame is removed: a crosshead screwdriver; a couple of blunt straight point screwdrivers for easing rubbers into place; washing-up liquid and a brush;

62

woodworkers' sash cramp are all that are needed — unless any screws have to be drilled out in which case an electric drill, sharp bit and coolant will be needed.

Safety

Always take care when handling glass — wear gloves. Removing broken glass is especially hazardous but new glass can crack if handled carelessly.

Nowadays, many insurance policies include something they call "windscreen cover" as an added bonus. However, many drivers are still not covered by this type of policy in which case a broken screen can shatter the bank balance, too. Both they and others who wish to convert to laminated or tinted windscreen could do worse than follow the advice given by Windscreen Services Ltd. of Worcester who fitted a new screen for the author, the screen having been removed from the car and taken to the specialists for their attention. If you wish to be your own "specialist" take special note that the tougher and much safer laminated glass is less forgiving when being worked with than the toughened variety and tends to split if not handled carefully.

Following the first part of the section entitled "Front Wing Removal" for details of how to remove the screen with frame from the car. Then . . .

WS2.   Take out the two outer crosshead screws from each end of the top rail of the frame. Note the two rivets by the fitter's left hand — on later cars these are screws, too, which should be left in place.

WS3.   It is not unusual to find an immovable screw. When this happens, the only recourse is to drill off the screw head, drill out the remainder of the screw after the frame has been disassembled and clean up the thread with a tap.

WS4.   Bottom screws (2 each side) are found beneath the rubber sealing strip which must first be pulled out of its seating and removed.

WS5.   The side frame slots into the top and bottom rails and can be pulled off with all the screws removed. Top and bottom screws are of different lengths — make a note of where they come from!

⇨

WS1.   The bottom bracket of the centre steady will have been disconnected when the screen was removed. Take off the domed nut which holds the top of the steady to the frame bracket.

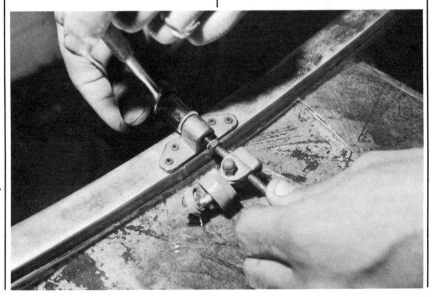

WS6.   Frame joints are often tight and have to be tapped apart with a wooden mallet.

WS7.   With both side frames removed, pull off the top rail, starting at one end and pulling the sealing rubber out of the frame as it is removed.

WS8.   Remove the bottom rail in the same way. Note how a padded stool makes an ideal "work surface".

WS9.   Take off the sealing rubber taking care not to be cut by any pieces of broken glass . . .

WS10.   . . . and clean all the old, hardened sealer from the rubber.

WS11.   Take this opportunity to clean the frame and to grease threads before reassembly. Remember that care must be taken not to twist the screen and so cause it to crack.

WS12.   Use a proprietary brand of screen sealer (available from motor factors) and inject a bead of sealer into each side of the rubber strip which has now been placed around the new screen.

WS13.   Brush liquid detergent (washing-up liquid) around the outer edge of the rubber sealer . . .

WS14.   . . . and also inside the top and bottom rail channels.

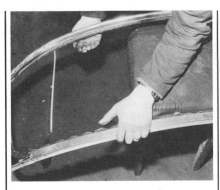

WS15.   Push top and bottom rails onto the rubbers (ease them on slowly). They will push out the excess sealer as they go.

WS18.   If it is found difficult to pull the top and bottom rails sufficiently together, use a woodworkers sash cramp, but tighten SLOWLY – give the excess sealer time to ooze out.

WS21.   The bottom rail to car body sealing rubber has to be fitted properly with the contours of the rubber fitting the contours of the bottom of the frame and the lip shown held open here, wrapped around the edge of the frame.

WS16.   Slot the side rails into place.

WS19.   Replace top and bottom screws. Make absolutely certain that the correct screw lengths are used in the corresponding holes.

WS22.   Only apply liquid detergent to the frame if the rubber will not go in dry. If it goes in too easily, it will come out easily as well.

WS17.   Ensure that the screw holes line up properly. Bang the side rails into place with the open hand if necessary.

WS20.   Scrape off the excess sealer from around the screen. Paraffin (kerosene) used on a rag will remove what remains.

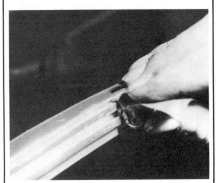

WS23.   Slide the leading edge of the rubber into the slot on the bottom of the frame and push it to the end.

WS24. *Work the rest of the rubber into place with a blunt screwdriver. You can see why Windscreen Services only employ fitters with four hands!*

WS25. *Apply a good, heavy bead of screen sealer towards the front of the rubber . . .*

WS26. *. . . place the rubber corner seals in place and apply more sealer to the bottom of the corner rubber before refitting to the car.*

Body Finishing and Spraying

It is the oldest truism in the bodyshop that the quality of a newly sprayed car's finish depends on the quality of the body preparation that was carried out before the car went near the spray booth. This is as true of an MGB as of any other car — perhaps more so than most because every 'B ought to be something of a "looker". Moreover, it would be a terrible shame if a car on which a great deal of time, effort and money has been spent was let down by second-class finishing.

The major problems are two-fold for the home restorer. Firstly, the higher quality the respray, the *more* blemishes and ripples beneath the surface will show up. A mirror-like finish exposes every slight undulation and poorly prepared bodywork becomes a dreadful and obvious eyesore. And secondly, (and really, this is the reverse of the former problem) surfaces which are matt such as those left by filler or paint primer disguise blemishes and ripples, making it absolutely essential that correct techniques are used to ensure a truly flat, smooth surface, after a new panel or repair panel has been fitted.

There is very little involved in the finishing and spraying of the MGB that is not common to all other cars and so the information given here is something in the nature of an overview of the procedures involved.

The steps shown here apply to finishing and spraying following rebuild but they apply equally to the respraying of a complete car with sound bodywork or even to the respray of a single panel; simply miss out those steps not relevant.

It cannot be over-emphasised that a good class respray cannot be carried out without the removal of all trim, lights and ancillaries. In order to achieve the very highest quality respray it will be necessary even to remove all the old paint, but unless Concours trophies are the aim this highly time consuming process is by no means essential.

It is well worth going to the trouble of ensuring that working conditions are "right". Achieving a truly flat, ripple-free finish is impossible unless the work area is adequately lit and the presence of even a small amount of dust or damp laden air can ruin a respray. There can hardly be better, or more pleasant circumstances in which to prepare a car's bodywork for respray than out of doors on a warm summer's day — although every silver lining has a cloud round it, for hot sun can cause problems with filler going "off" too quickly and airborne dust and flies with a kamikaze attraction for sticky cellulose mean that the actual spraying is usually best carried out indoors with plenty of light and ventilation.

Tool Box

Sanding rubber (for folding abrasive paper around — available motor factors or stores); single-cut file; coarse production paper; coarse to fine grades of wet or dry or equivalent all-dry papers (*e.g.* 200, 400, 500 grades); wooden block around which to wrap production paper; Perspex (Plexiglas) straight-edge (or similar); plastic-based filler; good quality primer/filler; top coat; thinners; the best spray equipment available; masking tape; newspaper; plenty of light, from all angles.

Safety

Principal dangers come from: filler dust (ESPECIALLY when fibreglass strands are mixed in). Use a mask when sanding — and remember not to work near children or pets — and from dust and fumes when spraying. ALWAYS use a suitable mask and ensure that the work area is well ventilated. Thinners presents a fire risk.

BF1. Use an angle-grinder to grind down any high welding beads or an appropriately tough disc on an electric drill to grind back excessively high brass if a brazed joint has been made. Surface rust will form within a very short space of time on the surface of new panels, especially next to the area where welding has been carried out. Any such surface rust MUST be removed before any filler is applied.

Dent and dings, welded or brazed areas and rippled panels will have to be filled smooth. Some prefer to use lead but its use is difficult and time consuming. Plastic filler is an excellent material when used over a sound base.

BF2. Mix the filler according to the manufacturer's instructions. If the weather is hot, filler will go "off" (hard) very quickly indeed. In these circumstances, mix in rather less hardener than normal and mix a small quantity of filler at a time. Ensure that filler and hardener are mixed together thoroughly. Mix the filler on a flexible surface so that hard filler can be "flexed" off but make absolutely sure that no small, hard pieces of old filler are picked up in subsequent mixes of paste — they will cause deep scours in the newly applied surface of the paste as they are pulled along by the spreader.

BF3. Spread the filler carefully and as evenly as possible over the surface to be flattened.

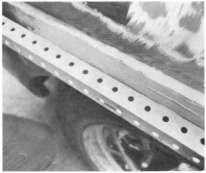

BF4. If the surface receiving attention is fairly level, use some sort of straight-edge (NOT the Perspex (plexiglas) straight-edge) to roughly check this first layer of filler for level while it is still soft. Add extra filler to the low points.

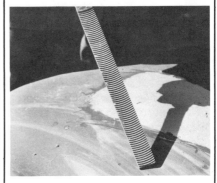

BF5. A good, sharp file will remove filler rapidly and easily and is capable of producing a fairly flat surface. Use it in alternating directions so as not to produce ripples on the filler.

BF6.   An electric drill mounted sanding disc removes filler even more quickly but great care has to be taken not to produce ridges. It is advisable to always take off the last skim of filler with a hand held body file or sanding block.

BF7.   Orbital sanding paper can be used with a rubbing block or with a large, flat sheet of wood. Alternatively a belt sander belt, with a large wooden block slotted in to it gives an even flatter finish although it is more cumbersome in use.

BF8.   Obtain or make a really straight straight-edge from Perspex (plexiglas) or some other flexible material. Flex it against the contour of the new or filled panel and check for rippling.

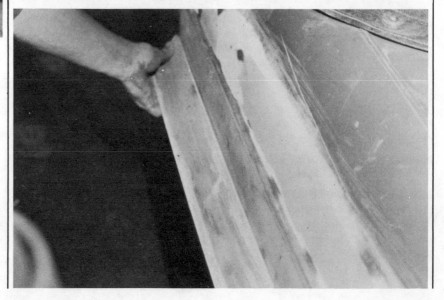

BF9.   Check also in the horizontal plane. It is surprising how many small imperfections this method will reveal. Carefully fill any imperfections revealed, this time spreading on a much smaller amount of filler . . .

BF10. . . . and flat down once again. Here a proprietary tool is used for gripping appropriately sized production paper.

BF11. Where a moulding such as that above the chrome strip over the rear wheel arch has to be shaped with filler — when a rear wing bottom panel is replaced, for instance — it is a good idea to place a line of masking tape along the line of the moulding as a guide.

BF12. To sand the inside of a concave curve, roll the production paper into a tube of the correct curvature.

BF13. When the panel has been made flat and true, the score marks left by earlier stages should be removed. Use a coarse grade of wet-or-dry or one of the newer types of dry rubbing paper wrapped around a block similar to the one shown upon the MGB bonnet. Such paper is made to be economically folded into four before being cut into strips, each strip then exactly fitting the rubbing block and its grips.

BF14.   If a new panel has been fitted before spraying, now is the time to drill holes for the chrome trim fixings: after spraying, a slipping drill could wreak havoc!

Carefully take note of the position of the rest of the trim and body mouldings and mark out along the centre line of the trim to be fitted.

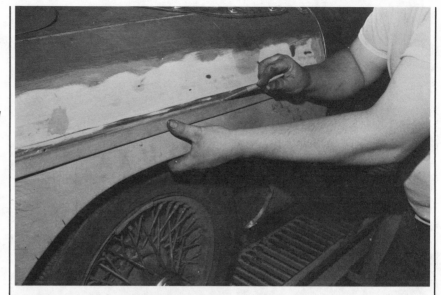

BF15.   Lightly centre punch and drill (⅛ inch) at approximately 6 inch intervals along this line. For the time being no more needs to be done.

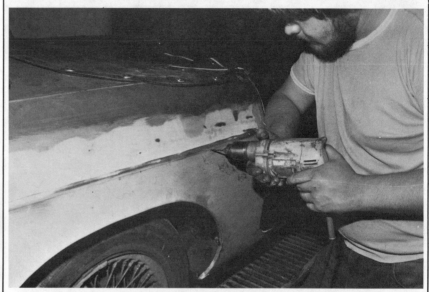

BF16.   Now that the panel is flat, true and smooth a coat of primer/filler should be sprayed on. Mask off any areas such as wheels or adjacent panels which are not receiving attention.

BF17.   Flat-off with an intermediate then with a fine grade of wet-or-dry leaving the panel really smooth.

BF18.   Here the car is shown ready for spraying in a professional spray booth. It is self-contained with heating, all-round lighting, a tidy, dust-free layout and an air extraction system beneath the car – to draw particles down and away from the bodywork. With the exception of the latter point the home sprayer should attempt to emulate these conditions as closely as possible. A useful tip is to spray water onto the garage floor using a watering can before the car is brought in. This tends to stop dust rising and being deposited on the car as the sprayer moves around it.

BF19.   First of all, spray the insides of the doors and the door shut panels on both sides.

BF20.   Partly close the doors, but leave them slightly ajar and go to one of the rear quarters. Spray in lines reaching front-to-back, covering the whole rear of the car, one overlapping strip after another.

BF21.   Spray the side, one panel at a time, following the same front-to-back pattern . . .

BF22. . . . working in lines, from the bottom-up. (Note the spray in the air here, making an adequate face mask absolutely essential to health. Protective clothing is also advisable.)

BF23. The same spray pattern is continued up and down the bonnet and along the other side. The second coat, however, is entirely put on AT RIGHT ANGLES to the first, experience proving that this gives the best cover. Subsequent coats are applied as desired, each at right angles to the last, rubbing down with fine grade paper between coats if necessary.

BF24. Once the spraying is finished it's time to put trim and ancillaries back in place, such as chrome strip clips which are held on with pop rivets.

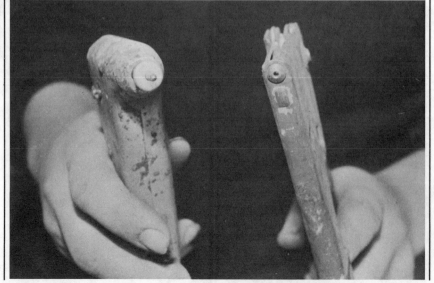

BF25. One of the clips is shown here ready and placed upon a pop rivet on the gun on the left. It CANNOT be applied with the type of gun shown on the right. Its nose is too short to reach inside the dish of the clip.

BF28. Other fittings such as lights, badges and number plates can now be fitted but take this opportunity to paint, rust-proof and preserve each part before it is fitted back into place; much of it out of sight, out of mind, but not out of the way of corrosion!

BF29. The author, sitting in his newly rebuilt '69 Roadster is highly delighted with the results, the outcome of a great deal of planning, effort, and yes — expenditure, although the one sure way to keep the cost down is to do-it-yourself and perhaps farm out the more complex work having done as much preparation as possible at home. It is important the no one should be blinded by the light of mystique in which most professionals like to surround their work — ANYONE can do ANYTHING if they are prepared to work at it, but for most people the pleasure is gained from obtaining a useable end result within a reasonable amount of time and it is strongly advised that the owner considers farming out at least the final stages of jobs which are most complex or skill-based or which require sophisticated equipment.

For others, and the author has included himself among their number, the only real satisfaction comes from doing it ALL themselves.

More strength to their elbows!

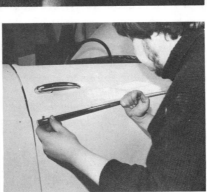

BF26. Once the clips are in place, the trim is lined up with them and hooked over the end clip from beneath . . .

BF27. . . . before being lightly "popped" onto the clips, one by one with the clenched fist, as shown.

Rust Prevention

Having spent a great deal of time and money on rebuilding an MGB's bodywork — or on finding and buying that elusive 'B with the beautiful body — it would be the height of folly to allow the action of the elements to eat into your investment. Even cars which are never taken out in the wet weather and are stored in a heated garage will, without fail, rust from the inside-out as water vapour from the air condenses on the inner panel surfaces. (Just about the only exceptions to this rule are those cars kept in the driest states of the U.S., Australia or similar areas).

Sometimes cars are "protected" against rust when, shortly after new delivery, rust inhibiting fluid is injected into their box-sections. This is often shown to be worse than useless and should not be relied upon to give lasting protection. There is no substitute for a conscientious DIY-job by the enthusiast owner. The process detailed here should be regarded as body-servicing and carried out, religiously every year. It ought to take almost a whole day to do this job properly, but the consolation to be gained is that the car will be as corrosion-free as it is possible to make it.

Several rust inhibitors are on the market usually with their own applicator, but the author has only had experience of Waxoyl and this is fairly pleasant to use, easy to clean off with white spirit and harmless to paintwork and trim.

No detailed guidance has been given on the use of conventional underseal. Many people prefer to paint the underside of their car after steam-cleaning it, while others prefer to spray on oil. Provided that the underside is steam-cleaned, inspected and re-treated every year it really does not matter which system is used. Most corrosion comes from *inner* sections and these will be protected if the prevention sequence is followed.

Tool Box

2 gallons of Waxoyl or similar protectant will be needed to give a first treatment. Protectant applicator kit. Electric drill, bit and appropriate grommets. Jack and axle stands or ramps.

Safety

Remember the safety rules about working underneath a car. Most protectants are flammable particularly before drying out — make sure that ALL welding is complete before treating the car. Otherwise when welding near newly applied protectant an internal fire can start which will be very, very difficult to put out.

RP1. Finnigan's Waxoyl (available in U.K.) has been found to work effectively by the author and other countries must have similar proprietary products. It is a yellow, waxy liquid which dries to a firm film. At average British temperatures it is generally found to be too thick to spray but standing it in a bowl of hot water makes it much thinner. In cold weather it is easier to use if thinned down with white spirit (turpentine substitute).

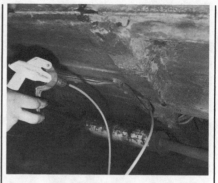

RP2. Finnigan's sell an applicator which consists of a gun, or pump, which pulls fluid out of the can, along a pipe and then through the injector pipe. At the end of the injector pipe is a 360° spray nozzle. Here, the crossmember is being injected with fluid through one of the existing holes. The injector pipe is pushed into the hole and right along to one end of the crossmember. It is then withdrawn slowly while copious amounts of fluid are injected into the member. The pipe is then re-inserted in the opposite direction and the process repeated.

It is a simple matter to test the gun's spray pattern by constructing a short cardboard "box-section" and spraying fluid into it. This can be opened up and the quantity of fluid injected examined, if separate blobs have been deposited, thin the fluid down with white spirit.

The side rails which extend forwards from the crossmember should be injected in the same way. It may be necessary to drill a hole on some cars. The gearbox crossmember is usually protected by stray engine oil but should have fluid sprayed onto its top surface in the case of clean cars.

RP3. The applicator comes with an optional spray nozzle which screws onto the gun. This should be used to spray fluid behind both front and rear aprons.

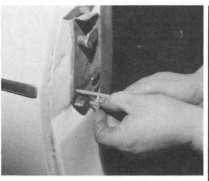

RP5. The door shut pillar can be approached by removing the trim behind the pillar. Alternatively, remove a door catch screw and insert the injector pipe first up then down, injecting fluid in both directions.

RP6. Most cars have a hole in the top of the outer sill (body rocker) as shown. Insert the injector pipe and inject fluid in both directions.

RP7. A hole drilled in the outer sill at the rear of the door opening will have to be plugged with a grommet as it is fully visible. It does have the advantage that the drill has to pass through both the swept-forward part of the door pillar (visible) and the recessed part of the outer sill (hidden) and so the small gap between them can be injected with fluid if the pipe is positioned with care.

RP4. The wedge-shaped boxes which live at the tops of the inner-wing areas should be very thoroughly sprayed with fluid as they are very prone to corrosion. They are not always this accessible, dependant on the model of car and how much equipment is in the way. It may be necessary to use the injector pipe (n.b. This box usually rusts from the outside; it should be regularly hosed off from under the wing). The underside of the flange to which the wings bolt and the joint between the flange and the wing should also be sprayed.

RP8.   Insert the pipe around the door hinges to inject the hinge pillar. The long inner-sill is injected after drilling a hole beneath the rubber or carpet near the door hinge pillar . . .

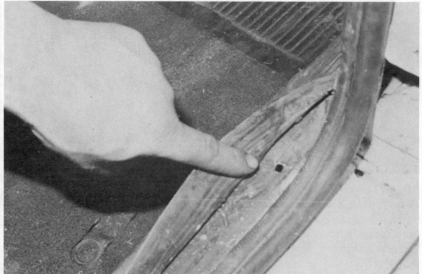

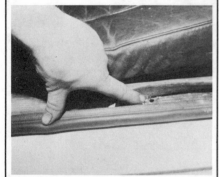

RP9.   . . . and near the line of the seat backrest.

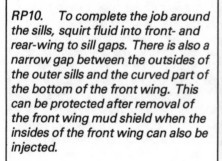

RP10.   To complete the job around the sills, squirt fluid into front- and rear-wing to sill gaps. There is also a narrow gap between the outsides of the outer sills and the curved part of the bottom of the front wing. This can be protected after removal of the front wing mud shield when the insides of the front wing can also be injected.

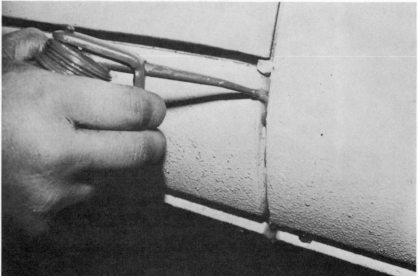

RP11.   Chassis rails running inside the boot have to be drilled before the pipe can be inserted.

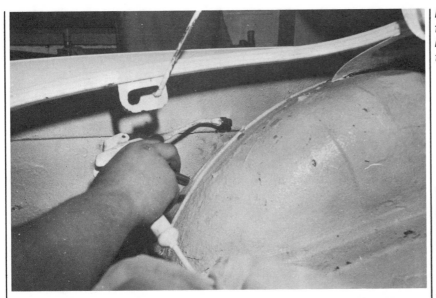

RP12. Squirt copious amounts of fluid all around the joint between inner and outer wing as found inside the boot.

RP13. "Hull" shapes at the base of the rear lights are prone to rusting and, again, are approached from inside the boot.

RP14. The injector tube can be threaded through the bootlid bracings via the boot lock aperture.

RP15. In the case of the GT, the different side- and cross-member structure will require injection through the holes which are, in most cases, already provided. The tailgate door must also be injected.

RP16. Although aluminium bonnets do not need to be injected (except the MGC's which corrodes where the trim and badges are fitted) steel bonnets can be injected through existing holes in most cases.

RP17. Doors are best protected after removal of the trim panel. The door-skin fold should also be sprayed with fluid.

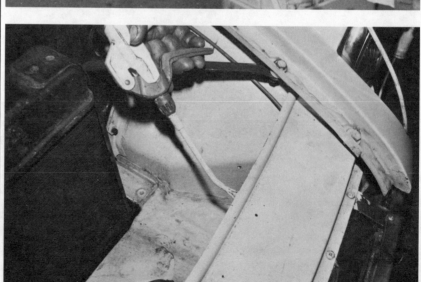

RP18. The panel onto which the bonnet shuts and the section beneath it onto which the oil-cooler is bolted should be protected from beneath.

RP19. Front and rear bumpers should be thoroughly sprayed after scraping off any mud which may have accumulated there.

RP20. Over-riders are expensive to replace and should also be protected.

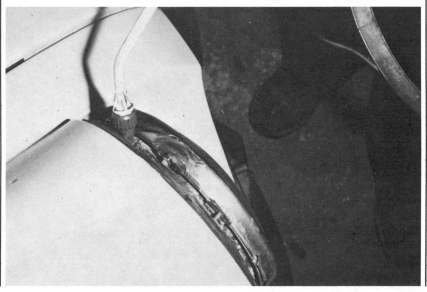

RP21. After removal of the headlamp bezel, fluid can be injected around the headlamp bowl. If there is any doubt that fluid is reaching its target, take out the headlamp. Inject fluid between the wing and headlamp bowl flange, too.

RP22. Before replacing the bezel, coat its inner face with fluid.

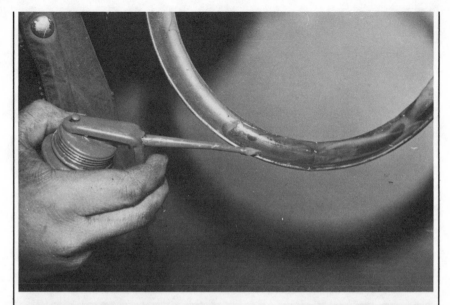

RP23. Inject fluid into the heater plenum chamber.

RP24. Carefully run fluid behind all badges, trim and chrome trim using the oil can.

4 Interior & Hood

This is probably the area which most worries d.i.y. enthusiasts. The reason is simple enough to understand. Someone with an aptitude for working with solid materials can be forgiven for feeling intimidated by flapping plastic hood material or seat fabric. For that reason, the stages shown here are even more detailed than for other sections of the book — no foreknowledge of the use of these materials has been assumed. The section on seat re-covering is lengthy and detailed, not because the task is difficult but because it happens to contain a large number of small, easy steps with which the great majority of enthusiasts are unfamiliar.

Steering Wheel Removal

Tool Box

Two hammers; the correct size socket to remove the steering wheel nut (usually but not always 1⅛ inch); an extra pair of hands!

Safety

AT LEAST one of the two hammers should be of soft metal. Two toughened steel hammers hammered together can throw off splinters of hardened steel at enormous velocity with obvious danger to eyesight.

SWR1. Snap away the centre of the wheel, or take out the grub screw from the side of the wheel boss and remove the horn push (earlier models). Undo the nut until level with the top of the column. One person pulls the wheel with hands and knees while the other person holds the soft hammer just a little way away from the top of the steering column while striking it as hard as possible with the second hammer. The wheel usually pops free after several such blows.

Fascia (Dashboard) Removal

Several different styles of fascia have been fitted to U.S.-market MGBs for cars in this category. The following removal instructions can only provide a guide to their removal.

Safety

The rear of an MGB fascia is a knitting box of wires and cables. Careless disconnection could cause instant fire at any point. ALWAYS disconnect the battery(ies) before working on the fascia.

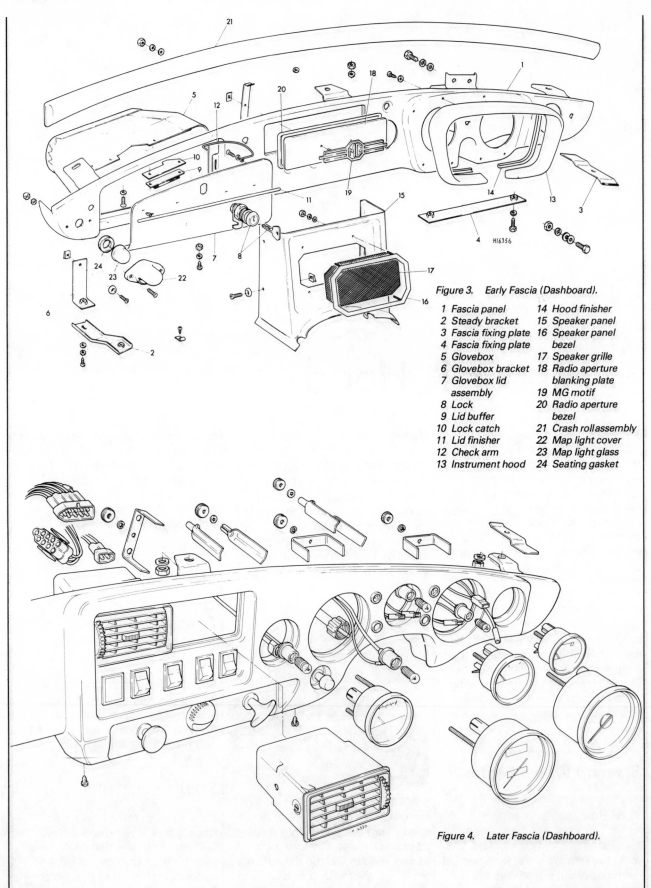

Figure 3. Early Fascia (Dashboard).

1 Fascia panel
2 Steady bracket
3 Fascia fixing plate
4 Fascia fixing plate
5 Glovebox
6 Glovebox bracket
7 Glovebox lid assembly
8 Lock
9 Lid buffer
10 Lock catch
11 Lid finisher
12 Check arm
13 Instrument hood
14 Hood finisher
15 Speaker panel
16 Speaker panel bezel
17 Speaker grille
18 Radio aperture blanking plate
19 MG motif
20 Radio aperture bezel
21 Crash roll assembly
22 Map light cover
23 Map light glass
24 Seating gasket

Figure 4. Later Fascia (Dashboard).

The early dashboard
(See Fig 3)

1) Remove the speaker panel (15), disconnect the steering column and lower it.

2) Remove the heater controls by pressing in the plungers in their shanks. Undo the nuts which hold the controls in place and pull them out from behind the fascia.

3) Disconnect the choke cable, the oil pressure pipe and the screenwasher pump.

4) Undo the dashboard mountings at 2, 3 and 4 and at A, B, C and D. Pull the dashboard forwards and disconnect wires and lamps, labelling them as they are disconnected to assist later re-assembly. (Pieces of masking tape can be used to tag wire ends and can be written on clearly in biro).

5) Carefully and slowly lift the dashboard away, feeling and looking carefully for wires or other fittings which may have been missed.

The later dashboard
(See Fig 4)

1) The lower fascia panels should first be removed (three retaining screws) and the two fixing screws removed from the lower edge of the dashboard. Unscrew the securing nuts on the heater control knobs and remove the knobs and controls. Disconnect the choke cable at the carburettor.

2) Take out the tachometer (rev. counter): Undo the knurled fixing nuts, remove the earth wire and the bridge-shaped retaining bracket. Disconnect the wiring.

3) Take off the trip recorder reset knob by removing its retaining nut.

4) Each end of the fascia is held with screws, which have to be removed, and the fascia top is held with six fixing studs from which the nuts must be removed.

5) Pull the fascia away, disengaging the top fixing studs. Take care to lift it clear of the steering column switch. Remove the switch wiring and tag each lead for identification as previously described.

Seat Re-covering

Most people who work on their cars are quite at home with mechanical components, are willing to tackle bodywork but fight shy of any kind of re-upholstery work. Most upholstery jobs *can* be successfully carried out at home provided that work is carried out methodically and carefully — just as though body panels are being worked upon, but with soft, deformable sheet materials being used rather than hard, stiff metal sheet.

The cost of having a worn seat re-trimmed can be very high indeed and so this is the area which is perhaps the most profitable for a beginner to develop and exercise his or her skills.

The basic principles involved are the same no matter which type of cover is fitted. In the UK John Hill's re-upholstery kits are available for every type of seat, even leather (although these kits *are*, naturally, rather expensive) but unfortunately some of the original colours are no longer available.

Information on re-covering an MGB seat is not available anywhere other than in these pages and therefore what follows is a highly detailed step-by-step guide to what is involved.

Tool Box

Straight point screwdriver; Crosshead screwdriver; Soft-faced mallet; Pop-rivet gun and long-head pop-rivets; Sharp scissors; Craft knife; Delayed-set contact adhesive (*i.e.* one with "shuffling" time — to allow for adjustment); Paint brush; Pencil; Light hammer; Boxes for keeping clips and fittings in after removal.

Safety

Contact adhesive is highly flammable and also gives off dangerous vapour. Always work in a well ventilated area.

SE1(A).   Slide the seat to be re-covered back along its runners as far as it will go. A soft-faced hammer may be found useful!

SE1(B).   Remove the screw in each runner holding them to the floor. Slide the seat to the foremost position and remove the equivalent screws at the rear. Lift out the seat, remove runners and the various packing pieces left on the floor for safe keeping.

SE2. Place the seat on a table or bench with its base uppermost and begin removing the spring clips holding the upholstery to the frame tube.

SE3(A). Often an over-cover has been slipped on and held with the same clips. This has to come off first.

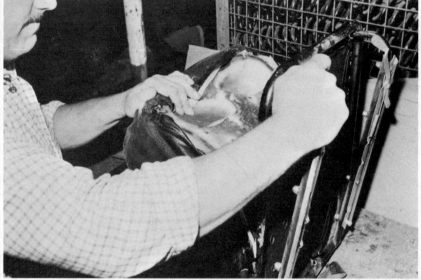

SE3(B). With all clips removed — including those from the rear of the seat — the foam rubber squabs and cover can be peeled away from the base and removed.

SE4. The rubber diaphragm is held to the frame tubing via spring clips. Short, thin steel rods are pushed into thickened edges of the diaphragm and these often slip out, allowing the seat to sag — a point worth checking if the seat feels a little bottomed-out.

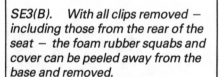
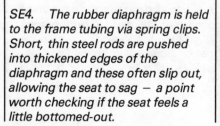

SE5. A rod should bridge the gap shown opened up here — it is through this gap that the spring clip fits.

SE8. The handle itself is usually a tight fit and requires some "persuasion" to remove.

SE11. Lift the bottom fold of the back panel out of the way and remove the spring clips holding the backrest front panel onto its frame tube.

SE6. It is usually possible to simply push the rod back into place but if the diaphragm is badly damaged it will have to be renewed. Don't forget to hook the spring clip back on through the adjacent hole in the steel frame.

SE9. Remove the self-tapping screw which holds the side trim in place a few inches below the back rest adjuster handle.

SE12. Using a craft knife or scissors, cut out the old backrest rear panel.

SE7. Unscrew the crosshead screw holding the seat reclining back rest adjuster handle into place (where fitted).

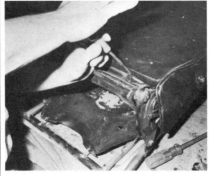

SE10. Unclip the spring clips holding the backrest back panel onto the frame.

SE13. Cut out the metal bezel set into the top of the backrest through which the seat headrest support is slotted (if fitted).

SE14. *Place the scrap of cloth with the bezel set into it onto the bench, turn it over and turn the tabs up which hold it onto its backing plate . . .*

SE15. *. . . leaving the three components as shown. The one in the centre is the now-redundant piece of cloth.*

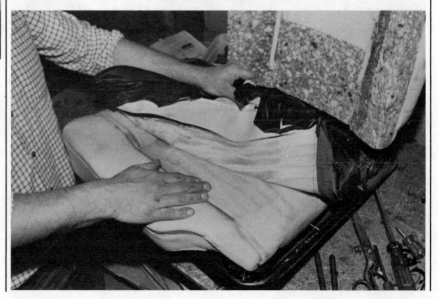

SE16. *Carefully peel the backrest cover from its sponge rubber squab, easing the two apart so that they separate without tearing large chunks out of the squab.*

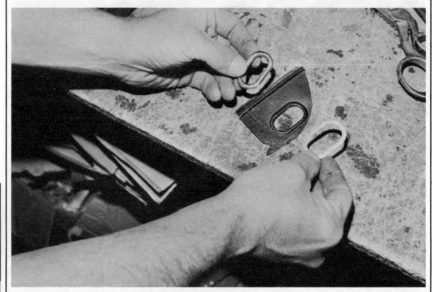

SE17. *Then repeat the procedure with the seat squab and cover.*

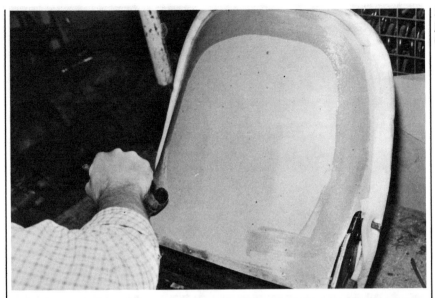

SE18. Coat the outer couple of inches of the rear of the backrest with adhesive . . .

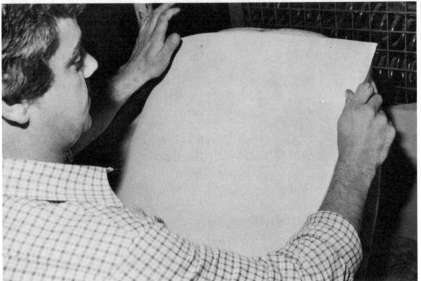

SE19. . . . cut out an appropriately sized rectangle of thin foam, paint the matching surfaces with contact adhesive and stick it in place covering the rear of the backrest.

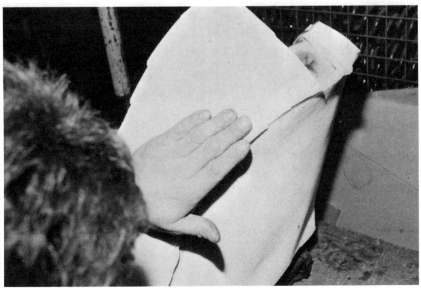

SE20. Trim the foam to the shape of the backrest. It is important to be neat, but engineering accuracy is not essential!

SE21. Glue pieces of thin foam rubber to the edges of the backrest leaving a gap where the headrest slots into place . . .

SE22. . . . and again, trim to shape after fitting. These side pieces should only extend down to just above the recliner shaft (if fitted), or about two thirds of the way down in any case.

SE25. Don't forget to leave that headrest slot clear!

SE28. Push the bezel into place from above . . .

SE23. Coat the top shoulders of the backrest with adhesive and . . .

SE26. Mark with a pencil on the new seat cover the position for the headrest slot bezel which has been removed from the old cover. Draw around the insides of the aperture taking care to locate the exact centre of the cover.

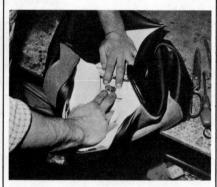

SE29. . . . turn the cover upside down, open it up like a shopping bag on the bench .

SE24. . . . glue on some thin plastic sheet. An unwanted plastic bag, opened up is ideal.

SE27. Carefully and accurately snip out the oval shape you have marked out.

SE30. . . . place the backing plate over the tabs and lightly hammer them down, holding the bezel tightly in place.

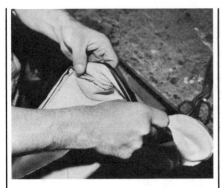

SE31. Turn the whole cover inside out, including the Micky-Mouse ear-shaped flaps at the lower part of each side panel.

SE35. Lick the glue brush into each flap to make sure that the card stays in place.

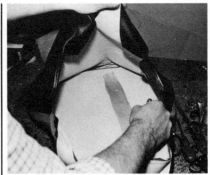

SE37. Brush two equivalent strips down the inside of the backrest cover, but only on the inside of the front panel, matching those on the seat. This gives the cover the correct shape when fitted and prevents it stretching straight across the backrest shoulders.

SE32. Carefully trim off as much of the excess material outside the stitching around each of these flaps.

SE36. Brush a strip of glue about 3 inches wide down each side of the central panel of the front of the backrest.

SE38. Pull the cover onto the seat back.

SE33. Cut out a piece of really thick card to fit snugly into each flap . . .

SE34. . . . and push each one into place.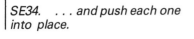

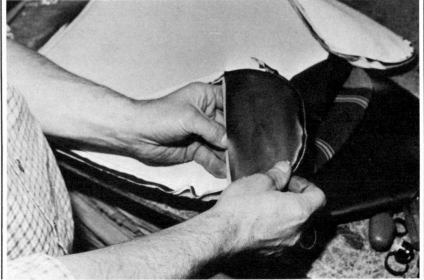

SE39. Ensure that all wrinkles are pulled out. The plastic sheet previously fitted now helps the cover to slide into place.

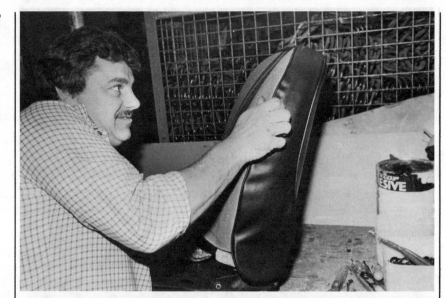

SE40. Remember to push the centre panel strips together. Smooth the cloth down with both hands, starting from the top.

SE41. The backrest back panel has a flap at the bottom which is shown here folded up inside like folding a flap into an envelope.

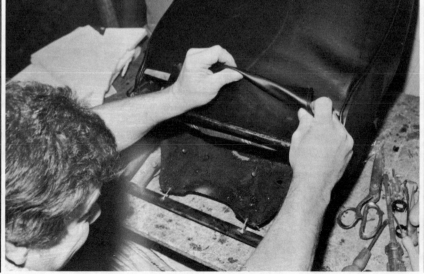

SE42. The flap from the backrest front panel is pulled tightly through, just in front of the rearmost tube.

SE43.   It is folded smoothly around the pivot tube and held in place with spring clips.

SE44.   The excess is then pulled back out . . .

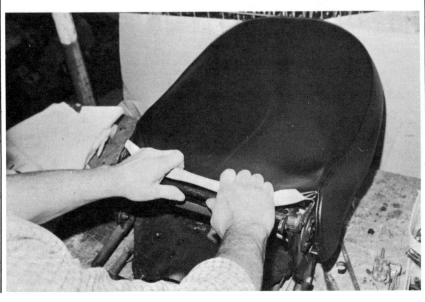

SE45.   . . . and cut off with scissors.

SE46.   The back panel flap is then pulled back out and stretched lightly downwards − but not by so much as to cause stretch marks.

SE47.   This fold is held by spring clips to the innermost of the three tubes and the excess trimmed off as before.

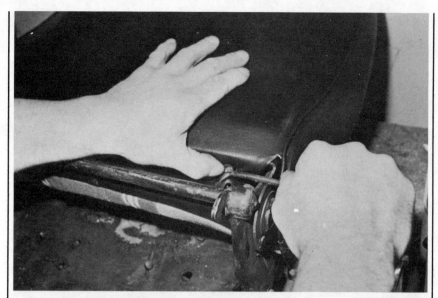

SE48.   Behind the flaps at the bottom of each side panel is a hole from which a self-tapping screw was removed. The position of the hole through the trim is ascertained by measuring and a bradawl or small drill used to make a hole through the thick card which has been glued into place. The screw and cup washer can be replaced or, if preferred, a pop-rivet and washer can be used.

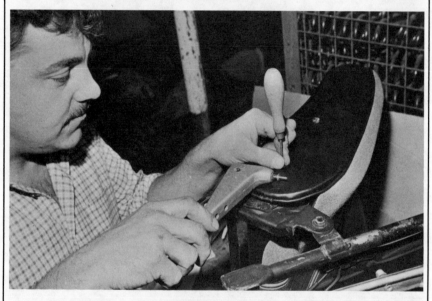

SE49.   The bracket adjuster shaft is found by feeling through the cloth and is then lightly tapped with a hammer. This action neatly and accurately cuts a square out of the cloth exactly matching the shape and size of the adjuster shaft.

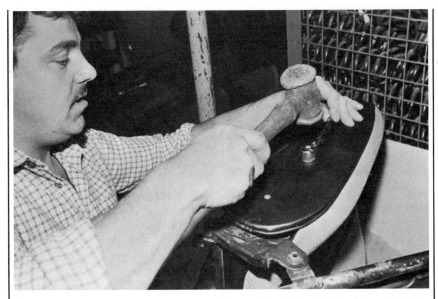

SE50. The adjuster lever is then carefully driven back on with a soft-faced hammer and screwed into place.

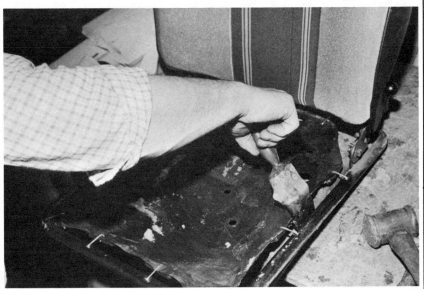

SE51. With the backrest complete brush adhesive around the seat base frame, around a corresponding area on the bottom of the seat squab and glue the squab down onto the frame.

SE52. Cover the entire seat squab with thin foam in the same way as detailed for the backrest. Ensure that the foam is glued down in such a way that it follows the contours of the seat base, and that the side pieces extend to the back of the seat.

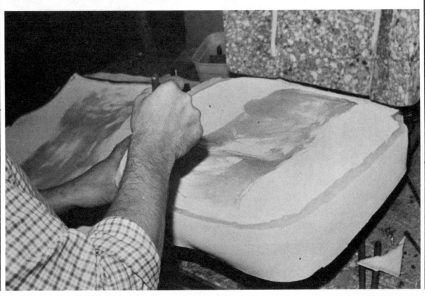

SE53. Apply adhesive to the centre panel of the seat base and to a corresponding area of the seat base cover, after first having turned the cover upside down and inside out.

SE54. Align the rearmost part of the seat cover and drape it forwards.

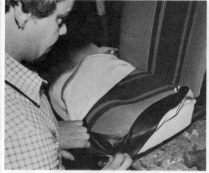

SE57. . . . pulling forward one front corner . . .

SE60. Apply adhesive to this section . . . and fold it under making a neat edge. This shot shows how long the first scissor cuts needed to be.

SE55. Make absolutely certain that the cover is properly aligned all round before . . .

SE58. . . . and then the other, smoothing the edges down as the job is done.

SE61. Work carefully here to ensure a neat finish.

SE56. . . . tucking in the rear flap . . .

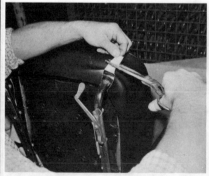

SE59. Snip the cloth in line with the outer edges of the base frame supports and cut off most of the redundant centre section.

SE62. Apply adhesive to the front flap and the front horizontal base tube and glue the flap around the tube. Pull the front sufficiently taut to give a smooth, crease-free finish.

94

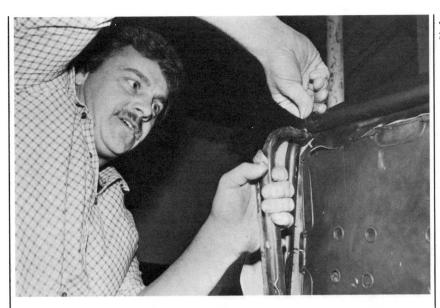

SE63.	Finish off by clipping the front edge down neatly.

SE64.	Cut the side panel at its rear quarter in such a way that the cut is in line with the backrest supporting the tilt pivot.

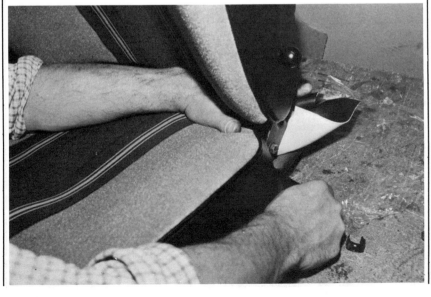

SE65.	Push the back flap through and out of the way.

SE66.   This view is of the seat from below. The position of the cut in the side panel can be seen straddling the backrest tilt pivot. The frontmost section of the side panel is neatly flapped and glued as shown before being clipped down to the side rail.

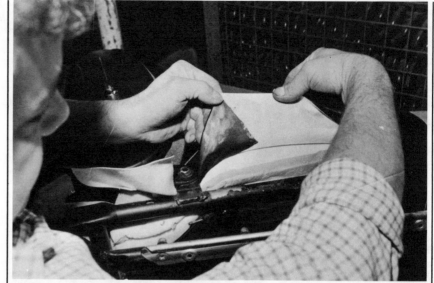

SE67.   The rear flap, protruding between backrest and seat base (with the seat folded forward again) is again flapped at its ends, pulled taut and clipped down.

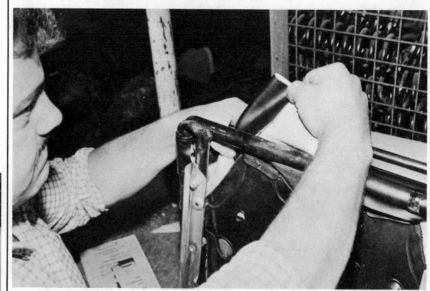

SE68.   Obviously the latch for the catch which holds the seat backrest in place (i.e. when not tipped forward for rear access) must not be covered over. The panel is cut, flapped from both sides to make a tube . . .

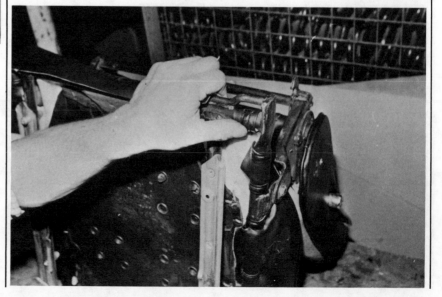

SE69.   . . . wrapped around the seat frame and neatly clipped down leaving the latch clear.

SE70. Steve Langdell, the man who carries out John Hill's MGB Centre's upholstery, looks highly pleased with the finished results.

SE71. Replacement leather covers are so expensive that utilising leather panels from a scrap leather seat makes strong economic sense. Snip the stitching, resisting the temptation to tear it apart – old, brittle leather will rip as easily as card – and sew the replacement into place using twine from an upholsterers or saddlers, passing it through the existing holes.

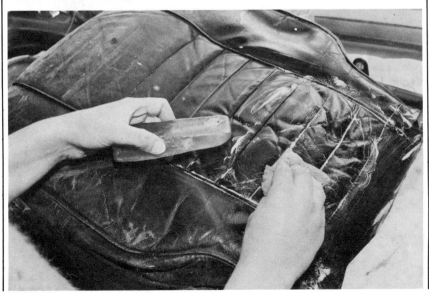

SE72. Old leather can be reconstituted. First, clean it with the foam (and as little water as possible) from saddle soap, applied with a sponge. Then treat the leather to several "sittings" of hide food to restore suppleness. Leather can also be re-coloured with specialist Connolly kits.

97

Carpets – general

Unless you are lucky enough to find some of the originals, matching carpets to the original type is very difficult indeed, especially for the earlier models.

Replacement carpets are widely advertised at very low prices but they are simply not worth having. They fit where they touch and that, often, is not in many places! The alternatives are, unfortunately, none too hopeful. New mass-produced carpets are heat-formed to fit transmission tunnel curvatures and these are all but impossible to reproduce. It is possible to cut darts in the carpets, dressmaker style and to slit and stitch the carpet but some experience is useful here and good quality carpet provides an expensive learning medium.

Regretfully, fitting really top-quality carpets may best be left to an upholsterer, unless top-class replacement carpets can be purchased. If the latter are available, be sure to fit carpet clips (similar to those shown in the "Fitting a Hood" section). Nothing is worse than loose-fitting carpets which slip and slide around the inside of the car.

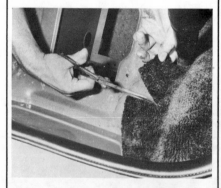

CG1. Where a roll-cage is fitted, carpets all HAVE to be trimmed around it. When carpet material is purchased be sure to buy the non-fray variety. Ordinary domestic carpet is of no use in this respect and foam-backed carpet becomes sodden and its backing quickly disintegrates.

Fitting a Hood

Watching "Smiling" Steve Langdell is a revelation! He makes fitting a hood to an MGB look like child's play – and it's not! But you CAN fit one yourself and avoid a nighmare of sags, draughts and flapping vinyl by working carefully and methodically, as shown in the following step-by-step instructions.

The first job and probably the most important one, is to buy the best hood that you can afford. If you can get an original factory hood the advantages are that it is very likely to fit much better than those made by outside concerns, it may be better made and it will be constructed of the correct material. The disadvantage of a factory fresh hood is that it is likely to cost a great deal. If you have to buy one from one of the hood specialists try, if you can, to avoid buying without seeing first (there are some horribly mis-shapen offerings) and get yourself a hood with the clips and stud fastenings already fitted if possible. The small extra cost saves a lot of work – not to mention the risk of getting it wrong!

Do ensure that the hood is (a) the right one for your car, and (b) that it fits, before removing the old one or attempting to alter the new one. The fit can be checked by the simple expedient of draping and smoothing it over the old, erected hood and checking for shape and size. There will be some useful sized overlaps where the manufacturer has allowed for adjustment during fitting.

Tool Box

Tape Measure; Chalk; Awl; Drill; Screwdrivers (various); Craft knife; Pop-rivet pliers; Delayed set contact adhesive; Glue brush; Light hammer; Scissors.

Safety

Contact adhesive is highly flammable and also gives off dangerous vapour. Always work in a well ventilated area.

H1. Work methodically and – provided that the hood is a good one – there shouldn't be any problem. Choose a warm day so that the vinyl (if that type of hood is being fitted) is supple but avoid the heat of high summer for then the hood will be too soft and easily over-stretched. Laid out in the foreground here are all the materials necessary, plus the two earlier types of hood sticks used prior to the Michelotti design fitted to the subject car.

H2. First step is to open the doors, fold the hood back, remove the rubber cant-rail sealing strip and drill off the pop-rivet heads found beneath.

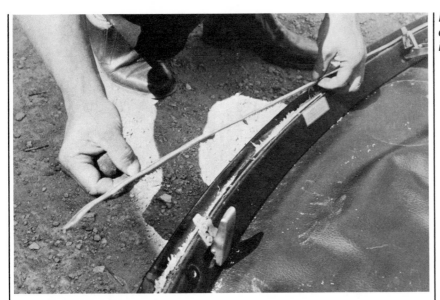

H3.   Lift away the aluminium channel being careful not to distort it.

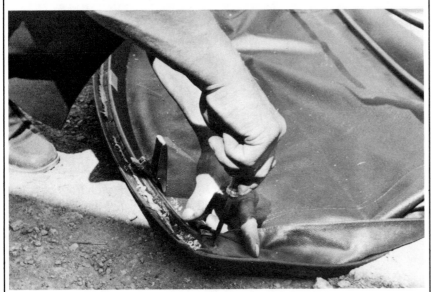

H4.   Unscrew the hood where it is folded and held down to the ends of the cant rail. Only a coat of adhesive stands between cant rail and removal of the front of the hood — peel them apart. Rub the cant rail down and re-paint it to give a smooth finish under the new hood.

H5.   Slip the steel bar (which clips onto the two chrome ''claws'' on the rear bodywork) out from the old hood and, right away slide it into the new hood — before you forget which way round it goes!

H6. Refit the bare cant rail to the top of the screen frame.

H9. Apply glue, with a brush, to the central third of the cant rail . . .

H12. Make absolutely certain that the sides of the hood line up with the closed door glasses.

H7. Clip the rear of the hood in place, after fitting the hood frame (if not Michelotti, in which case it will be attached to the cant rail) . . .

H10. . . . and to the corresponding part of the inside of the hood.

H13. Fold back each front corner, apply glue to it and the cant rail.

H8. . . . and after folding the front-most part of the hood back on itself, measure with a tape and mark the centre of the hood with chalk.

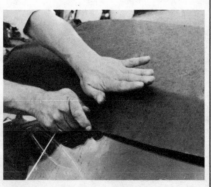

H11. Pull the hood forward, aligning the chalk mark with the windscreen steady bar and ensuring that the hood is taut.

H14. Stretch each corner forwards just enough to get rid of any sags or wrinkles — but not so much that you will need a team of three to close the hood on a cold day when the material has contracted!

H15. Fold the draught excluder corners down onto the cant rail, pierce them with an awl and fit them into place with the crosshead screw and cup washer removed earlier.

H18. Pop-rivet it back down then refit the draught excluder rubber . . .

H21. . . . then cut off the surplus with a craft knife.

H16. Glue the flap at the front onto the face of the cant rail which sits on the top of the screen frame.

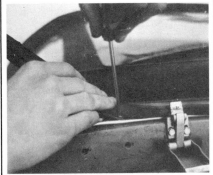

H19. . . . carefully easing it into the channel with the aid of a screwdriver.

H22. Press-stud clips known in the trade as "cocks and hens" . . .

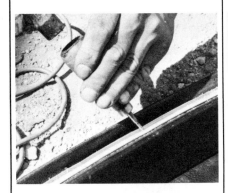

H17. Glue down the draught strip channel in order to prevent leaks behind the strip itself remembering to line up the holes with an awl before the glue dries.

H20. Snip the surplus hood material around the front frame clips . . .

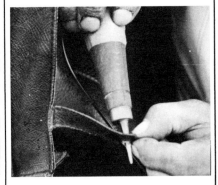

H23. . . . have to be fitted to the tags provided one on each side, at the bottom of the window aperture. First, pierce with an awl . . .

H24. . . . push in the "cock" from beneath, place the "hen" on top and spread the hollow tube on the cock with a centre punch and hammer, using another hammer as an anvil beneath. Although fitting the press-studs with the hood in place is awkward, it is the only way of ensuring that they align with the buttons on the car.

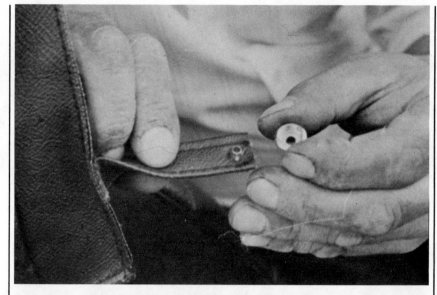

H25. If at all possible, buy a hood with the rear clips already fitted. If this is not possible, pierce the cloth as shown on this sample and push the claw part of the clip into place through the material.

H26. Place the material on the bench with the claws sticking upwards through the material and locate the retaining plate over the claws before bending them inwards with a light hammer.

5 Mechanical Components

Before carrying out any of the restoration jobs listed here, a complete set of tools should be bought or hired — and there will still be money to spare when compared with the cost of having main-dealer work carried out! In addition, a Haynes Owners' Workshop Manual should be regarded as a vital — and inexpensive — part of any toolkit. It gives all the fine detail, dimensions, clearances etc. not included here. This chapter is aimed specifically at the older-car owner who is confronted with dirty, worn and possibly difficult-to-remove components. As a friend of the author's once pointed out, "You should never despair when mechanical things are a problem to repair. You just have to remember that they were built to be taken apart, so you've *got* to win in the end!"

This chapter aims to pick out the problems you are most likely to encounter in advance.

You're almost there!

"Now — take the strain . . ."

Engine/Gearbox Removal & Engine Strip

The following picture sequence demonstrates the removal of the engine alone, followed by removal of the engine and gearbox as a unit. It is not possible to remove the gearbox while leaving the engine in situ.

Clutch replacement can be carried out after removal of the engine but many enthusiasts prefer to remove engine and gearbox together and split them when out of the car. This takes a little longer but makes engine-clutch-gearbox realignment much easier and greatly reduces the risk of damaging the gearbox first-motion shaft.

ER1.   1971 U.S.A. specification MGB engine compartment, when twin SUs were still standard. Note emission control system fitted. (Picture: Steve Glochowsky).

Tool Box

A good range of open-ended, ring and socket spanners. Straight point and crosshead screwdrivers. An

engine sling and block and tackle capable of lifting the considerable weight of engine and gearbox combined. Crowbar. Trolley jack. Axle stands. Boxes or bags in which to keep small components. Handwiping rags. Cloths for wing (fender) protection.

Safety

If garage roof timbers are used as a mounting for the hoist, ensure that they are REALLY strong. If in doubt, support them on either side of the car with 4" × 4" timbers used as vertical baulks. Ensure that all lifting gear is sound and efficient. Watch out for trapped hands or fingers − engines rarely come out in one sweet movement − and keep children, pets and yourself from beneath the power unit whilst it is in the air. Make sure the batteries are disconnected.

Engine In Situ

The following jobs can be carried out while the engine remains in the car. Removing and refitting:
1) the cylinder head;
2) the sump;
3) the timing chain and gears;
4) the big-end bearings;
5) the pistons and connecting rods;
6) the camshaft.

However, renewal of any of the last four items generally indicates a degree of wear which is best attended to − other than temporarily − by a complete engine overhaul.

Engine/Gearbox Removal

ER2.   Begin by marking around the hinge brackets with a scriber, so that the bonnet can be accurately refitted. Whilst an assistant and the bonnet prop support the bonnet, remove the two bolts which hold the hinges on each side before disconnecting the automatic bonnet prop at the inner wing mounting (later models). Place rags under each bonnet corner to prevent bodywork damage.

On U.S. cars and others fitted with the earlier type of emission control equipment the air pump air cleaner (Fig 5, item 4) is removed after disconnecting the hoses and removing the two nuts and washers. The pump itself (item 5) is removed after loosening the pump bolts and removing the drivebelt, then removing the top adjusting link bolt and the mounting bolt after which the pump is free.

On later cars, the restricter connection (Fig 6, item 9) must also be removed from the rocker box cover and other components removed before the basic engine ancillaries become accessible for removal.

ER3.   Continue by removing the water temperature gauge sender being careful not to damage the transmission tube.

ER4.   Coil the tube and place the whole unit out of harm's way in the rear corner of the engine bay.

ER5.   Disconnect and remove both heater hoses and both radiator hoses after draining the radiator and engine block, when a tap is fitted.

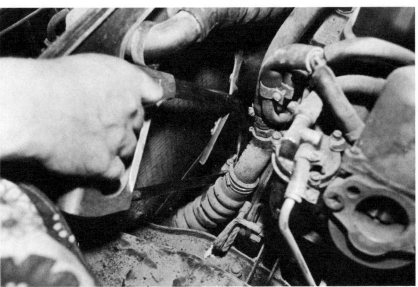

ER6. Hoses frequently bond themselves on, over a period of time, and if they are to be renewed cut them through with a hacksaw to save time.

Figure 5. Typical Early Emission Control System.

1 Air manifold
2 Filtered oil filler cap
3 Check valve
4 Air pump air cleaner
5 Air pump
6 Relief valve
7 Crankcase emission valve
8 Vacuum sensing tube
9 Gulp valve

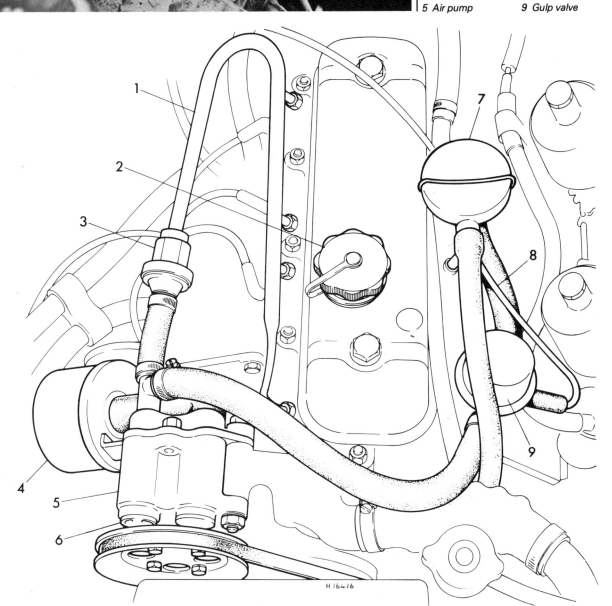

H 16416

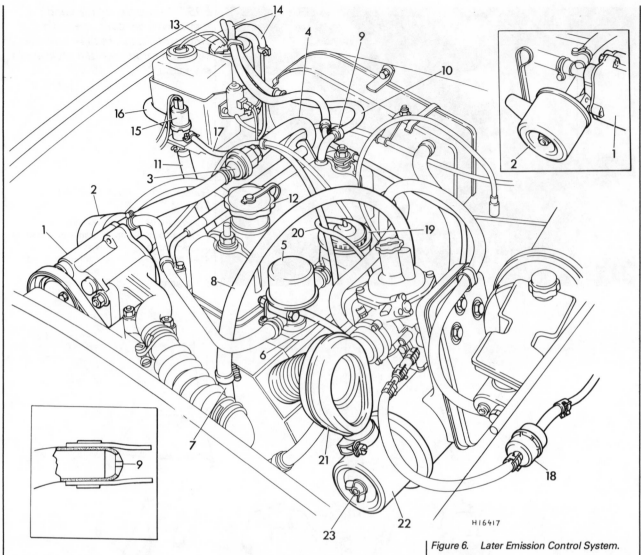

Figure 6.   Later Emission Control System.

1 Air pump
2 Air pump air
   cleaner
3 Check valve
4 Air manifold
5 Gulp valve
6 Sensing pipe
7 Oil separator/
   flame trap
8 Breather pipe
9 Restricted
   connection
10 Purge line
11 Air vent pipe
12 Oil filler cap
   (sealed)
13 Absorption
   canister

14 Vapour lines
15 Running-on
   control valve
16 Running-on
   control hose
17 Running-on
   control pipe
19 Exhaust gas
   recirculation
   valve (EGR)
20 EGR valve hose
21 Air temperature
   control valve
22 Air cleaner case
23 Wing nut retaining
   air cleaner cover

ER7.   If the oil cooler is to be left in
place, the union mounted on the
top must be locked with a spanner
while the pipe nut is undone,
otherwise the top of the unit will
shear off around the nut.

ER8. After removing the oil pressure connection (seen between spanner head and distributor) undo the oil cooler pipes at the engine block and oil filter. (If access is found to be difficult, remove the distributor first.)

ER9. Remove the radiator and shroud complete by taking out the outer bolts and by removing the steel steady straps from the wing mountings.

ER10. The oil cooler can be removed still attached to its pipework. The whole assembly should be placed safely to one side.

ER11.   Remove the two air
cleaners from twin S.U. carbs.
noting that the long retaining bolts
screw into a U-shaped bracket
behind each carburettor flange.
Then remove both carburettors
after taking off the 2 nuts and
washers from each one.

ER12.   The emulsion blocks and
heat shield are then removed. The
latter can become brittle and
cracked as shown.

ER13.   Remove the six nuts and
washers from the inlet and exhaust
manifolds, take off the inlet
manifold and tie the exhaust
manifold back to the inner wing
after lifting the exhaust pipe
mounting flange onto the side-
member. The exhaust manifold can
be removed complete but only after
taking off the six nuts holding the
pipes to the manifold. They are very
inaccessible and prone to shearing,
however.

ER14. Take off the generator wires, loosen the mounting and adjustment bolts, remove the fan belt then disconnect and remove the generator. Note that the distributor cap and plug and coil leads have been removed.

ER15. Remove the oil filter assembly complete.

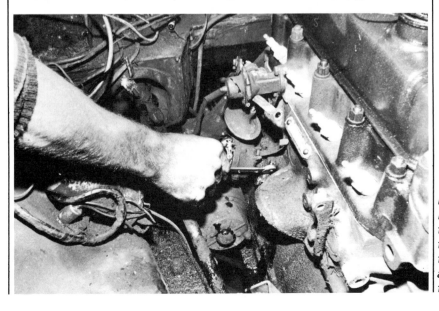

ER16. Take out the distributor. Loosen the pinchbolt and pull out the distributor if you don't mind timing being disturbed, or take out the two bolts which fit through the adjuster slots if you want to keep the ignition timing.

Before proceeding further check that:

1) The engine oil is drained;
2) The heater control cables are disconnected;
3) The starter wiring is disconnected;
4) The earlier, mechanical drive-type tachometer is disconnected;
5) The exhaust pipes are disconnected form the catalytic converter, where fitted;

North American Models:

6) The wire from the induction manifold heater is disconnected;
7) The manifold pipe (Fig 6, item 17) is removed from the running-on control valve (Fig 6, item 15).

ER18.   Place very strong rope or chains around the engine, front and rear. Lift a little with the block and tackle, simultaneously jacking the gearbox a little. Draw the engine forwards until it is clear of the first-motion shaft, then tilt the engine sharply upwards at the front to clear the crossmember.

ER19.   Make absolutely sure that the weight of the engine is not taken on the first motion shaft as it is withdrawn.

ER17.   Use a ring spanner to hold the engine mounting bolts while the nuts are undone. Note that some engines have a packing plate under the left-hand mounting and this should be saved for subsequent refitting. Ensure that the earth straps are free and unlikely to foul on the engine. **If it is intended to remove the engine and gearbox together move straight to the instructions given in ER20.**

Place a jack beneath the front of the gearbox. Remove the starter motor and remove all the bellhousing bolts and nuts.

ER20.   It is recommended that a bracket is made, which can be bolted to the engine via the rocker box bolts. Alternatively a chain can be bolted across the engine using suitable engine bolts.

Unbolt the clutch slave cylinder (leaving the hydraulic pipe in place). Disconnect the exhaust front-pipe bracket.

ER21.   Undo the propshaft bolts at the gearbox flange, "telescope" the propshaft splines backwards and lower the shaft to the ground.

ER22.   Disconnect the gearbox mountings then place a jack beneath the gearbox crossmember. Ensure that the speedometer drive is disconnected from the gearbox (use a large pair of pliers if the knurled nut is tight) and remove the wiring from the reversing light and overdrive, if fitted. See Fig 7 and loosen the nuts at the rear of the engine restraint rod (item 1) (later models) then remove the rearmost nut (item 3) and the plate and buffer (items 4 & 5). Remove the front, vertical nut and bolt and remove the restraint rod.

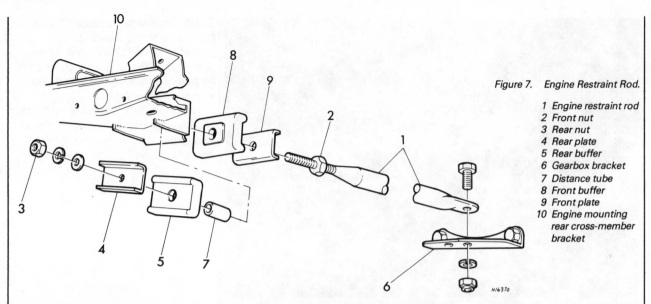

Figure 7. Engine Restraint Rod.

1 Engine restraint rod
2 Front nut
3 Rear nut
4 Rear plate
5 Rear buffer
6 Gearbox bracket
7 Distance tube
8 Front buffer
9 Front plate
10 Engine mounting
    rear cross-member
    bracket

H16370

ER23. Take out the two bolts at each end of the gearbox cross-member lower the jack so that the gearbox rests on the fixed cross member, ease the whole unit up (with the block and tackle and a jack on the gearbox) and forwards, clear of the crossmember. Then, lower the rear of the gearbox to the floor. Lift the power unit upwards at an acute angle. Note the position of the hoist on the engine bracket. It is here that a crowbar carefully used, can help to keep the unit clear of obstructions.

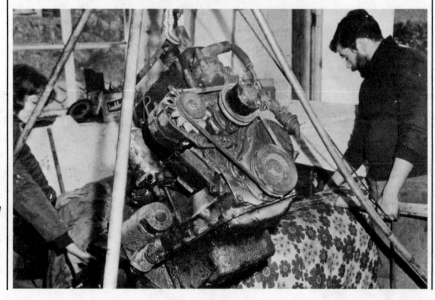

ER24. The engine is lifted high and the car's body is pushed back from under the gantry. Here, Shan, the author's wife, steadies the rear of the gearbox as the car is pushed from under the combined units.

ER25.   The author moves the engine/gearbox unit with the aid of a friend who balances the heavier, engine-end on a trolley jack while the author lifts the gearbox, using the trolley jack as a "roller skate".

ER26.   Having scraped off any rust with an old wood-chisel and painted on primer-sealer with a brush the author takes the opportunity to rub down and prepare the engine bay for spraying. Note that the wing (fender) is still protected with a large cloth.

Engine Strip

This section shows how to strip a worn engine, once removed from the car. Since very few home-mechanics own an engine dismantling stand, the engine is shown being dismantled on the floor — emphatically the safest place for it.

For details of how to recondition the engine, see the Haynes MGB Owners' Workshop manual. There simply is not enough room here to give details of clearances, reassembly, torque

figures, and so on. Enough information is given to enable the home-mechanic to strip the engine and send the block and crank off to a machine shop for reconditioning and to know which parts to purchase to enable a thorough rebuild to be carried out.

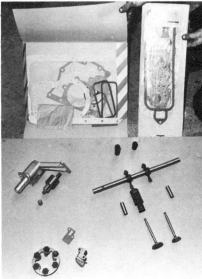

ES1.   New parts needed for a thorough rebuild, in addition to the pistons and rings, main and big-end shells and, if necessary, camshaft bearings usually supplied by the engine reconditioners, are: at the top of the picture, the top- and bottom-end gasket sets; the left hand group is the oil-pump assembly (12H (1429); beneath it is the timing chain tensioner assembly (17H 6680) and a new flywheel lock-washer (12H 1303); while the right hand group (purchased as necessary) include tappets (1H 822 pre-18V engines; 2A 13, 18V engines-on), rocker shaft (11G 82), rocker assembly (bushed) (12H 3377), inlet valve guide (12H 2222), exhaust valve guide (12B 1339) outer valve spring (12H 1679) and inner valve spring (12H 176).

The pushrods (12H 3357) should be examined for pitting and replaced if necessary. Inlet valves (12H 435) do not usually require renewal but exhaust valves (12H 436) are occasionally so badly burned that they do need renewal. It may also be necessary to renew the timing chain (2H 4905 — double; 3H

2127 — single) the camshaft gear (11G 203 — double; 12H 4200 — single) and crankshaft gear (12A 1553 — double; 12H 4201 — single). Numbers in brackets are B.L. parts numbers and can be used for positive identification when ordering parts.

ES2.   First tighten, then remove the cylinder head nuts (Fig 8) in the order shown. Undo the four rocker shaft nuts and lift off the whole assembly.

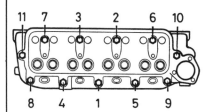

Figure 8.   Cylinder Head Nuts — Loosening & Tightening Sequence.

ES3.   Pull out the push rods (severe internal oil sludging may make them difficult to get out) and push them through eight numbered holes in a piece of card so that they can be returned from whence they came when the engine is being rebuilt.

ES4. Tap the cylinder head under the thermostat housing with a soft-faced hammer, to free the cylinder head gasket bond.

ES5. Lift off the cylinder head.

ES6. Examine the waterways for clogging (as shown here) and the valves, after their removal, for burning. Excess carbon should be scraped from the combustion chambers.

ES7. Run two cylinder head nuts down a head stud, lock them together with a pair of spanners then, place a ring spanner on the bottom nut and turn anti-clockwise. The stud will unscrew out of the cylinder block. Take all the studs out.

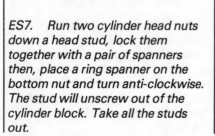

ES8. Knock back the flywheel tab washers with a cold chisel. Lock the crank with a spanner on the crankshaft front nut and undo the flywheel bolts (or nuts, according to model).

ES9. Take off the flywheel. Note the condition of the starter ring, especially on earlier models, and the clutch face on all models.

ES10. Clean off the engine backplate and especially around the recessed bolts, with a wire brush.

ES11. Knock back the tab washers, unbolt and remove the oil seal retaining plate.

ES12. Unbolt and remove the engine backplate . . .

ES13. . . . and take out the oil seal.

116

ES14. Take out the countersunk-head screw from beneath the distributor pinch-bolt plate . . .

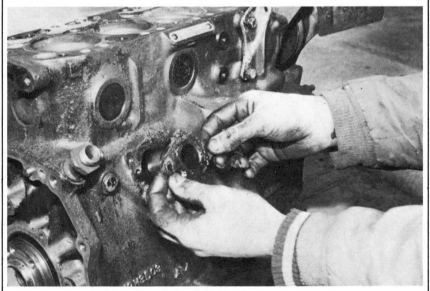

ES15. . . . lift out the distributor housing . . .

ES16. . . . and pull out the driving spindle, skewing it in a clockwise direction to remove it from the gear drive.

ES17. Unbolt the fan and spacer, where fitted . . .

ES18. . . . and lift off the water pump pulley.

ES19. Unbolt the water pump and remove it.

ES20. Take off the tappet covers — one bolt per cover.

ES21. Lift out the tappets by pushing a finger into each one, like a thimble, and then lifting it out of the block.

ES22. Knock back the tab washer on the pulley bolt.

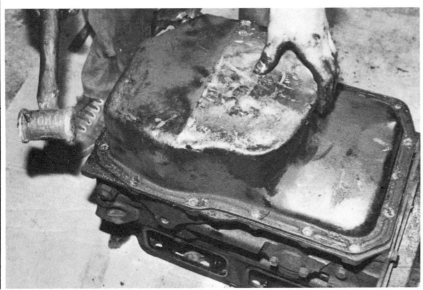

ES23. Kneel by the side of the block and carefully "roll" it over, onto its top face, pushing away rather than towards yourself.

ES24. Take out all the bolts from around the sump and tap the sump loose with a soft-faced hammer.

ES25.   Unbolt the oil pump and filter and remove it.

ES26.   Place a block of wood between the crank webs and the side of the block, place a socket spanner and bar on the pulley nut and hammer the nut loose. Use a large hammer: one or two sharp blows should free it.

ES27.   Unbolt the timing chain cover and take it off.

ES28.   Unbolt the camshaft gear nut after knocking back the tab washer.

ES29.　Unbolt and remove the timing chain tensioner . . .

ES30.　. . . and pull off the gears and chain complete. Remove the Woodruff keys from the two shafts and put them in a safe place.

ES31.　Unbolt the camshaft locating pin . . .

ES32.　. . . and carefully work out the camshaft.

121

ES33.   Unbolt the engine front plate . . .

ES34.   . . . not forgetting that the engine mounting plate is bolted to the front plate and the side of the block.

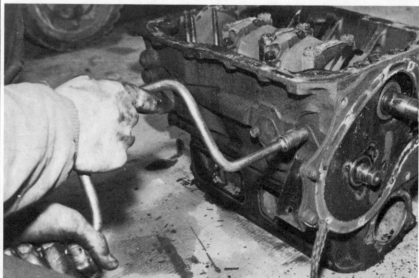

ES35.   Lift away the front plate.

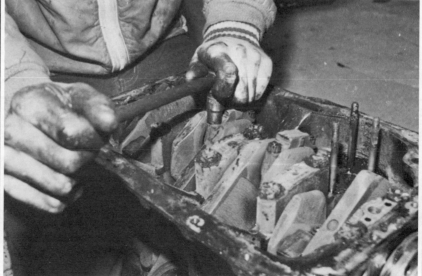

ES36.   Unbolt the big end caps.

ES37.   Place the block on its side and push the pistons upwards, lifting them up through the bores.

ES38.   Place each cap back onto its connecting rod as it is replaced. It is vital that the caps are not confused.

ES39.   Unbolt the main bearing caps. They are often extremely tight and difficult to pull out of the block. Then end caps can be tapped upwards but it may be necessary to fabricate a puller made to use the threaded hole in the centre of each end cap.

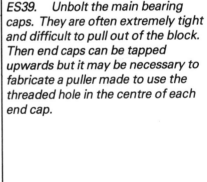

ES40.   Mark each main bearing cap so that their order of assembly cannot be confused. Scored crank journals are obvious signs of wear as are ridges around the tops of the cylinder bores. A thorough check can only properly be made with an internal and an external micrometer however − equipment which any good machine shop will possess.

Single Zenith/Stromberg Carb Cleaning & Adjustment (USA models only) *with John H. Twist of University Motors, Michigan*

It is recommended that this section is used in conjunction with Haynes MGB Owners Workshop Manual.

Tool Box

½ and ⅝ inch AF wrench; straight and crosspoint screwdrivers; needle-nosed pliers; aerosol carb. cleaner; light lubricating oil; grease.

Safety

Gasoline is highly volatile, highly flammable – DON'T SMOKE!

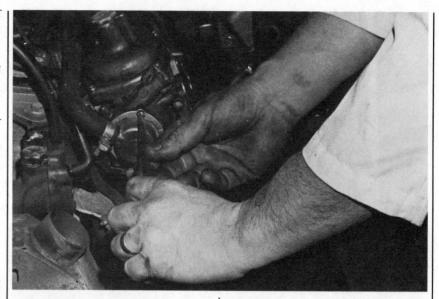

Z1. Remove the air cleaner with a ½ inch wrench. Be certain to disconnect the spring between the rear of the air cleaner can and the throttle return cam at the right side of the carb (not shown).

Z2. Before removing the cam from the engine compartment, it will be necessary to release the wing nut holding the air filter in place. Inspect the filter and note that the filter gets dirty from the inside out. If there is any question about the filter, replace it with the correct filter, GFE 1062.

Z3. Remove the three screws holding the water jacket and bi-metal spring assembly to the auto choke. These are fine thread screws

and can be easily stripped! Loosen the hose clamp at the top of the water jacket, allowing the hose to rotate freely.

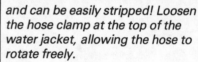

Z4. Then withdraw the jacket and carefully remove the black bakelite insulator from the choke assembly.

Z5. Using a pair of needle nosed pliers, remove the small rubber plug immediately above the outside screw, holding the choke assembly to the carb body. This makes access to the choke easier.

Z6. In this picture, the water jacket/bi-metal spring has been tied back with a piece of mechanics' wire so that it will not interfere with the rest of the process. Remove the three screws holding the choke assembly to the carb body. These have a $^{10}/_{32}$ or 2BA thread, but if one is lost, $^{10}/_{32}$ will act as a suitable replacement.

Z7. Withdraw the choke assembly and the orange gasket holding it to the carb body. Be certain NOT to tear the gasket. A new one is not easily obtainable!

Z8. *Carefully inspect the base of the choke assembly. The brass plug sealing the mixture valve is often loose. When loose, or when the plug has dropped away, fuel can drip onto the catalytic converter — and if the converter is red hot as it often is while on a cold start, a FIRE can result.*

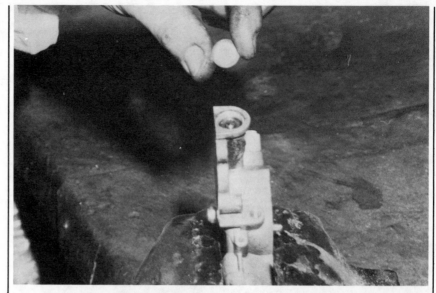

Z9. *If the brass plug is loose, tap it into place with a small hammer. If the plug is missing altogether, inspect the left frame rail, as it is sometimes found there, after dropping out.*

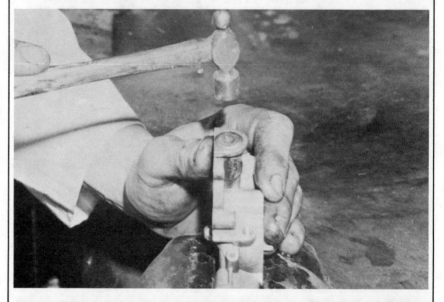

Z10. *Spray the choke assembly well with carb cleaner, working the "finger" on the choke mechanism all the time.*

Z11.   Then lubricate the assembly with very light lubricating oil, or silicone based lubricant.

Z12.   Replace the choke assembly onto the carb body after lightly greasing the orange gasket. Get the screws TIGHT. Remember to replace the small black rubber plug. It will be necessary to hold the throttle part-way open while fitting the choke assembly to the body. Then again open the throttle, position the "finger" at about a 2:00 position (as shown) and rotate the black insulator anti-clockwise by about 60 degrees — so that the finger can be seen from above.

Z13.   CAREFULLY, refit the water jacket/bit-metal spring onto the choke assembly ensuring that the finger is inserted into the hook on the bi-metal spring. Rotate the plastic insulator clockwise and align the three marks — on the choke housing, the insulator and on the water jacket (as shown). In colder climates rotate the water jacket slightly clockwise to richen the starting mixture.

Figure 9.   Zenith Type 175CD 5T
Carburettor.

1 Damper assembly
2 Air valve piston
3 Float chamber plug
4 Float chamber
5 Float
6 Needle valve
7 Top cover
8 Spring
9 Air valve unit
10 Diaphragm
11 Air valve grub screw
12 Idle air regulator
13 Idle air regulator
14 Throttle quadrant
15 Locating plate
16 Automatic choke operating lever unit
17 Outer spring
18 Inner operating lever
19 Inner spring
20 Automatic choke
21 Water jacket
22 Sealing rim
23 Heat mass
24 Insulator
25 Vacuum kick piston cover

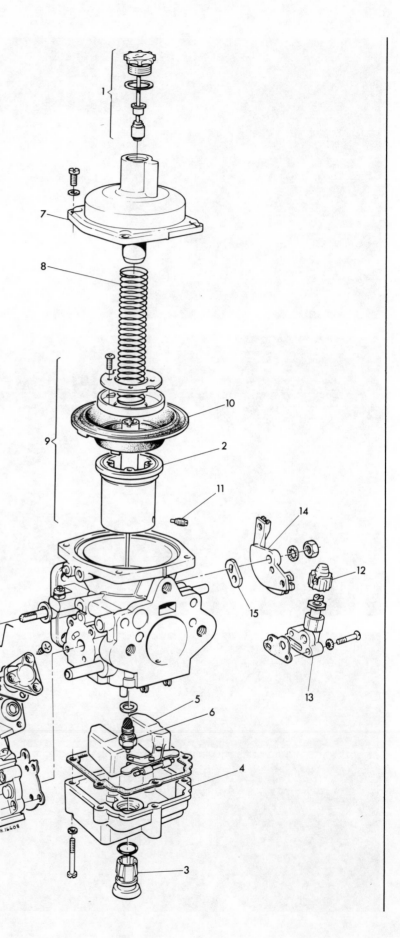

Z14. Remove the two screws holding the air regulator valve to the right side of the carb. Take care with the orange gasket.

See Fig 9. Dissemble and clean all idle air regulator parts (item 13). Then screw the ⅝ inch hex white plastic adjusting nut into its housing until it bottoms. Unscrew the nut then by two turns. Then screw the brass adjusting pin into the white plastic nut until it bottoms out, then unscrew it by two and a half turns. Grease the gasket, and reinstall the bleed valve to the side of the carb.

Z15. Remove the dashpot (Fig 9, item 7) (or suction chamber as it's called by the Stromberg people). Often the crosshead screws are too tight to allow easy removal. Tap lightly on the end of the screwdriver and they'll loosen easily.

Z16. Remove the cover, spring, piston and diaphragm. Note the tag on the left of the diaphragm and its corresponding relief in the carb body.

Z17.   Remove the diaphragm from the piston prior to cleaning. Remove the 4 crosshead screws. Use spray carb cleaner and a rag to wipe the varnish and soot from the carb. This process may take quite a time as the carb is usually very, very dirty. Similarly clean the piston, cover, spring etc. – but do NOT allow the carb cleaner to contact the diaphragm – or the diaphragm will expand and a new one will be needed. Additionally, inspect the diaphragm for perforation. A new diaphragm is available as BLM 225 480.

Z18.   Replace the components into the carb body, again ensuring that the tags on the diaphragm are in their respective slots and that the two vacuum holes at the base of the piston are at the rear of the carb throat.

Z19.   Fill the dashpot with oil (any excess will quickly be pushed out).

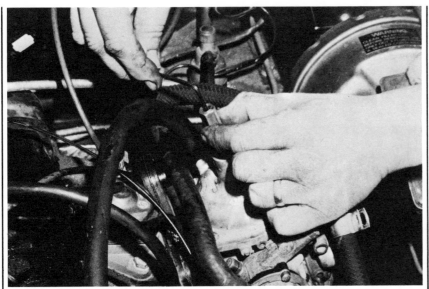

Z20.   Start the engine and allow it to come to operating temperature. The idle should be set at about 800rpm and the mixture adjusted as for an SU carb, i.e. raise the piston slightly. If the idle speed increases dramatically, the mixture is too rich. If the idle speed drops, the mixture is too weak. There should be a slight increase, then steadying (or slightly dropping back) of the idle speed, if the mixture is correct. To make the mixture adjustment, a special adjusting tool is necessary, available in the USA as BLT 0020100. If the tool is not available, then a ⅛ inch Allen wrench can be used, but the piston MUST be kept from turning (or a torn diaphragm will result). Sometimes a thumb, placed against the piston will prevent rotation. Sometimes it is necessary to remove the suction chamber top, remove the piston, hold it in hand, make the adjustment, then replace it. If the air pump is in place, the catalytic converter MUST NOT glow red hot at idle − if it does, the mixture is too rich. If in spite of re-adjustment the mixture remains too rich, replace the needle. Part No. AAU 7092.

Clutch Operating Mechanism − Examination & Overhaul
with *John Twist, University Motors, Michigan*

There should be little free play in any of the clutch parts, and rattles and vibrations should be eliminated. This attention to detail gives the finishing touches to any rebuild and helps to make the car feel like new again.

Renewal of the clutch cover, clutch disc and release bearing is straightforward but renewal of these parts alone will not always prove satisfactory in removing the freeplay or vibrations in the clutch pedal. Each part should be examined, as follows, and renewed if worn.

1) Examine clutch pedal − does it have a great amount of side play? If so then tighten the fulcrum bolt ($^9/_{16}$ inch). If the bolt is tight, and there is still movement, replace the pedal bush. (Fig 10, item 2).

Tool Box

Bench vice; ball pein hammer; cross-head screwdriver; impact screwdriver; brake bleeding tube, jar and fluid; range of AF spanners.

Safety

Take note of basic workshop procedures shown in the Appendix. Remember when working on hydraulic internals that cleanliness is the key word if you want to avoid an early failure. If in doubt, wash parts in clean brake fluid.

CL1.   The fulcrum bolt wears as well as the bush, as the nearer of the two shown here indicates. Replace it with a new one like that in the background.

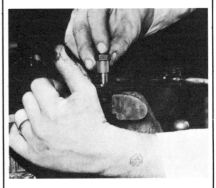

CL2.   Slide the new bush onto the bolt and place the bolt into the existing bush.

CL3. Place the fork over an opened vice and drive the new bolt and bush downwards with a hammer until the old bush is driven out and drops away leaving the new one in its place.

Figure 10. Clutch Operating Mechanism.

1	Clutch pedal	27	Locknut
2	Bush	28	Lockwasher
3	Pedal rubber pad	29	Copper washer
4	Distance tube	30	Pipe clip
5	Spring	31	Pipe clip
6	Clevis pin	32	Banjo connection
8	Master cylinder	33	Banjo bolt
	and reservoir	34	Sealing washer
9	Cap	35	Sealing washer
10	Seal	36	Slave cylinder
11	Boot		body
12	Circlip	37	Spring
13	Pushrod	38	Piston cup filler
14	Secondary cup	39	Piston cup
15	Piston	40	Piston
16	Piston washer	41	Boot clip – small
17	Main cup	42	Boot
18	Spring retainer	43	Boot clip – large
19	Spring	44	Pushrod
24	Metal pipe (RHD)	47	Clevis pin
25	Metal pipe (LHD)	49	Bleed screw
26	Hose		

2) Examine pedal free play — the pedal should have about ½ inch freeplay and be spring loaded rearwards. If the movement is greater, the pedal/clevis pin/master cylinder pushrod (Fig 10, item 1,6,12) may be worn.

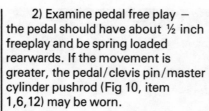

CL4. Remove the pedal box cover (four crosshead screws). If the screws will not loosen easily, dig out the "cross" in the screw head, place a crosshead screwdriver (long shank) into the screw and strike it with a hammer. This seats the

screwdriver into the screw, and jars and screw loose from the captive nut below. Examine the pushrod and pedal for elongation and the clevis pin for wear. If worn the pedal can be welded up and redrilled; the clevis pin and the pushrod can be replaced.

3) Examine hydraulic pressure — the clutch pedal should easily disengage the clutch. If there is trouble entering reverse, or if the MGB creeps away from a corner, clutch depressed, it's rebuild time! Rebuild as follows:

3a) open the bleeder on the slave (Fig 10, item 49) and pump the system dry.

3b) Fill the cockpit with newspapers and remove the circlip holding the pushrod into the clutch master cylinder (Fig 10, item 12). Remove the piston, cups and spring (Fig 10, items 14 to 19). DO NOT

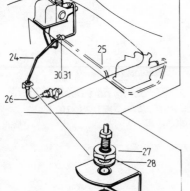

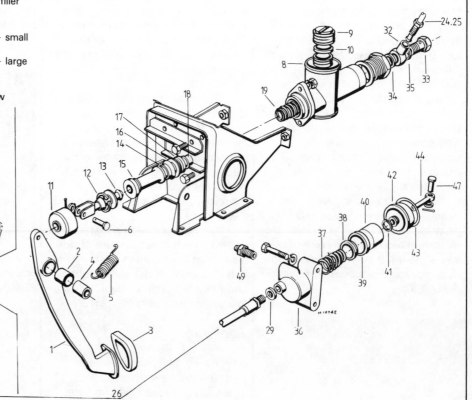

HONE the cylinder. It is not necessary to remove the cylinder from its position, as it can be rebuilt in place.

3c) Fit the seals, coated with brake fluid or brake grease, and reinstall the pushrod. Coat the new clevis with grease and connect the pedal to the pushrod.

3d) If the slave cylinder leaks, it is faulty, but even if the slave cylinder is not faulty and you are rebuilding the master cylinder, it is best to rebuild the slave as it frequently gives up in sympathy if not rebuilt. Loosen the hose (Fig 10, item 26) from the cylinder (⅝ inch or ⅜ inch BSF) and remove the two bolts holding the cylinder to the gearcase (⁹/₁₆ inch). Unscrew the cylinder from the hose and place in a vice. Remove the metal ring holding the pushrod boot (Fig 10, items 42,43) then shake the cylinder until the piston (Fig 10, item 40) falls away (or use air pressure CAREFULLY!) The inside of the slave may be honed, or at least rubbed clean with a fine grit paper. Wash thoroughly and reassemble the spring, cup, piston and pushrod seal. Screw into the hose until almost tight, secure to the gearcase, then tighten the hose. Remove the bleeder to ensure that it is clean.

3e) Bleeding the system: Fill the master cylinder, remove the bleeder screw and with an assistant in the drivers seat; depress the pedal; place your forefinger on the bleeder hole; release the pedal; wait ten seconds; remove the finger; depress the pedal; replace the finger on the bleeder hole. Then again, remove finger, depress pedal, replace finger, release pedal, wait ten seconds. (The time interval is to allow the vacuum created to draw brake fluid into the clutch master cylinder bore). After doing this about five times and after a stream of fluid has begun to move when the pedal is depressed, hold the pedal down, replace the bleeder and continue as above several more times, tightening and loosening the bleeder screw instead of using the finger. Every five or six strokes, the assistant should inspect the fluid in the master cylinder and top it up. It is vital that the fluid level is not allowed to fall too low or extra air will be drawn into the system.

Trying to bleed with the bleeder screw in place for the first number of strokes is sometimes futile, as the air pressure created cannot escape through the bleeder.

4) Rattles and vibrations from within the clutch unit: Always replace the spigot bush in the rear of the engine crank when doing a clutch job. Always replace the release bearing fork bushes and the fork bolt, as looseness in the release bearing fork can transmit rattles to the pedal — and allows the release bearing to contact the thrust face of the pressure plate without being properly centered.

Parts List

Note part numbers are B.L. except those in brackets which are Lockheed.

Pedal Bushing: AAA 4129
Clevis Pin: CLZ 0514 (⁵/₁₆ × ¾ inch)
M/c Pushrod: 17H 7985 (93548)
Pedal return spring: BHH 1387
M/c rebuild kit to 1977: 8G 8424 (KL 71534)
M/c rebuild kit from 1977: BHM 7127
Slave rebuild kit: 8G 8420 (KL 71525)
Slave Hose: ACC 5509 (KL 49301)
Spigot Bush 3 main: 1G 765
Spigot Bush 5 main: 22H 1416
Fork Bush: 11G 3195
Fork Bolt: 11G 3196

Note: The hydraulic hose rarely has to be renewed.

Front Suspension strip & overhaul

"Clonks" when starting away or braking, vibration from the front end at speed, lack of front-end adhesion and "pattering" transmitted through the steering wheel, steering stiffness or vagueness — all are symptoms of things going wrong in the front-end Steering & Suspension Department. Nothing, not even an engine that isn't "on song" takes more of the "sports" out of a sports car than bad handling and on an MGB there is a lot more to give trouble at the front end than at the rear — although most of the trouble comes from lack of maintenance rather than any inherent weakness. So, when the work detailed here has been carried out be sure to lubricate the front end *at least* to the manufacturer's schedules and preferably even more regularly.

Carry out the tests detailed in the Buying chapter to enable specific faults to be pinpointed before dismantling commences. Do ensure that the front suspension is jacked-up under the bottom suspension arms so that when the wheel is off the ground, the suspension is in its usual, on-the-road position, (*i.e.* the one that is most badly worn) and so that the spring tension does not disguise wear in any of the components.

Tool Box

Trolley jack or purpose-built suspension coil-spring compressor. Set of AF socket spanners and ratchet or ring spanners. Axle stands. Large bar to act as a drift. Hammer. Large paraffin (kerosene) bath for washing dirty suspension parts. ⅛ inch drill bit or metric equivalent.

Safety

Follow the usual safety rules on working under a car such as NEVER going under a car supported by a jack alone; always use soundly based axle stands. Be more than wary of the energy contained within a front suspension spring. It can, quite literally, be a killer if released suddenly.

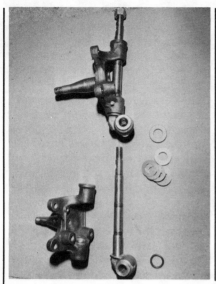

FS1.   This is where trouble frequently lies with the MGB's front suspension — with the kingpins. The stub axle, shown top assembled onto the kingpin, turns about the kingpin to give steering while the wheel — via the wheel bearings — is mounted onto the stub axle which protrudes left. The two parts are shown disassembled below, illustrating the problem of getting sufficient lubrication onto the top and bottom bearing surfaces. All too often water beats the grease to it, causing rapid wear or kingpin seizure.

Early cars were not fitted with a bottom grease point and it is conceivable that new kingpin and bush assemblies have subsequently been fitted without the manufacturer's recommended modification detailed in Fig 11. It is a simple matter to have a firm of engineers carry out the drilling accurately if it is beyond the scope of the home mechanic.

Figure 11.   Modification to add Grease Nipple to Swivel Axle.

Dimension $C = \frac{1}{16}$ in (1.6 mm)   Angle $E = 6°$
Dimension $D = \frac{3}{4}$ in (19 mm)   Angle $F = 12°$

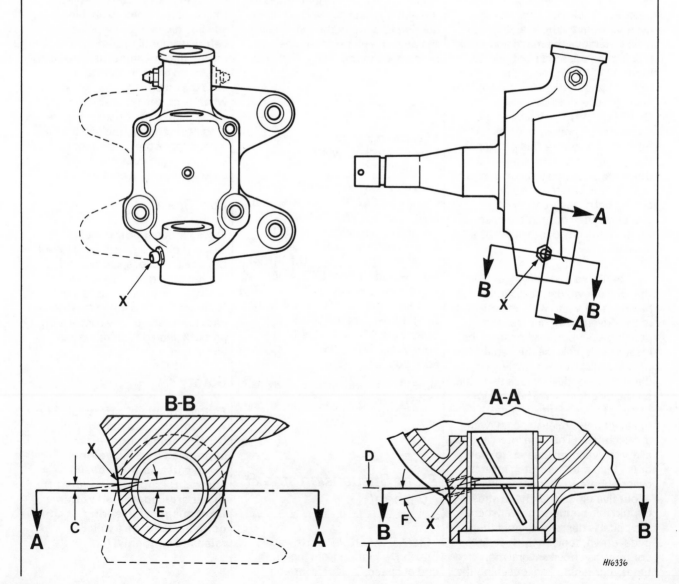

B-B

A-A

HI6336

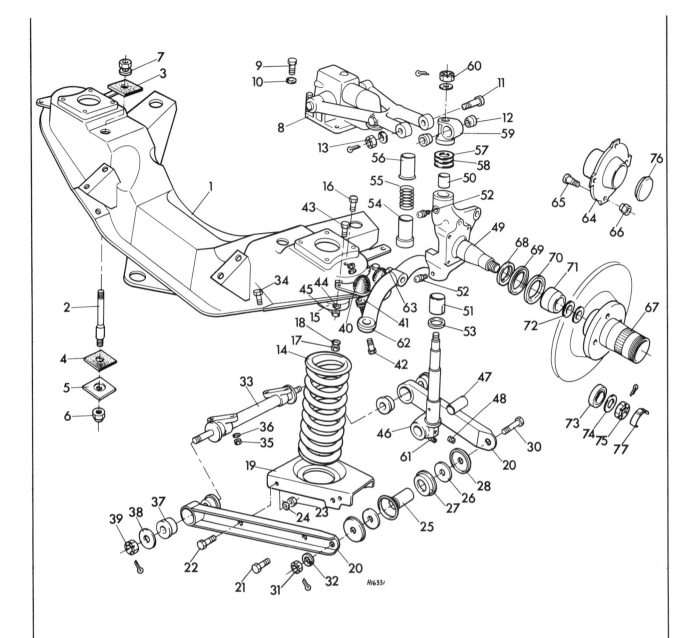

Figure 12.   Front Suspension (MGB).

1 Crossmember	14 Coil spring	30 Pivot bolt –
2 Bolt – cross-	15 Spigot for spring	wishbone to
member to body	16 Screw	swivel pin
3 Upper mounting	17 Nut	31 Nut
pad (rubber)	18 Washer	32 Spring washer
4 Lower mounting	19 Pan assembly	33 Wishbone pivot
pad (rubber)	20 Wishbone arm	34 Wishbone pivot
5 Plate	21 Screw –	retaining bolt
6 Nut	wishbone to pan	35 Nut
7 Plain washer	22 Screw –	36 Washer
8 Hydraulic shock	wishbone to pan	37 Wishbone pivot
absorber	23 Nut	bush
9 Bolt	24 Washer	38 Washer
10 Spring washer	25 Distance tube	39 Nut
11 Fulcrum pin	26 Thrust washer	40 Rebound buffer
12 Bearing	27 Seal	41 Distance piece
13 Nut	28 Seal support	42 Bolt
		43 Screw

44 Spring washer	57 Thrust washer	68 Collar for oil seal
45 Nut	58 Floating thrust	69 Oil seal
46 Swivel pin	washer – 0.052 to	70 Inner hub bearing
47 Bush for swivel pin	0.057 in (1.32 to	71 Bearing spacer
48 Grub screw	1.44 mm)	72 Shim – 0.003 in
49 Swivel axle	59 Trunnion	(0.076 mm)
50 Swivel axle upper	60 Nut for swivel axle	73 Outer hub bearing
bush	61 Lubricator nipple	74 Bearing retaining
51 Swivel axle lower	62 Steering lever	washer
bush	63 Bolt for steering	75 Bearing retaining
52 Lubricator nipple	lever	nut
53 Cork ring	64 Hub assembly	76 Grease cup (disc
54 Lower dust	(disc wheels fitted)	wheel fitment)
excluder tube	65 Wheel stud	77 Grease retainer
55 Dust excluder	66 Wheel nut	(wire wheel
tube	67 Hub assembly	fitment)
56 Upper dust	(wire wheels fitted)	
excluder tube		

FS2.   The MGC's kingpin assembly is very similar to that of the MGB. The ''saucer' on top is simply a bump stop platform but unlike the MGB which has its shock absorber acting as its top suspension link the top of the MGC's kingpin is connected to a torsion bar and anti-roll bar.

FS3.   If the front suspension is being rebuilt as part of a full restoration or overhaul the owner may wish to remove the whole subframe assembly which carries the complete suspension and braking systems.

To do so, remove the steering rack (as shown in the following section) remove the brake pipes and either catch the fluid or block off the pipes, support the crossmember (Fig 12, item 11) under the centre with a trolley jack (and remember

that the complete assembly is VERY heavy) and undo the four nuts and washers (Fig 12, item 7) from the tops of the body fixing bolts (Fig 12, item 2) before lowering the assembly to the ground. Engine oil, suspension grease and road dirt invariably mean that a lot of cleaning up will have to be done.

Figure 13.   Disc Brake (MGB).

1 Disc	11	Dust seal and
2 Bolt		retainer
3 Washer	12	Brake pads
4 Nut	13	Clips
5 Dust cover	14	Plug
6 Dust cover bolt	15	Bleed screw
7 Spring washer	16	Caliper bolt
8 Caliper, RH	17	Tab washer
9 Piston	18	Split pins
10 Seal, inner		

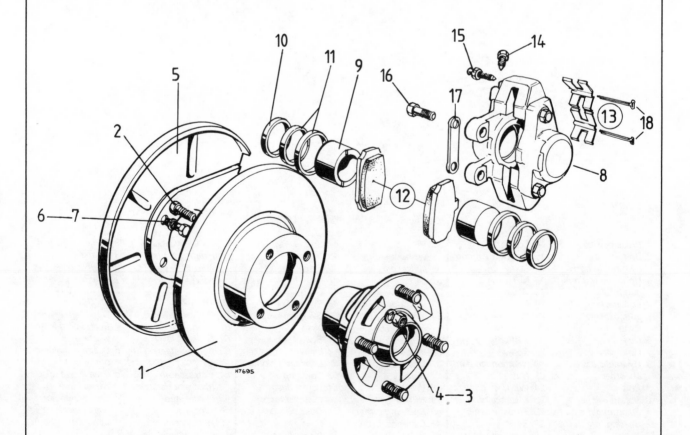

FS4. The disc brakes have be completely removed. Knock back the tab washers and undo the two calliper retaining bolts (Fig 13, item 16). Leave the brake pipe in place unless it is to be renewed.

FS5. Place the calliper out of the way on an upturned oil drum or some other support high enough not to put a strain on the brake pipe.

FS6. Disconnect the track rod end from the steering lever (Fig 12, item 62). Use a taper wedge or other proprietary t.r.e. removing tool. Alternatively, strike opposite sides of the steering lever hole simultaneously with two hammers. This distorts the hole and frees the taper. Sometimes both methods have to be used at once in stubborn cases.

137

FS7. Remove the dust cover, split pin and nut (75) holding the front disc in place and pull off the hub and disc unit. The disc, if replacement is needed, bolts directly to the hub. Access to the split-pin on wire wheeled cars is through the hole in the splines using long nosed pliers. The hub usually pulls off easily but it may be necessary to use a hub puller or a couple of tyre levers or strong screwdrivers if it "sticks".

FS8. The disc dust cover (Fig 13, item 5) is unbolted and removed and the steering lever arm (Fig 12, item 62) too.

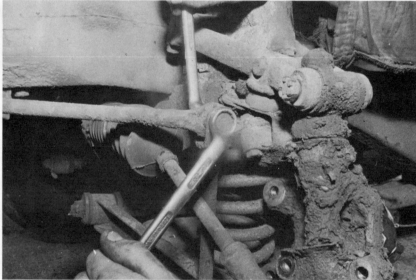

FS9. Disconnect the front anti-roll bar at its top mounting. It may be necessary to jack up the front suspension a little.

FS10. It is VITALLY IMPORTANT that the following section is not carried out without first fitting a spring compresser or placing a trolley jack under the bottom of the swivel pin (Fig 12, item 46). The fulcrum pin is unbolted (Fig 12, item 11) and drifted out with a steel rod or old screwdriver, as shown. If this is done without taking the safety precautions mentioned the assembly will fly apart, releasing a force of several tons and damaging both the mechanic and the car. N.b. Scissors or bottle jacks are not stable enough to be used in this operation.

FS11.   Swivel the assembly forwards . . .

FS12.   . . . and pull — or more likely, drift — both rubbers out of their housing.

FS13.   Undo the swivel pin nut (Fig 12, item 60) and tap off the top trunnion (Fig 12, item 59) by placing a bar through it.

FS14.   Lift off the whole stub axle assembly (Fig 12, item 49) . . .

FS15.   . . . and lift off the shock absorber after undoing the four bolts (Fig 12, item 9) that hold it in place.

FS16.   If only the shock absorber is to be renewed, incidentally, it can be removed after compressing the front suspension spring as described, removing the top fulcrum pin (Fig 12, item 11) and unbolting the shocker, as above.

FS17.   Carefully and slowly lower the jack ensuring that it is not likely to tip and when the spring pan (Fig 12, item 19) is lowered, remove the spring. If it is broken or its length is less than that shown in the manufacturer's specifications, renew it.

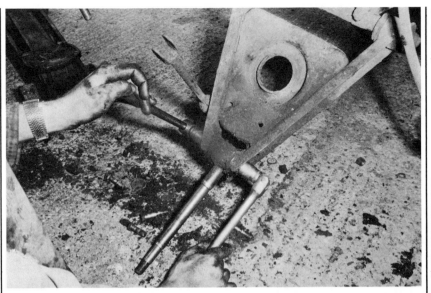

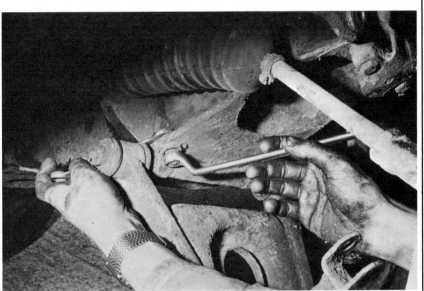

FS18. To remove the now denuded kingpin, undo and remove the bottom pivot bolt (Fig 12, item 30) . . .

FS19. . . . and remove it, taking care to keep washers and seals if they are to be refitted.

FS20. The spring pan assembly is removed complete from the subframe by removing the four fixing nuts and bolts (Fig 12, item 35).

FS21. It is less usual for the rear bushes to wear but if they have worn they are removed by undoing the wishbone pivot nuts and split-pins (Fig 12, item 39).

FS22. Replacement bushes and washers are available as a kit.

FS23. It is more usual for the pivot bolt (Fig 12, item 25) and distance tube (Fig 12, item 47) to seize in the swivel pin bush (Fig 12, item 47) through lack of lubrication. Movement then takes place in the wishbone arms (Fig 12, item 20), ovaling the front holes, as shown on the example on the left, and necessitating their renewal. Each is held to the spring pan with two bolts. (Fig 12, item 22-24).

FS24. A typical kingpin overhaul kit. New bushes will have to be pressed into place in the stub axle and reamered (Fig 12, item 49) by a B.L. main dealer or other similarly equipped workshop. If "sealed-for-life" blanking plugs are fitted, take them out with an Allen key and fit grease nipples. Take a small twist drill and clear out all grease routes in top and bottom trunnions after temporarily unscrewing the grease nipples.

FS25. Also replace both top and bottom pivot bolt and bush assemblies while the assembly is stripped, whether needed or not. Before permanently reassembling onto the car, first temporarily assemble the distance tube, pivot bolt and ancillary components onto the swivel pin and wishbone arms. The endfloat should be between 0.008in. and 0.013in. Replace the distance tube (not included in the repair kit) if the endfloat is not within these tolerances.

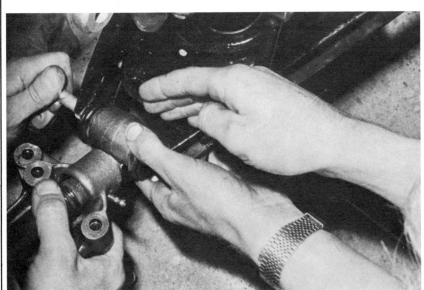

FS26. After refitting the spring pan assembly permanently assemble the bottom pivot bolt assembly, not forgetting the split pin.

FS27. Place the jack under the unit as shown and jack it up, making absolutely sure that the jack remains stable, until . . .

FS28. . . . the top trunnion (Fig 2, item 59) is aligned with the shock absorber forks. Slip the fulcrum pin in to ensure that the rubber bushes are aligned . . .

FS29. . . . ensure that the bolt holding the shock absorber forks together is slackened to allow them to separate a little and give the uncompressed rubbers a little more clearance . . .

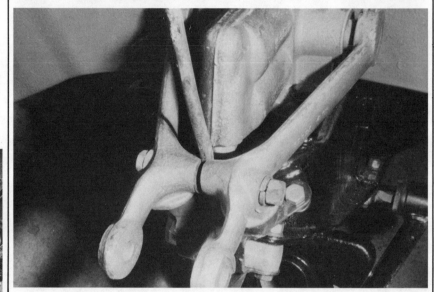

FS30. . . . and tap the top trunnion into place with a soft-faced hammer.

FS31. In practice, it will still be necessary to "encourage" the bushes to go all the way in and to align with the fulcrum pin but two tips can help. 1) Smear the bushes lightly with brake fluid. This lubricates without damaging the rubber. 2) Before assembly, squeeze the bushes into the trunnion as far as they will go with a woodworker's G-cramp.

Finally, methodically check every nut and bolt to ensure that everything is tight. A rebuilt front suspension assembly can restore the sort of taut handling for which the MGB is famed and increase its safety factor greatly, and yet, in relative terms, its cost is low.

Some enthusiasts find that the wishbone bushes on their MGBs have a relatively short life before they revert to their "clonking", worn-out state. They are increasingly turning to MGB GT V8 bushes which are very much dearer but much longer lasting as they have metal inserts and solid rubber bushes that have to be pressed in place with a vice prior to fitting.

Another modification, this time suggested by Peter Laidler, is to drill the distance tube (Fig 12, item 25) that fits between the bottom pivot bolt (Fig 12, item 30) and the swivel pin bush (Fig 12, item 47). In its standard form, the bearing surface between distance tube and bush is lubricated but the static surface between pin and tube is not. In theory, lubrication in this area is not essential but in practice the distance tube and the pivot bolt weld themselves together with rust, making removal of the pivot bolt, which should be straightforward into a frustrating, cussifying affair. The distance tube, incidentally is not part of the bottom swivel repair kit and has to be purchased separately. (Part Number BHH 1773).

See Fig 14. The new tube should be ground around its full circumference, half way along its length to remove the case hardening (which is a hardened outer skin, too hard to be penetrated by a twist drill). A ⅛ inch hole should be drilled right through the tube at right angles to the tube, which allows a little of the lubricating grease injected into the trunnion when it is grease, to enter the distance tube and prevent a future annoying seizure.

The MGC

The front suspension is the only area, apart from the engine, that is

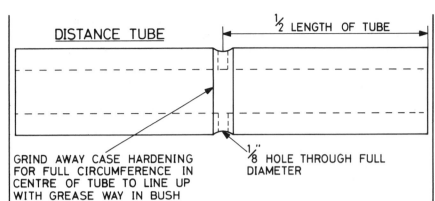

DISTANCE TUBE

½ LENGTH OF TUBE

GRIND AWAY CASE HARDENING FOR FULL CIRCUMFERENCE IN CENTRE OF TUBE TO LINE UP WITH GREASE WAY IN BUSH

⅛" HOLE THROUGH FULL DIAMETER

Figure 14.   Modifications to Distance Tube (see text).

radically different on the MGC. The reason for this modification is that the MGC engine was so deep that the MGB's front suspension crossmember could not be accommodated. Obviously, therefore, the MGC owner does not have the option of removing the complete front suspension as a unit.

FS32.   An MGC front suspension unit, completely rebuilt. Note the "frame" clamped around the top pivot which leads to the anti-roll bar and the torsion bar. The telescopic damper which all MGCs wear at the front is not fitted here. (Photo: Pearl McGlen).

Rear Suspension Axle – Strip & Overhaul

The MGB's rear end layout has been the butt of much criticism by independent rear suspension afficionados but it is one of the most

robust and long-lived parts of a generally robust and long-lived car – as well as being free of the hysterics suffered by some of its contemporaries when being cornered hard. The first type of rear axle known as the "three-quarter floating" or "banjo" type (because of its appearance) fitted up to chassis number G-HN3 132923 (wire wheels) and G-HN3 139215 (bolt-on wheels) plus a few earlier cars (Roadsters only) was virtually unchanged from that of the MGA and is capable of being stripped-down further by the home mechanic than its replacement, known as the "semi-floating" or, again because of its appearance the "tubed" type. This latter type, incidentally, is the only rear axle fitted to GTs. Popular myth has it that later axles cannot be fitted to earlier cars but in fact, as John Hill says, "It's the easiest job I know! It's a direct replacement."

The restorer has to decide how much of the rear suspension to strip down. If only localised faults are apparent it would probably be easier to carry out the work with the axle in-situ. If extensive renovation is the aim, the whole axle complete with springs should be removed.

Tool Box

As well as a trolley jack and axle stands, a good selection of ring and/or socket spanners will be needed. Releasing fluid. Socket extension. Hammer. 5/16 inch drift.

Safety

Ensure that the front wheels are chocked while the rear end is

supported on a pair of axle stands bearing on planks placed just ahead of the foremost rear-spring mountings. Take care when lowering the axle – it is surprisingly heavy.

RE1. One of the most common reasons for giving the rear-end some scrutiny is to rectify sagging springs. Measure the distance from the wheel arch to the centre of the wheel on both sides and compare measurements. Another common reason is to replace worn shock-absorbers.

RE2. MGB rear ends are generally very stiff and so the bounce-test to check whether the shock absorbers are doing their job does not always give the full answer. Rear end "clonks" usually come from the shock absorber link bushes – see on the right of the photograph – and these should be renewed if worn, bearing in mind that early, lower ride height cars have different lengths of link to the later, higher rubber-bumper cars (Fig 15, item 2). Shown to the left of the photograph is a telescopic damper, complete with fixing kit for the MGB (See "Modifications" section).

Common problems are leaking rear hub oil seals (Fig 16, items 53, 54), leaking piston seal (Fig 16, item 35) – both of which are often caused by a blocked breather assembly (Fig 16, item 11) while less often encountered are; broken halfshaft (Fig 16, items 40, 41) or worn and noisy differential. Wire wheels can also wear, giving a "clonk" on drive take-up, as can the half-shaft splines especially if dirt is allowed to get into the differential housing when it is being topped-up with oil. *N.b.* It is all too often possible to confuse worn propeller shaft universal joints with a worn differential. They, too "clonk" on drive take-up and frequently transmit the noise through the rear axle. Check them carefully before jumping to conclusions!

The following stages are each necessary in the removal of the whole rear-axle assembly, but can be taken as separate stages in themselves.

RE3. If you wish to remove the rear dampers do so by taking out the two retaining nuts, bolts and washers (Fig 15, items 3, 4, 5, 6). Slacken the first nut using a socket spanner with extension, to clear the wheel arch and hold the bolt head with a ring spanner. Then slacken and remove the second nut and bolt before returning to remove the first. Otherwise, if the first bolt is removed complete the whole damper unit will tend to rotate as a unit as the second bolt is undone. Disconnect the shock absorber link (Fig 15, item 2) and remove the shock absorber.

Springs can sag, as already described, and individual leaves can break. They should be renewed in pairs but, in an emergency, single second-hand springs can be fitted provided that the replacement is compatible with its new partner. If a single spring is to be replaced, the rear of the car should be supported with strong, stable axle-stands just ahead of the front spring shackles and the axle itself supported on the side on which the spring is to be removed.

RE4. Undo the four axle U-bolt nuts and remove the locating plate (Fig 17, item 18).

RE5. Disconnect the two nuts holding the shackle pin and plate (Fig 17, items 10 and 14) and tap out the pins. Lower the end of the spring to the floor.

RE6. *At the other end of the spring, undo and remove the eyebolt (Fig 17, item 21) and remove the spring. (Take care! It is surprisingly heavy!)*

Differential Assembly and Pinion Oil Seal

It is possible for the home mechanic to remove the complete differential and renew the pinion oil seal and change the spider gear washers on the earlier "banjo"-type axle but removal and replacement of the bearings and crownwheel and pinion is a far more ambitious project – the really determined are advised to work from the B.L. Workshop Manual although its instructions are directed, naturally, towards the fully equipped professional workshop complete with specialist service tools rather than the ragged trousered enthusiast! This is one of those cases where removal of the part and delivery to a fully equipped workshop would be the best course of action.

The later, more common "tubed"-type of axle requires the use of a special stretching tool to open up the differential casing before the differential unit can be removed. Moreover, when the pinion seal is removed it is often necessary to remove the differential unit complete because problems are often experienced with the bearing spacer behind the pinion. Some owners prefer to fit a second-hand axle complete if they experience severe trouble with their differential. Others may wish to save themselves the cost of garage dismantling by following the sequence on removing the axle and the following one on removing hubs and halfshafts before delivering the unit to their local specialist for attention by them.

Removal of the "Banjo"-Type Axle Differential

Remove the hub and halfshaft as detailed in the following sequence. Make a light hacksaw mark across the edges of the propeller shaft flange and pinion flange so that they can be reassembled in the same place and then split them. Drain the axle oil and pull on the parking brake to prevent the pinion turning.

Pinion Oil Seal Renewal

Take off the nut which holds the pinion flange in place (Fig 16, item 2). (It may be necessary to gain extra leverage on the socket spanner being used with an extension arm). Tap off the flange with a soft-faced mallet and take off the steel dust cover (Fig 16, item 5). Prise out the old oil seal (Fig 16, item 6) with a screwdriver. When fitting a replacement seal place the lip facing inwards taking care to lubricate it on all its running surfaces. Reassemble in the reverse order and retighten the end nut to 135 to 140lb.ft. The pinion seal number is 88G 320.

Changing the Spider Gear Washers

RE7. *When the washers under the differential and pinion gears (spider gears) wear, the gears are able to twist, causing excessive strain on the halfshafts, eventually breaking them. Replacement also removes certain clunking noises from the differential assembly.*

RE8. *Drive out the dowel pin (Fig 16, item 25) holding the pinion shaft (Fig 16, item 26) in place. Use a long ⅛ inch punch and work from the crownwheel side. It may be necessary to drill out the metal peened over the entry hole with a 3/16 inch drill.*

RE9. Gently tap out the pinion and remove all four gears and washers (Fig 16, items 19, 24).

RE10. The washers (arrowed) are to be replaced. Use new washers (No. ATB 7072 and IG 7445); two of each. Replacing the gears can be facilitated by using a liberal amount of grease on the gears and their washers to hold them in place during assembly.

RE11. When the unit is reassembled, "stake" the dowel pin hole with a small chisel so that there is NO CHANCE of the pin working loose.

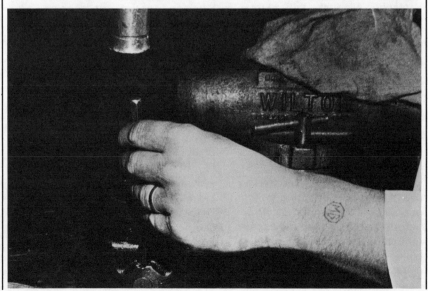

Removing Rear Axle Complete

RE12. *Jack up the rear of the car, place soundly based axle stands just ahead of the rear spring front mountings, disconnect the hydraulic brake at its tee-piece, mounted on the axle and seal off the hydraulic pipe to prevent the fluid from draining from the master cylinder.*

Disconnect the handbrake linkage (at the handbrake end) and remove the shock absorbers, as already described.

Remove the check straps from their TOP mountings. (The lower ones have a greater propensity to shear.) If an anti-roll bar is fitted to the rear, disconnect it at its end fittings (Fig 15, item 14) by removing the mounting bolt and nut (Fig 15, items 15, 16). Disconnect it from the bodywork at the rubber bearings (Fig 15, item 9) removing the nuts, bolts and washers (Fig 15, items 17, 18, 19) from the bearing bracket. (Unless a new anti-roll bar

is to be fitted, leave the locators (Fig 15, items 10, 11) in place).

Place a trolley jack under the differential casing, remove the rear shackle pins (Fig 17, item 10) as already detailed, and lower the rear of the springs carefully to the floor.

Figure 15.   Rear Shock Absorber & Anti-Roll Bar. (Courtesy John Hill's MGB Centre).

1 Shock absorber – rear	10 Upper locator
2 Link	11 Lower locator
3 Bolt	12 Locator screw
4 Nut	13 Spring washer
5 Spring washer	14 End fitting
6 Plain washer	15 End fitting bolt
7 Anti-roll wind up bar	16 Stiff nut
8 Lock nut	17 Screw
9 Roll bar bearing	18 Spring washer
	19 Nut

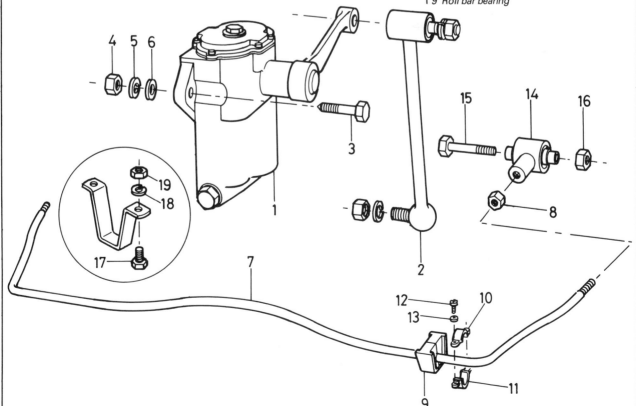

RE13. If the check straps are due for replacement, cut them off with a hacksaw rather than risk shearing the attachment bolts. The lower nut can be removed with the assistance of heat (even a butane blowtorch can make all the difference) and releasing fluid, once the axle is away from the car's fuel tank. With the jack still in place under the differential, undo the eyebolts (Fig 17, item 21) from the fronts of the springs and lower the complete assembly to the floor. If the wheels are refitted before removing the eyebolts, the whole axle assembly – which is very heavy, can be easily wheeled around the workshop.

Eyebolts are often very stubborn to remove. As a last resort be prepared to hacksaw through them and renew BUT ensure that replacements are readily available, first. They have a stepped shank and are NOT standard bolts.

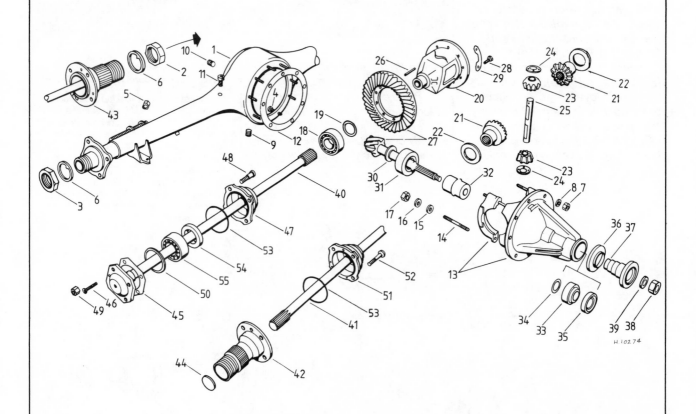

Figure 16. Rear axle "Banjo"-Type.

1 Case	21 Differential wheel	38 Nut	47 Hub assembly (disc wheels)
2 Bearing nut (RH thread)	22 Thrust washer	39 Spring washer	48 Wheel stud (disc wheels)
3 Bearing nut (LH thread)	23 Differential pinion	40 Axleshaft (disc wheels)	49 Wheel nut (disc wheels)
4 Gear carrier stud	24 Thrust washer	41 Axleshaft (wire-wheels)	50 Hub assembly (wirewheels)
5 Rebound spindle nut	25 Pinon shaft	42 Hub extension, RH (wirewheels)	51 Hub assembly (wirewheels)
6 Locking washer	26 Pinon peg	43 Hub extension, LH (wirewheels)	52 Wheel stud (wirewheels)
7 Nut	27 Crown wheel and pinion	44 Welch plug (wirewheels)	53 Oil seal
8 Spring washer	28 Bolt – crown-wheel to differential cage	45 Joint	54 Oil seal
9 Drain plug	29 Lockwasher	46 Screw, shaft to hub	55 Bearing
10 Filler plug	30 Thrust washer – 0.112 to 0.126 in (2.85 to 3.20 mm)	35 Oil seal	
11 Breather assembly	31 Rear pinion bearing	36 Dust cover	
12 Gasket	32 Bearing spacer	37 Flange	
13 Differential carrier	33 Front pinion bearing		
14 Stud	34 Shim – 0.004 to 0.030 in (0.102 to 0.762 mm)		
15 Plain washer			
16 Spring washer			
17 Nut			
18 Differential bearing			
19 Packing washer – 0.112 to 0.126 in (2.85 to 0.254 mm)			
20 Differential cage			

Figure 17.   Rear Suspension.

1 Main leaf
2 Bush
3 Second leaf
4 Centre bolt
5 Distance piece
6 Nut
7 Locknut
8 Clip – third leaf
9 Clip – fourth leaf
10 Shackle and pin plate

11 Shackle plate
12 Shackle rubber
13 Nut
14 Spring washer
15 U-bolt
16 Nut
17 Bump rubber pedestal
18 Locating plate
19 Spring seating tab

20 Hydraulic shock absorber attachment bracket
21 Eyebolt
22 Nut
23 Spring washer
24 Rebound strap
25 Tube for rebound strap
26 Nut
27 Plain washer

28 Spring washer
29 Bolt – rebound strap
30 Nut
31 Spring washer
32 Bump rubber
33 Clip for second leaf*
34 Pad for second leaf clip*
35 Interleaf strip, 1-2, 2-3, 3-4*

*Later vehicles only

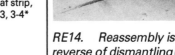

RE14.   Reassembly is NOT the reverse of dismantling! First attach the fronts of the springs to the car. (N.b. – the longer part of the spring from the centre, goes to the rear. Then, with the aid of a brawny assistant, slide the axle up the springs (it sits on top, of course) . . .

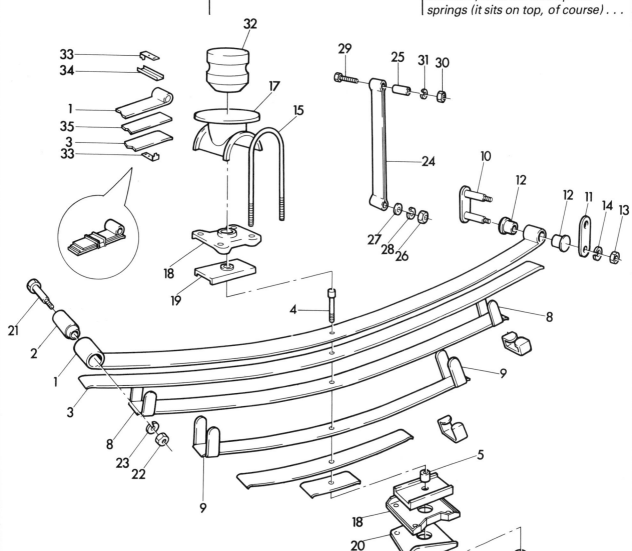

HI6333

RE15. . . . and fit the U-bolts, locating plate and other associated components. (See Fig 17 for order of assembly). Finally, jack up the axle unit and, with some inevitable difficulty, locate the shackle pins into the chassis and spring eye bush.

Refit the check straps, hydraulics (not forgetting to bleed the brakes), shock absorber linkage and handbrake cable. Fortunately much of the reassembly process is quite straightforward provided that new parts are fitted or those to be replaced have been thoroughly cleaned.

Swapping Axles

If banjo and tubed type axles are to be interchanged, it is important to note that the U-bolts for each are different. There are also four different types of handbrake cable, as detailed below. (Part numbers in brackets are B.L.)

"Banjo" axle, bolt-on wheels (AHH 5227)
"Banjo" axle, wirewheels (AHH 5228)
"Tubed"-type axle, bolt-on wheels (AHH 7391)
"Tubed"-type axle, wirewheels (AHH 7392)

Rear Hub/Halfshaft Strip

Oiled-up rear brakes are a common reason for British MOT test failure and are often caused by a failed rear axle oil seal. (Sometimes this, in its turn, is caused by a blocked rear axle breather causing a build-up of pressure inside the axle and this should be checked out). Heavy clonking at the rear end is occasionally the fault of halfshaft spline problems and as the process of stripping the hub/halfshaft is the same for both problems, both are dealt with here.

Tool Box

Jack and axle stand. Socket set. Long extension bar. Engineer's pliers. B.L. Special Tools number 18G 284, and 18G 284D — or, see text.

Safety

Remember the safety rules when working on a car supported off the ground. Securely chock the front wheels in both directions. Don't inhale brake shoe dust — the asbestos content can cause lung cancer.

HH1.   Remove the roadwheel (loosen the nuts or spinners before raising it from the ground).

HH2.   Slacken the brake shoe adjuster (at rear of backplate) then remove the brake drum after taking out the two crosshead set screws.

HH3.   Push in, twist, pull out the spring clips which help to locate the brake shoes using a pair of pliers.

HH4. Lever each brake shoe in turn off its stop so that the shoulder of the shoe rests on the stop. Take off the springs and remove the shoes.

HH5. Remove the splitpin and undo the hub nut. A torque wrench doubles admirably as a long-armed extension.

HH6. Pull off the driving flange complete with wheel mounting studs. Wire-wheeled cars' splines are a part of this unit.

HH7.   Disconnect the hydraulic brake line and handbrake cable and unbolt the backplate (4 bolts).

HH8.   The bearing cap, in which the oil seal is housed is lifted away next. The oil seal should be renewed whether faulty in the past or not. This is a common source of leaks and disturbing then refitting the old oil seal is asking for trouble!

HH9.   The halfshaft is removed by fitting an old brake drum to the driving flange, back to front, then temporarily bolting the driving flange to the end of the halfshaft. The old brake drum can be driven outwards, complete with halfshaft, with a soft-faced hammer.
        If this operation is carried out using one of the car's own brake drums there is a risk of dangerous but invisible hairline cracks forming in the drum which could cause failure later on with lethal consequences. The alternative is to use one of the B.L. Special Tools listed in "Tool Box".

Dual Circuit Master Cylinder Strip & Overhaul
With John Twist, University Motors, Michigan

The two most common failures of the dual circuit master cylinder are leaking from the front seal, which allows brake fluid to drip down along the brake pedal and onto the foot or floorboards, and, most common, internal leaking. The latter is evidenced by the pedal slowly sinking to the floor over a period as long as several minutes, with very light pressure on the pedal.

As a note here, a new type of brake fluid is on the market. This is a silicone brake fluid and is better for the MG for several reasons. Most importantly, it doesn't eat up paint work — a beautifully restored MGB can look terrible after a spill of brake fluid at the master cylinder, also it does not absorb moisture as does the conventional type — which means that the internal rusting common to brake systems is no longer a problem. It is about four times as expensive as regular fluid and worth every penny.

Tool Box

$^{13}/_{16}$ inch combination wrench; $^{3}/_{8}$ inch ratchet; $^{3}/_{8}$ inch drive extension with ½ inch swivel; ½ inch open-end wrench; crosshead screwdriver; "icepick"; $^{7}/_{16}$ inch line wrench — if available (sometimes needed to free up lines at master cylinder); $^{7}/_{16}$ inch open-end wrench; $^{1}/_{8}$ inch or $^{5}/_{32}$ inch punch; 90° pick; long nose circlip pliers, wide punch; hammer; the homemade jig.

Safety

Follow basic workshop procedures — see Appendix.

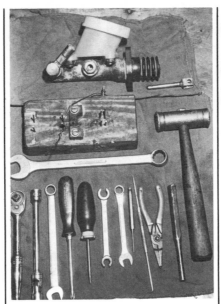

DCB1(A).   "Tool Box" illustrated.

DCB1(B).   Loosen a bleed nipple at the rear end and at the front of the car, and pump the master cylinder dry. Then, remove the four crosshead screws holding the pedal box in place. If the screws will not come loose, scratch the cross in the head clean, place the screwdriver into the cross, and strike heavily with a hammer. This will almost always remove a stuck screw. DO NOT round out the cross in the screw head, as then drilling will be the only solution to removal. If the screws must be renewed, use 2BA or $^{10}/_{32}$ inch. Lay the pedal box to one side.

DCB2.   Remove the split pin and clevis pin from the pedal and pushrod. If the clevis pin is worn, replace it with a $^{5}/_{16}$ inch × ¾ inch new one.

DCB3.   Push the operating piston rearwards and remove the pushrod.

DCB4.   Loosen and remove both brake lines ($^{7}/_{16}$ inch wrench). Bend them out of the way.

DCB5.   Push the spring and retainer rearwards with a pair of screwdrivers, while a helper removes the spring type clip from the piston. Place these items on the workbench for later cleaning.

Use a ½ inch swivel socket and a long ½ inch open-end wrench and loosen and remove the two $^{5}/_{16}$ inch bolts holding the master cylinder to the pedal box. Then remove the filler cap (an oil filter wrench sometimes is necessary). Now push the piston into the master cylinder, turn the cylinder slightly and lift out of the pedal box area.

DCB6.   Use a $^{13}/_{16}$ inch wrench and remove the brake line fittings on the side of the master cylinder. Remove the plastic valves and springs found under the fittings, making a note on paper of their assembly order.

DCB7.   Remove the crosshead screws holding the reservoir to the cylinder. Here some extra leverage may be needed as the screws can be very tight.

DCB8.   Remove the top circlip.

DCB9.   CAREFULLY, use an "icepick" and a hammer to smash the white washer into a million pieces, making repeated holes in it. DO NOT allow the "icepick" to damage the master cylinder or the piston!! This method is about the only method which consistently works. The workshop manual says to shake it out, but you could be shaking for a hundred years!

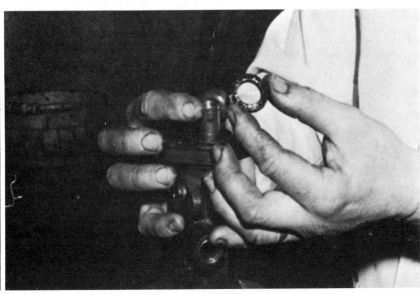

DCB10.   Remove the seal with a 90° pick.

157

*DCB11.   Remove the thin washer
— it's easiest to remove the cylinder
from the vice and shake it, when the
washer will drop out.*

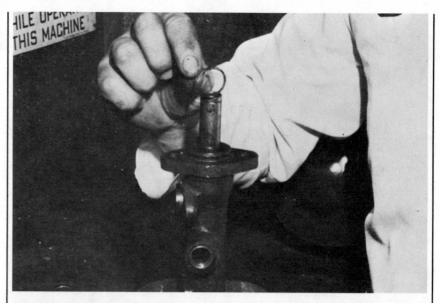

*DCB12.   Reach deeply into the
master cylinder bore, while pushing
the piston down, and carefully
grasp the bottom circlip and remove
it. DO NOT gouge the bore or
piston!*

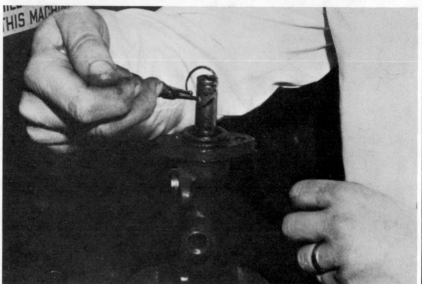

*DCB13.   Remove the thick metal
washer and withdraw the piston
assembly.*

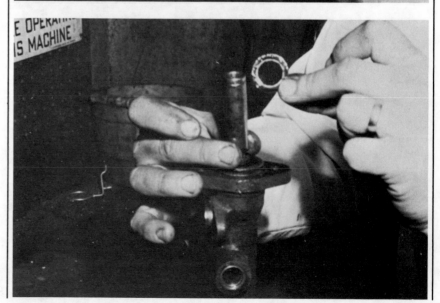

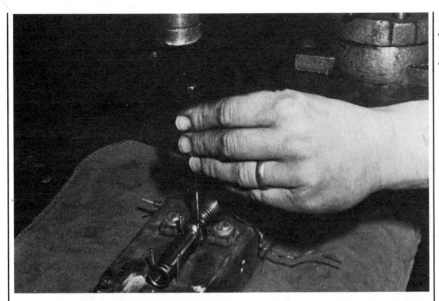

DCB14. Fasten the piston assembly in a homemade jig, and drive the front peg (roll pin) out with a ⅛ inch or ⁵⁄₃₂ inch punch.

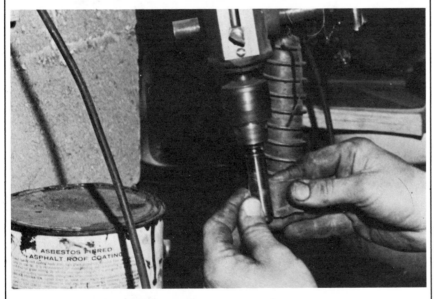

DCB15. Chuck the front piston into a drill or small lathe and polish the surface, ridding it of any gouges or lines caused by removal of the white washer. Polish it finally with a 600 grit paper — ensuring that it is as smooth as possible.

DCB16. Use a honing tool and make several passes through the master cylinder bore. It is essential that the larger part of the bore (the front), is well honed and smooth.

159

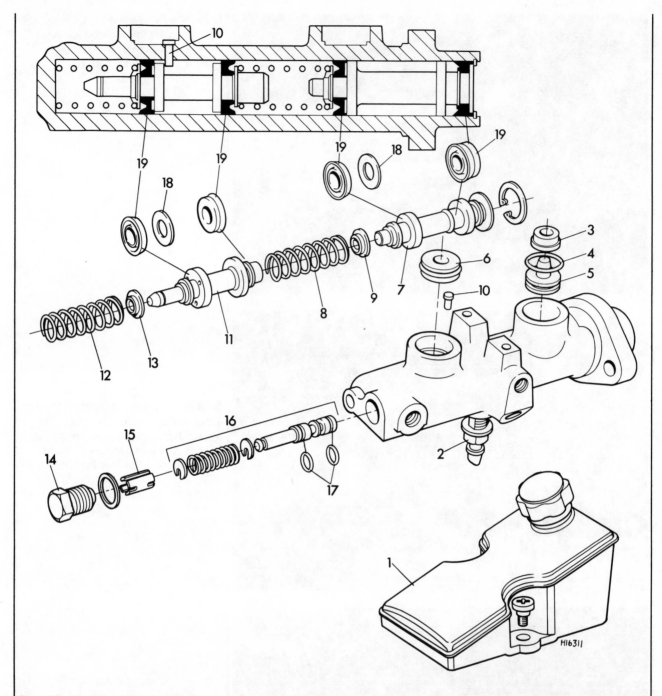

H16311

Figure 18.   Dual Circuit (Tandem) Master Cylinder & P.D.W.A.

1 Fluid reservoir	5 Primary feed port adaptor	9 Cup	15 Distance piece
2 Pressure failure switch	6 Secondary feed port seal	10 Stop pin	16 Pressure differential unit
3 Primary feed port seal	7 Primary piston	11 Secondary piston	17 O-ring
4 Primary feed O-ring	8 Return spring	12 Return spring	18 Shim washer
		13 Cup	19 Seals
		14 End plug	

Replace the seals on the two pistons, place the assembly in the jig and replace the peg (roll pin) with the larger punch. Coat the seals with brake grease (NOT the ordinary type), or with brake fluid and reassemble in reverse order, as shown in Fig 18.

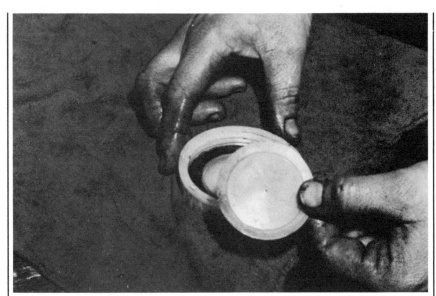

DCB17.   Replace the seal in the filler cap by prising the centre away first.

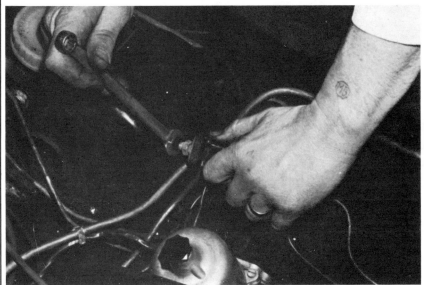

DCB18.   Having replaced the master cylinder into the pedal box, connected the lines and bled the system (rear first) fit the pedal box cover and adjust the brake light switch. The further the switch is screwed into the cover, the less freeplay the pedal will have. It should have at least ½ inch freeplay.

Steering Rack Removal & Steering Column U.J. Overhaul

Steering rack removal and refitting is relatively straightforward on earlier cars, without a collapsable (energy absorbing) steering column. Where the latter system is used, a B.L. alignment tool must be used — see MGB Haynes Workshop Manual for further details.

Tool Box

Long nose pliers. Ball joint splitter and/or two 2lb hammers. Set of ring or socket spanners.

Safety

Ensure that the car is held safely and securely and that the rear wheels are locked when its front wheels are held off the ground. Ensure that all steering connections, particularly at the U.J., are secure after re-assembly.

R1.   A worn U.J. will cause M.O.T. failure in Britain and gives ''sloppy'' steering. It is secured to each half of the steering column by splines and held by pinch bolts.

After supporting the front of the car off the ground with axle stands placed under the spring pans, the wheels are removed. After removing the split pin and nut, steering arm ball joints are freed with the aid of a ball joint splitter and/or a pair of hammers. These are used to strike both sides of the ball joint taper hard and simultaneously, distorting it briefly, which allows the ball joint to spring free. In practice, the ball joint gaiter is invariably struck and split usually necessitating renewal of both ball joints (which should be replaced in pairs). A ball joint splitter works out cheaper in the long run!

R2 & 3. *These shots, taken of a* ▷ *car with a stripped engine bay, show the two bolts at each end of the steering rack which hold it to the body frame. The two nuts and spring washers found at their opposite ends should be renewed, leaving the rack held only by the U.J. When removing the rack be sure to retain any shims which may have been fitted.*

The rack is finally removed after unbolting and removing the pinch bolts. (Note that they pass through slots in the column and must be taken out before the splines can be slid apart).

When the rack or a replacement is fitted, attach it at the U.J. end first. Note carefully whether there is a gap at either of the rack-to-bodyframe mountings and if so, pack it with shims so that as the mountings are tightened, no sideways pressure whatever is applied to the universal joint.

Electrical Components

This section, in being aimed at the restorer, complements the relevant repair sections of Haynes MGB Owners' Workshop Manual.

Tool Box

In addition to the basic tool kit, some "odd" sized spanners are sometimes needed (see Text for details). Engineers and long-nosed pliers. Heavy duty soldering iron.

Safety

ALWAYS disconnect the battery(ies) before working on any electrical part of the car. A short can destroy parts of the wiring system in a second or even start a car-wrecking fire.

Starter Motor Overhaul

See "Tool Box" & "Safety" at start of chapter.

Although different types of starter motor were fitted to the MGB, rebuilding the "electrical end" (as opposed to the starter dog end) is basically similar on all models.

SO1.   The unit is held by two bolts to the engine backplate/ gearbox bellhousing. It is VITAL that the battery(ies) are disconnected before removal.

SO2.   Remove the band surrounding the brush inspection holes.

SO3.   Remove the two long screws holding the case together.

SO4.   Remove the two brushes connected to the field coils and withdraw the rear plate.

SO5.   Remove the armature and the front housing.

SO6.   Use a $^9/_{16}$ inch tap to remove the CE (commutator end) bush. This tap will screw into the bush then, when it bottoms out, will lift the bushing out as the tap is turned — or the whole thing will come free.

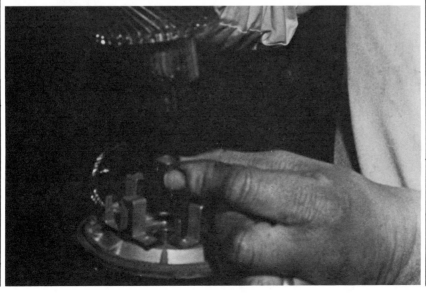

SO7.   Place the new bush (soaked in oil for several hours — the workshop manual suggests 24) into the rear housing and use the armature to drive the bush into place.

SO8.   Tap the armature carefully, driving the rear (CE) bush in and turning the armature each time it is struck.

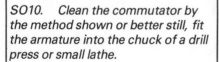

SO9.   Drive the DE (drive end) bush into place (which also drives the old bush out) by using the same technique. Tap carefully.

SO10.   Clean the commutator by the method shown or better still, fit the armature into the chuck of a drill press or small lathe.

SO11.   Solder new brushes to the rear plate and to the field coils. The field coils are usually aluminium and brushes cannot be soldered directly to the available post. DO NOT completely cut the old brush wires away, but use them to solder the new brushes to.

Starter Solenoid Overhaul

See "Tool Box" & "Safety" at start of chapter.

Two types of pre-engaged starter have been fitted to the MGB. The first, from Chassis No. G-HN4 138401 (Roadster) and G-HD4 139472 (GT) was used from 1968 to 1971. The second type was fitted to all "18V" engines from 1972 on.

The earlier type is identifiable by having two 3 inch mounting studs beneath the bellows and its body is parallel throughout its length.

The later type has a mounting flange with two threaded holes in it and tapers down towards the commutator end. Its armature has a black plastic cover. This solenoid also has a spade terminal (smaller than the actuating terminal) which allows battery voltage to be drawn from the copper actuating bar when the starter is being operated. (This is for those MGBs which run with an 8 volt coil, using battery voltage when starting-up).

When the ignition key is turned to the "START" position, current passes through two electromagnets in the solenoid core. One electromagnet is connected to earth, one to the "STA" (starter) terminal and is grounded (earthed) through the starter brushes. This pulls the piston into the magnet, and by lever action causes the toothed gear on the armature to engage the flywheel. At the same time, it presses the contact bar against the battery and starter posts, allowing battery current to flow into the starter.

Both solenoids CAN be installed upside-down on the starter, causing the battery to drain through the electromagnets and burning up the solenoid, starter, some of the wiring and possibly even the whole car! ("I've seen it happen", says John Twist). ENSURE that the "STA" terminal is connected to the starter.

SS1. Having disconnected the batteries, withdrawn the solenoid from the starter and cleaned it thoroughly, remove the two crosshead screws from the end on which the electrical contacts are mounted.

SS2. With an electrical soldering iron heat the soldered connections on the end cap while pushing up on the cap. Eventually the solder will melt sufficiently and the cap will come free. There is only one connection on the earlier type-M 418G starter motor solenoid (1967-71) and two on the later type-2M 100 (1971 on). On the earlier solenoid, the nut on the starter terminal marked "STA" must be removed prior to lifting the cap.

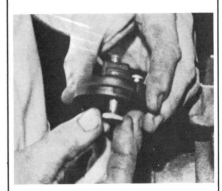

SS3. The single post on the cap of the earlier type has a ¼ inch Whitworth nut...

167

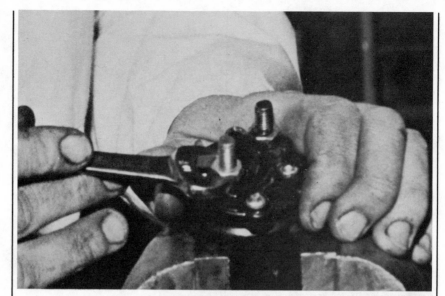

SS4. . . . while the later two-post type has 13mm nuts.

SS5. Place the cap to one side and heat the wires which protrude from the solenoid case to remove the blobs of solder that remain. There is one wire on one side and there are two on the other.

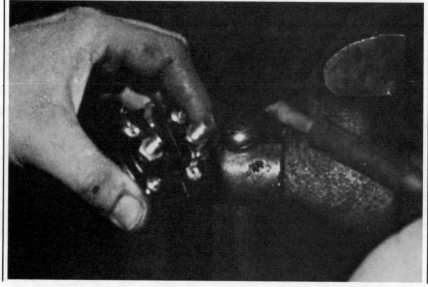

SS6. Clear the spade terminal holes through which the wires normally pass, in the cap. Either heat them with a soldering iron and shake out the molten solder (take care not to splash molten solder into the eyes) or drill out the old solder with a $^3/_{32}$ inch or ⅛ inch drill. (Freeing the holes enables the wires to be reinserted on reassembly).

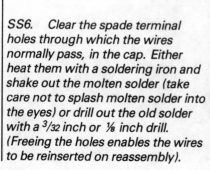

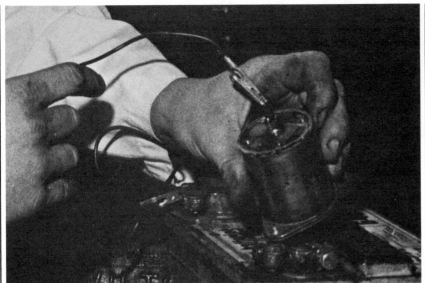

SS7.   There are two coils within the solenoid. One is connected between the actuating terminal (in the centre) and ground (earth). Here the solenoid is being ground (earthed) on the negative part of a battery while a test lead is taken to the positive terminal. The other coil is checked by attaching the positive terminal as shown, to the actuating terminal, and the "STA" wire to the negative post.

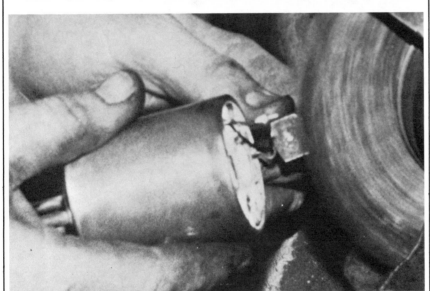

SS8.   Clean the two contact posts and the copper actuating bar on a wire wheel. (Wear goggles and remove loose clothing). Here, the earlier type solenoid "STA" terminal is being cleaned . . .

SS9.   . . . while the other terminal can be cleaned separately.

SS10.   Replace the actuating bar and spring.

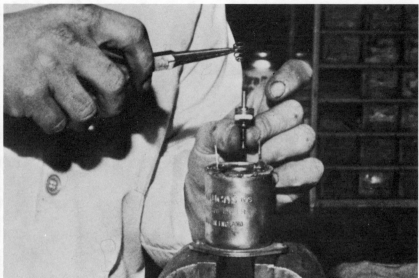

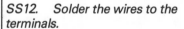

SS11.   Place the cap onto the solenoid base. Make absolutely certain that the double wire from the coil is fitted into the actuating terminal and that the single wire (later solenoid) is fitted to the "STA" terminal (i.e. the one that goes to the STArter).

SS12.   Solder the wires to the terminals.

SS13.   Test both coils of the solenoid by placing the plunger in the bore and first testing the actuating terminal to ground (earth) connection, then the terminal to "STA" post. In both cases the plunger should be pulled forcefully into the bore of the solenoid.

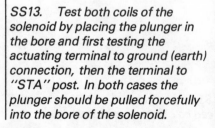

SS14. *Wrap the joint between the barrel and the cap with insulating tape to make it watertight . . .*

SS15. *. . . and spray the unit with black aerosol to prevent it from rusting, ensuring that the electrical terminals are protected.*

Heater Motor Overhaul

Older MGBs are not noted for the efficiency of their heating systems. This is generally because either: the heater radiator is blocked; the heater tap is badly adjusted or the cable is seized; the heater flaps have jammed or broken; the heater tap mounted on the engine has filled with deposits (especially in a "hard" water area) or simply, the engine is running too cool.

An over-worked heater motor, too, can break down or simply become tired and slow, reducing the volume of warm (or cold) air available to feet or screen. The following sequence shows how to overhaul the unit.

See "Tool Box" & "Safety" at start of chapter.

EHM1. *The heater unit can be removed as a unit after undoing the screws that hold the brackets and flanges to the bulkhead. Also, disconnect the heater hoses and wiring to the heater motor.* ▽

EHM2. *The box which protrudes down into the bulkhead incorporates the control flap, which is vulnerable to water ingress and corrosion. Here the cable mounting has broken off the heat control flap.*

EHM3. *Remove the heater motor after taking out the three screws around the mounting flange. Tag one of the wires with insulating tape, either side of the bullet connector before pulling the connection apart to identify the original wiring order and thus fan direction.*

EHM4.   Hold the body of the motor carefully in the vice and on earlier models, remove the nut holding the fan to the fan motor armature.

EHM5.   On later models (fitted with a plastic fan) prise off the slip ring with a thin screwdriver poked between the fan blades.

EHM6.   Lubricate the shaft with penetrating oil, hold the armature with vice-grips between the fan and motor and work the fan loose from the shaft. Then, tap the shaft through the fan as shown.

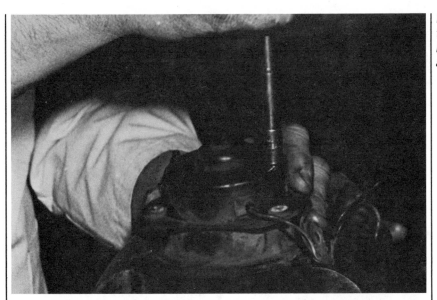

EHM7.   Loosen the 2BA nuts at the back of the motor then tap the body apart and withdraw the armature.

EHM8.   Spin the commutator by holding it in the chuck of an electric drill, as shown, cleaning it with fine glasspaper. Undercut the insulators.

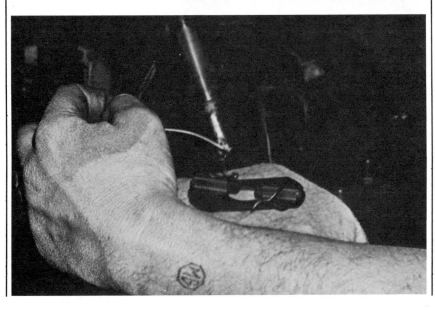

EHM9.   Solder new brushes onto the plate. Older units use a ¼ × ¼ inch brush, while newer units (those fitted with plastic fans) use a $^{5}/_{16}$ inch brush. Reassemble the unit having placed several drops of oil in the front and rear bearing. AFTER the unit has been re-installed, try the wiring on both of the alternative combinations and select the one offering the greatest air movement.

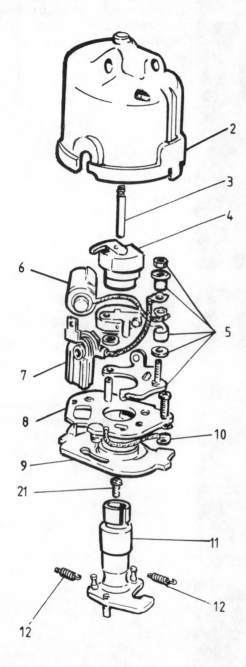

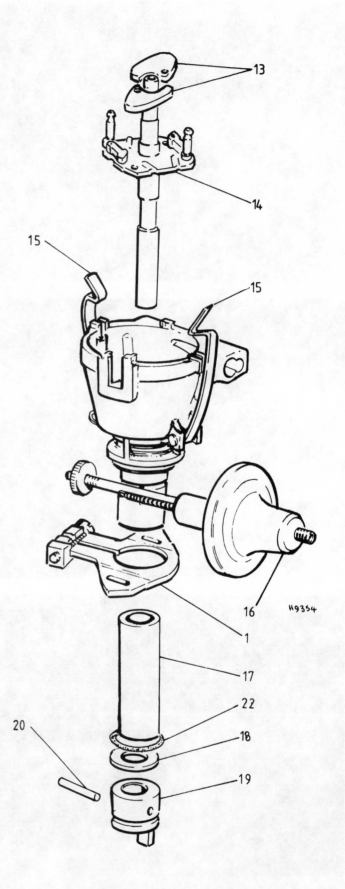

Figure 19.   Lucas 25D4 Distributor.

1	Clamping plate	12	Automatic advance springs
2	Moulded cap	13	Weight assembly
3	Brush and spring	14	Shaft and action plate
4	Rotor arm	15	Cap retaining clips
5	Contacts (set)	16	Vacuum unit
6	Capacitor	17	Bush
7	Terminal and lead (low tension)	18	Thrust washer
8	Moving contact breaker plate	19	Driving dog
9	Contact breaker baseplate	20	Parallel pin
10	Earth lead	21	Cam screw
11	Cam	24	O-ring oil seal

Distributor — general

Many parts of the distributor wear and malfunction. In particular the following points should be checked:

1) The vacuum unit perforates and no longer functions.
2) The plates holding the points wear, allowing the points to contact the distributor cam on an angle — and causing the vacuum unit to work in jerky motions.
3) The mechanical advance seizes (freezes).
4) The cam develops freeplay (sideways) on the distributor shaft.
5) The distributor shaft wears in the bushing of the body.
6) The points and condenser fail.

All these items conspire to create a spark at the wrong time, or to give the spark to each cylinder at a different degree (the sparks should be separated by 90°).

Lucas Parts List

Bush (421 998)
Top plate (422 318): This plate has a vertical brass shaft for holding points.
Top plate (54 412 154): This has only a short shaft for holding the Quickafits.
Base plate (54 419 792): This wears in the curved slot.
LT lead (54 413 549): An excellent low tension connection is essential.
Cap (54 412 472 DC1) — early models — uses screw in distributor terminals.
Cap (54 417 214 DC6) — later models — uses push on terminals.
Rotor (400 051 RA1)
Points/Cond. (600 41 004 TK50)
Spacer (1G 2673): This keeps the wires apart on the DC1 cap but is no longer available.
Suppressors (60 460 666): The present Lucas suppressors are made in Italy.
Vacuum Unit: These are differentiated mainly by "carb vacuum" or "manifold vacuum", depending on their connection on the left side of the engine. Early models will have carb type (54 411

985) & later models Manifold type (54 425 359). There are, however, about ten different vacuum units, depending on the year and model (Roadster or GT). Consult the local Lucas dealer for the proper listing.

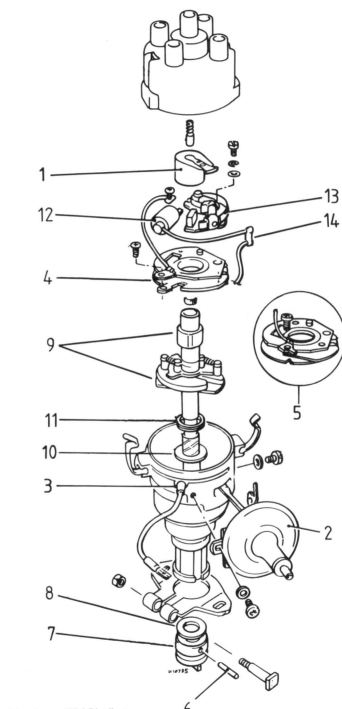

Figure 20.   Lucas 45D4 Distributor.

1 Rotor arm	5 Baseplate (early cars)	9 Cam spindle and automatic advance weights assembly	11 Spacer
2 Vacuum unit			12 Capacitor
3 Low tension lead	6 Retaining pin — drive dog		13 Contact set
4 Baseplate	7 Drive dog	10 Steel washer	14 Low tension lead connector
	8 Thrust washer		

Variations for the 1975 on Distributor

Plate assembly (60 600 540).
Points (54 423 769 CS8).
Condenser (54 425 179 C 4).
Rotor (54 422 803 RA4).
Cap (54 427 109 DC8).
Vacuum Unit (54 525 516): It should be noted that the vacuum unit in the 1975 MGB (USA), was not connected, but better performance can be achieved by connecting it directly to the manifold.

D1. Access to the distributor retaining bolts is rather cramped. It is best removed by loosening the pinch-bolt as shown, leaving the two bolts which hold the pinch-bolt plate to the block in place.

Lucas Horn Overhaul

Tool Box

Bench vice; $^3/_{16}$ inch drill; screwdrivers; wire brush.

Safety

Refer to the notes on "Safety" at the start of this chapter.

EH1. Hold the horn in the vice as shown, and drill off the six rivet heads with a $^3/_{16}$ inch drill.

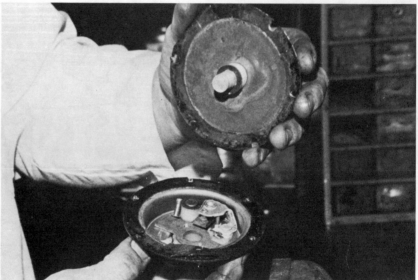

EH2. Separate the diaphragm and base from the top.

EH3. Free up the 2BA basic adjusting screw (Note — It has a LEFT HAND THREAD and unscrews clockwise).

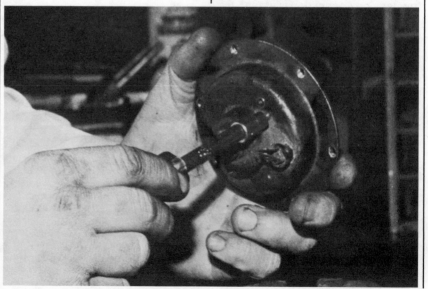

EH4. Free the locknut and remove it and the tone adjusting screw. Wire brush the screw so that it will work freely in the assembly.

EH5. Clean the contact points with fine sandpaper.

EH6. With a $^3/_{16}$ inch bit, drill out the insulators holding the electrical spade terminals to the body.

EH7. Replace the spade terminals with a 2BA crosshead screw, or its metric equivalent.

EH8. Ensure that the end of the screw is well insulated from the horn body by using new insulating washers or portions of the old spade-terminal base.

EH9. Tighten the screw and nut assembly, making absolutely certain that, when tight, there is NOT A SHORT between the post and the horn body. A double spade terminal, such as that fitted to a Lucas coil, can be added later.

EH10.   Reassemble the diaphragm and cover to the base.

EH11.   Replace the rivets with 2BA screws and nuts, or their metric equivalent. Sometimes one side of the nut has to be filed down so that it clears the body of the horn.

EH12.   Connect the horn terminals to a 12 volt battery and adjust the basic and note screws by half a turn each until the proper note is found, then make a final adjustment with the tone screw.

Wiring Loom — general & Courtesy Light Switches

Tool Box

Small open-ended spanners; crosshead screwdriver; wire brush; hammered-finish paint; small paint brush; 2 pairs of pliers for separating stubborn bullet connectors.

Safety

Refer to the notes on "Safety" at the start of this chapter.

With care an older cloth covered loom can be cleaned to make it appear new and fresh. CAREFULLY remove the loom, noting the location of the clamps which hold it in place and, to speed up renewal, fold a piece of masking tape double leaving an inch at the end single and sticky. Wrap this around the end of a wire as it is disconnected and write its location on the masking tape. Wire brush the clamps and repaint them with a hammered metal finish paint. Coil the wiring loom and place it into a shallow pan with warm soapy water. SQUEEZE, BUT DO NOT SCRUB the loom until it is as clean as it will get before it begins to unravel, then hang it in the garage to dry. The PVC wires can be cleaned to almost new lustre by spraying a rag and the wires with aerosol carb cleaner, and wiping the sludge and grease from the wires. The newer looms, incidentally, are wrapped in a light blue PVC tape.

As a rule, the wires themselves do not fail. The ends may lose contact with the wires but the wires themselves rarely break. Any splicing or correction to the loom should be made outside the wrapping. There should be no connections within the loom itself. If changes are made in the loom, solder Lucas bullet connectors to the wires and use the black female connectors of the type used with the rest of the system.

NOTE: Prior to removing the loom from the car, remove ALL the black female connectors as they impede the free movement of the loom through the bulkhead, boot etc. Prior to replacing the loom in the car, clean each bullet connector with fine sandpaper to ensure a good connection.

The interior light switches in the door pillars become bent and corrode so that they do not work. Remove them from the pillar and from the purple/white wire. Wire brush them so that they will make good contact to the pillar and to themselves. Straighten a bent plunger with pliers.

7 Modifications

Information on tuning and modifying the MGB could easily fill a book in itself! This section offers advice to U.S. owners who would like their cars to go as fast as its designers intended, information on converting earlier cars to negative earth (ground) so that modern radios, cassette players and alternators can be fitted and then a general section on go-faster tuning and performance accessories.

De-toxing (USA MGBs)

North American MGBs were fitted with progressively more strangulatory exhaust emission control regulations which, though initiated for the most commendable of motives, did nothing for the sporting character of the MGB. The North American owner who wishes to ''de-tox'' his or her car may gain the following advantages (although nothing can be guaranteed):

mileage may be better; acceleration can improve; deceleration too, should be sharper (there will be generally more positive throttle response); there'll be no more ''popping'' or red hot converters; the engine looks ''cleaner''; the front spark plug will no longer be hidden from view.

NOTE: de-toxing in some states may be illegal. Responsibility for compliance with the law must rest with the individual owner.

Procedures DT2 to DT15 are for the 1975-80 MGBs & DT16 to DT20 for 1969-74 models.

Tool Box

$5/16$ inch combination spanner; $3/8$ inch drive ratchet; $3/8 \times 6$ inch extension; Allen wrench for pipe plug; $1/2$ inch socket; $5/8$ inch deep socket (for injector bolts); $1/2$ inch open-end wrench; $7/16$ inch open-end wrench; $1/4$ NPT tap and tap wrench; four $7/16$ inch bolts; one $1/4$ inch (Allen driven) NPT pipe plug.

Safety

Remember when working on, or around, fuel systems that gasoline is volatile and highly flammable. DON'T SMOKE!

DT1(A). ''Tool Box'' illustrated.

DT1(B). Before starting, the bonnet (hood) must be removed or held aloft with a stick as the factory slide is too short and both fenders should be covered with large cloths or old blankets.

DT2. Remove the two hoses to the air pump. Remove the long bolt (½ inch wrench) holding the air pump to the thermostat cover and remove the bolt from the adjusting strap (½ inch).

DT3. Remove the pump and the fanbelt.

DT4. Remove the four air injectors with a $^7/_{16}$ inch wrench. If the injectors will not unscrew, cut the tubing at the injector and use a $^7/_{16}$ inch socket. Remove the bolt holding the injector to the rear right head nut.

DT5.   Remove the air pump adjuster bracket. If this is left in place, and if it should loosen, it could foul the alternator fan. Use a ½ inch wrench.

DT6.   Replace the air injectors with ⁷/₁₆ inch fine bolts or Allen screws, and tighten snugly.

DT7.   Hold the tall nut at the thermostat cover with a ½ inch wrench to keep it from spinning and remove the bolt at the top.

DT8.   Remove the thin black vacuum line from the manifold to the TCSA switch on the master cylinder box.

DT9.   Remove the two bolts holding the gulp valve to its bracket ($^7/_{16}$ inch wrench and socket).

DT10.   Lift the gulp valve 90° fitting and hoses away. It may be necessary to twist the 90° fitting to facilitate removal.

DT11.   Remove the bolt holding the gulp valve bracket (^{15}/$_{16}$ inch socket) discard the bracket and the thinnest of the two copper washers. Then replace the bolt and one washer snugly.

DT12.   Tap the hole from the 90° fitting ¼ NPT. There will be metal shavings and it's best to grease the tap before cutting the threads so that the chafings will remain on the tap, or better still, to remove the manifold first.

DT13.   Fit a ¼ NPT plug or Allen screw to the hole. To stop possible vacuum leaks, wrap the threads with teflon tape, or use jointing compound.

DT14.   Move the vacuum advance line from the TCSA switch directly to the intake manifold. MGBs fitted with the TCSA switch allow the distributor vacuum advance to work only in fourth gear.

DT15.   The detox is now completed. At University Motors, John Twist says, ''We find that setting the timing at factory specs allows good acceleration without pinging''. John carries on, ''Further steps, which we don't do, could include removing the EGR line from the EGR valve (top of the manifold) and plugging it. The catalytic converter could be removed but that's best left for an exhaust job in the future. A 1975 (non-Californian) front pipe will eliminate the converter, although the manifold must be removed from the engine to remove the converter from the manifold. The carb can be removed and the spring loaded valve in the butterfly soldered shut. This allows even faster decelerations''.

DT16.   The manifold with the gulp valve and piping are removed.

DT17. Replace the vacuum fitting with a $5/16 \times 1/2$ inch bolt (fine) which can be found holding the air manifold to the head, or the air hose clamp to the thermostat cover nut.

DT18. Tap the centre hole ¼ NPT. Use grease on the tap to hold the shavings, or remove the manifold to be absolutely sure.

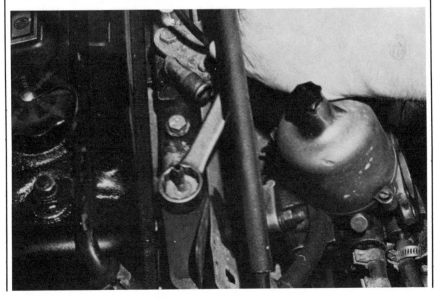

DT19. Use a $15/16$ inch wrench to remove the nut from the gulp valve bracket. Replace the nut and the largest copper washer.

DT20.   The final view of the carb side. DO NOT remove or block the hoses to the carbs from the front tappet inspection cover.

The detox on the 1968 MGB is the same as for 69-74, except that the 90° fitting in the centre of the intake manifold cannot be blocked, as a Smith's PCV valve is fitted there. Two options: leave a piece of hose on the T-fitting and block the hose with a bolt and hose clamp or, tap the manifold as suggested and instead of blocking it with a pipe plug, fit a ¼ NPT nipple, about 1½ inch long and reconnect the PCV valve.

Negative Earth Conversion (1963-1967 models) *With John Twist of University Motors, Michigan*

The GHN3 MGBs were supplied from the factory with a positive earth (ground) electrical system. The system was reversed in 1968 with the introduction of the GHN4 MGBs which used an alternator rather than a dynamo type generator and which continued until 1980 with the negative earth system. A modern approach to ownership often includes the fitting of a radio or tape player, both of which are difficult and cumbersome to wire with the existing system. Wired negative earth, the earlier MGBs continue to function properly.

Tool Box

AF spanners; engineers' pliers (use two pairs for parting stubborn bullet connectors); jumper wire; wire strippers; soldering equipment.

Safety

Refer to notes at start of chapter.

1) Disconnect the batteries, remove them from position, clean all posts and clamps and renew the connection from the earth strap to the body (left/nearside).

NE1.   While the batteries are removed, replace the Lucas ''cap'' style terminal ends with ''wrap around'' American style clamps. The Lucas terminal ends are sized to fit the battery posts, and since the positive post is larger than the negative, these clamps will no longer be satisfactory for use.

DO NOT CUT the old terminal ends from the wire, but melt them off with a small propane torch. Cutting the wiring, especially the cable from the batteries to the solenoid shortens it needlessly, and it may not reach the new battery position. Be certain to add the proper battery fixtures (clamp – AHH 6353; bolt – AHH 6750; rubber pad – AHH 6351), as excessive bouncing and shaking will take years off battery life. ⇨

Replace the batteries 180° from their old alignment, and connect the major power cable (solenoid to battery) to the positive post, then connect the intermediate cable (negative post of right battery to the positive post of the other battery). Finally, reconnect the earth cable to the negative post of the left battery.

2) Examine the ignition coil. The WHITE wire must be connected to the '' + '' or ''CB'' terminal; the WHITE & BLACK wire (distributor to coil) must be connected to the '' – '' or ''SW'' terminal. (''CB'' = contact breakers; ''SW'' = switch; reversed in this application since the batteries are now reversed).

3) Polarize the generator. Remove the BROWN/GREEN wire from the ''F'' (Field) terminal on the generator (the smaller spade). Use a jumper wire and make a momentary connection between this spade terminal and the live post of the starter solenoid (post with the BROWN wire).

A spark will occur as the connection is made. This procedure reverses the magnetic field in the generator. Reconnect the BROWN/GREEN wire to the generator and start up the engine. The ignition light should act as before – (ON when the ignition is ON, ON at very low RPM, OFF above about 1000 and OFF when the ignition is OFF). WARNING: If the ignition light remains ON when

the ignition is OFF, IMMEDIATELY disconnect the BROWN wires from the starter solenoid and check your work!

4) Check the heater blower operation. With the ignition ON, turn on the heater blower and judge the amount of air which is being blown into the footwells. Then reverse the wires at the heater motor (bullet connectors) and again judge the amount of air being blown. Use whichever connection affords the greatest air movement.

5) Converting the Tachometer to Negative Earth:

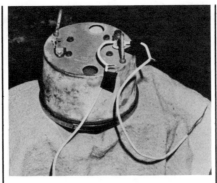

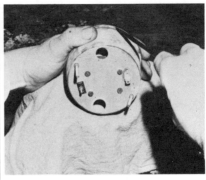

NE4. The white wires are now cut through and a section of insulation removed, and then reconnected to the OTHER white wires. The connections should be soldered, or Lucas bullet connectors soldered to all four ends and connectors used.

NE5. The chrome bezel is now loosened along its circumference.

NE2. Remove the tachometer from the car by undoing the two knurled nuts and taking off the lock washers and clips.

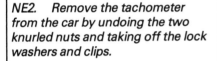

NE3. In this illustration one leg of the white wire loop is tagged with two pieces of electrical tape. This operation cannot be carried out as shown, as the white wire is part of the wiring loom — this is for illustration only.

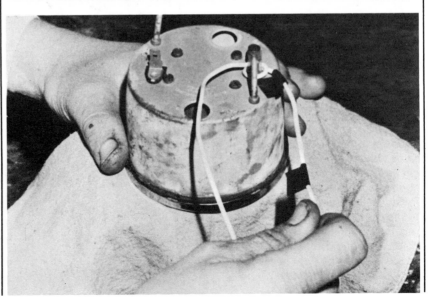

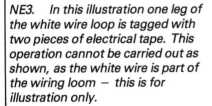

NE6. Once loosened, the chrome ring can be turned and removed.

NE7. The two screws holding the unit's internals (there are washers under the cheese head screws) can be removed and the internal working assembly will drop out.

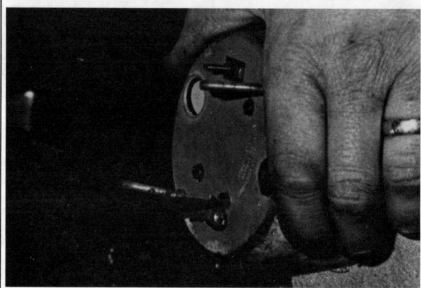

NE8. The power and earth wires must be cut and connected to the opposite terminals in much the same way that the white wires were cut and reversed. The resistor connected to the spade terminal must be unsoldered and connected to the post immediately to its left (pointer). At the same time the wire connected to the left terminal must be soldered to the right terminal. This illustration shows the wiring PRIOR to reversal.

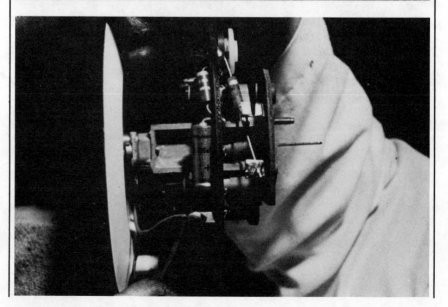

6) From a newer MGB, or by handlettering your own, place a warning label under the bonnet and on the battery cover: "WARNING – This vehicle wired negative earth".

V8 Engine Conversion – general

The fitting of a Rover 3500cc (ex-Buick, but considerably modified) V8 engine is an exciting prospect, but should only be contemplated where the basic car is very sound indeed and where the braking system has been uprated.

"He said it was running too juicy, so I took four of the plugs out."

The 135BHP Range Rover engine was fitted by B.L. while the earlier Costello versions used the higher output Rover saloon (sedan) units. Both were mated to a standard MGB gearbox and this proved to be the cars' Achiles heel. A far more attractive proposition would be an MGB with a Rover SD1 engine (which has an even higher output but with better fuel economy) and an SD1 5-speed manual-shift gearbox.

The V8 Conversion Company of Britain fit V8 engines to MGBs and can supply components for DIY fitting. They make the following points:

"The problems incurred with this conversion vary according to the particular model but basically the earlier the model the more difficult the conversion". Brief details of some of the problems are as follows:

1) Mating of the Rover engine to the

MGB gearbox by means of a special adaptor plate and crank adaptor (thus utilising the MGB flywheel and starter motor).
2) Specially fabricated tubular steel exhaust manifold and join pipes.
3) Body-engine mountings specially made.
4) Purpose-built engine mountings for the sides of the cylinder block.
5) Modified steering shaft to clear exhaust and engine mounting.
6) Bulkhead cut away to clear V8 heads.
7) Transmission tunnel modifications.
8) Flitch plates modified to clear exhaust.
9) Radiator mountings moved forward.
10) Electric cooling fans required.
11) Brake pipes rerouted.
12) Remote oil filtering required.
13) Change rear axle ratio.
14) Recalibrate instruments.
15) Modify clutch hydraulics."

To expand on a point raised by The V8 Conversion Company, later cars already have many of the necessary modifications carried out at the factory. Post-1975 cars are already satisfactory in respect of details 6, 7, 9 (and 10, in the USA) while inner flitch panels are correctly shaped on post-1973 cars.

Brakes – fitting the V8 type

This suggestion was made by Peter Laidler in the MG Owners' Club magazine. His idea is to use a combination of new, easily obtainable second-hand and existing MGB components.

Existing parts – MGB Callipers; MGB Disc shields (to be modified).

Second hand parts – Set of callipers from Triumph 2000.

New parts – V8 Discs × 2 (BTB 1319); Calliper seals × 2 (17H 4353); Set disc pads (GPB 212); Calliper to hub lock tabs × 2 (BTC 114); Calliper piston seal kit × 1 (8G 8641).

The most expensive parts

shown are, obviously the V8 discs but they are the essential ingredient in improved braking, being thicker and giving improved heat dispersal and thus increased efficiency.

The Triumph callipers are stripped and the outer halves disposed of along with the bridge bolts and seals. Hook out the metal rings holding the piston seals into the inner halves and bang the half-calliper down onto a block of wood until the piston falls out. Remove the inner seal, thoroughly clean the calliper halves, renew the seals and refit the pistons.

After removing and dismantling the MGB's callipers, the inner calliper halves are discarded. After renewing the outer halves' piston seals the Triumph inner and MGB outer halves are bolted together using the new components listed. The bridge bolts should be torqued up to 35-37lb/ft. The resultant callipers are hybrid replicas of the standard V8 callipers at a fraction of the cost!

Engine Performance Tuning – general

If it is true that the British are famous for making compromises, then it is equally true that they have made a famously successful one out of the MGB. Achieving the right balance between everyday "useability" and sporting flair is no mean feat but compromises, by definition, still leave a number of discontented customers. Those who want a less sporting car have a whole traffic-jam of other cars to choose from but those who want more performance have to bear in mind that, as they say in Yorkshire, "You don't get owt for nowt". More pennies produce more power, but the number of pennies required to produce – and to run – a Porsche or Ferrari are beyond most 'B owners. Moreover, the reliability factor of many high performance cars would drive many of those brought up on the MGB's long-stroke longevity to despair!

However almost any improvement in performance implies expense and some reduction in the everyday "useability" that makes the standard car so easy to own.

Gentle modification *can* undoubtedly add a little throttle "snap", tighten up the cornering and braking and make the MGB just a little more enjoyable without making a measurable difference to the car's reliability and even, in some cases, extending it. In addition, many owners enjoy expressing their own individuality in their cars and since differences in individuality and taste cannot be measured in terms of the length of the driver's seat adjustment, many cosmetic additions are frequently made to MGBs. The following sections show how mild changes can be made to both performance and appearance but owners are strongly urged to remember Abingdon's own motto, "Safety Fast". Cars weakened with rust or damage should NEVER be made to go faster and if engines are to be tuned to give a significant increase in power, then braking and suspension modifications should FIRST be made.

It would also be foolish to "hot-up" an engine which is worn without generally reconditioning it. The car's oil pressure when hot should be above 50lb/in² whilst running at moderate road speeds, each cylinder should give a compression of 150 to 160lb/in² when checked with a compression tester and, of course, oil consumption should be minimal and there should be an absence of threatening engine noises. (When checking cylinder compression, bear in mind that a low reading on adjacent cylinders usually means that the gasket between them has blown — often indicating cylinder head problems — while a single low reading usually indicates a burned out valve or piston rings, but do check tappet clearances before jumping to conclusions!

Before embarking upon the task of performance tuning your MGB, try a really thorough standard lube & tune job and compare

Standard Performance Figures

Speed (M.P.H.)	Time in Secs.			
	'60's Rdstr	'60's GT	'70's Rdstr	'70's GT
30-50 in top	9.0-9.5	9.5-10.0	9.0-9.5	9.0-9.5
40-60 in top	9.0-9.5	10.0-10.5	9.0-9.5	9.0-9.5
0 to 50	8.5-9.0	8.5-9.0	8.0-8.5	8.0-8.5
0 to 60	12.0-12.5	13.0-13.5	11.0-11.5	11.5-12.0
M.P.G.	28-30	28-30	24-26	24-26

performance before and after. Setting-up an engine correctly can make a great deal of difference.

Once the engine is correctly set-up it may be informative to find a stretch of dry, flat straight road and test the car against the stopwatch, provided that road conditions are safe. No two cars are the same because of the effect of cumulative differences in production tolerances, but the following yardstick can be applied as a general guide. However note that U.S. cars built since the early 'Seventies are markedly slower. For instance a 1979 U.S. Specification Roadster should take from 16.0 to 16.5 seconds to reach 60mph from rest and average around 20 miles per U.S. gallon.

Fuel Octane Ratings

Traditionally, tuning an engine has frequently included the raising of compression ratios. This necessitates the use of fuels with a high octane rating which have a high lead content. In the U.S.A. and, increasingly, in other parts of the world, high lead content fuels have been or are being phased out for very real health reasons and where a "standard" MGB (Compression Ratios of 8.8 to 1) gives "pinking" (pre-ignition) and pronounced "running-on" or "dieseling" because of the unavailability of high octane fuels, consideration should be given to *reducing* the compression ratios by machining out the combustion chambers.

Engine Performance Tuning Procedure

Stage One

It is possible to increase bhp at the flywheel by around 5% by fitting 1¾ inch S.U. carburettors and the appropriate manifold. The ignition timing should be set at 10° B.T.D.C. and the carburettors should be fitted with KP needles, "blue" springs and "100" jets.

Stage Two

If the following modifications are carried out in addition to those listed above, around 105bhp should be available at the flywheel. In addition, fuel economy and general smoothness may well improve. Smoothness may be further improved if the crank, flywheel and clutch assembly are professionally dynamically balanced.

The exhaust and inlet ports of the cylinder head should be lightly ground and polished using a flexible drive shaft driven from an electric drill or other suitable power source. Be careful not to grind too much of the port wall between the exhaust and inlet valve seats away (visible just inside the ports). This is where the water jacket has been brought as close to the valves as possible. Grind out any frazes from the combustion chambers and lightly polish them but do not enlarge the chamber walls because this may cause the head gasket to overlap

with adverse consequences. Aim for a smooth finish consistent with the removal of the minimum amount of metal.

The combustion chamber shapes can be improved in one respect and that is by removing some of the "pier" which protrudes into the top of the chamber as shown in Fig 21.

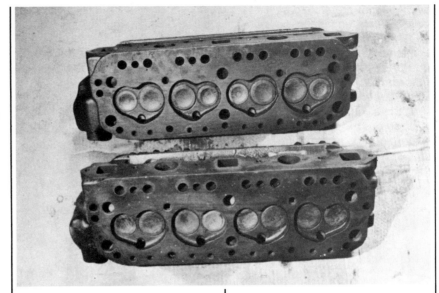

ST1. Later "12V" engines' cylinder heads have been modified from new to give this slight improvement in combustion chamber shape and therefore do not require any further attention in this respect.

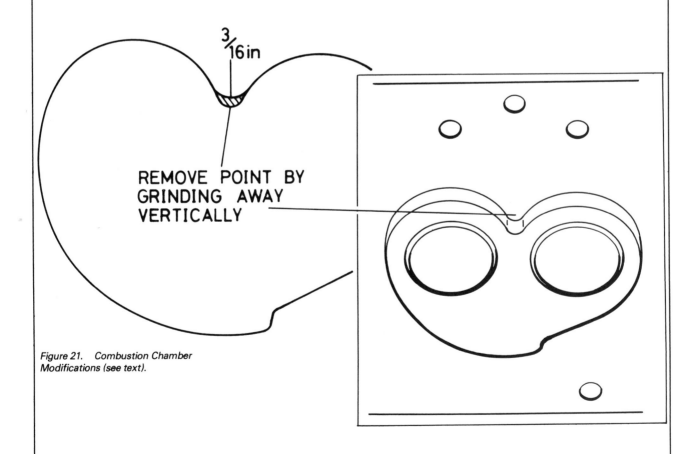

$\frac{3}{16}$ in

REMOVE POINT BY GRINDING AWAY VERTICALLY

Figure 21. Combustion Chamber Modifications (see text).

ST2. A new manifold gasket should be placed first on the head and then on the manifold and used as a template in relation to which all the ports should be ground to shape. Production line techniques mean that the fit between manifold and port is usually rather hit-and-miss, so this modification helps to smooth out the worst of the poor fitting.

ST3. If a steel manifold is fitted (giving better exhaust gas extraction), apply engineers' blue to the outer face of the manifold gasket and bolt the manifold onto the car, thus ensuring that the "spring" in the tubing is allowed for and that the manifold ports are shaped in accordance with its true position on the engine.

If the type of petroleum available permits it, have 0.27 inch skimmed from the cylinder head which increases the standard compression ratio to 9.2:1.

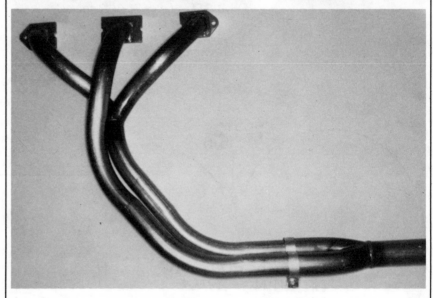

Weber Carburettor

The fitting of a Weber carburettor gives the potential for even more power but some experimentation is generally needed to obtain the best results, depending on local conditions, and if a rolling road is available, its use would be recommended. The 45DCOE Weber is the one to use and must be fitted with the appropriate manifold. The old, Special Tuning Department installation kit number, if some old-stock should be discovered, is C-AJJ 3312.

The Weber carburettor is mounted on synthetic rubber O-rings which absorb excessive vibration and therefore prevent disturbance of the fuel-to-air ratio. Each fixing nut should be locked with a double-coil spring washer and the nuts should be drilled and wired in pairs to prevent them from coming loose. The nuts should be tightened up fairly firmly but when the unit is gripped tightly, just a little free movement should be felt. A steady-rod should be made up and connected to the rear engine plate, similar to that shown in Fig 22.

Initial Weber 45DCOE carburettor setting should be:

Auxiliary venturi: 5.0mm
Chokes: 40.0mm
Main jet: 1.85mm
Air correction jet: 1.60mm
Emulsion tubes: F16
Idling jets: .60/F8
Pump jets: .60
Needle valve: 2.25mm (spring loaded)
Float/cover gasket level: 5mm

When the level between the float and cover gasket is measured, it is MOST IMPORTANT that the float is allowed to hang vertically. A false reading will be obtained if the lid is held horizontally.

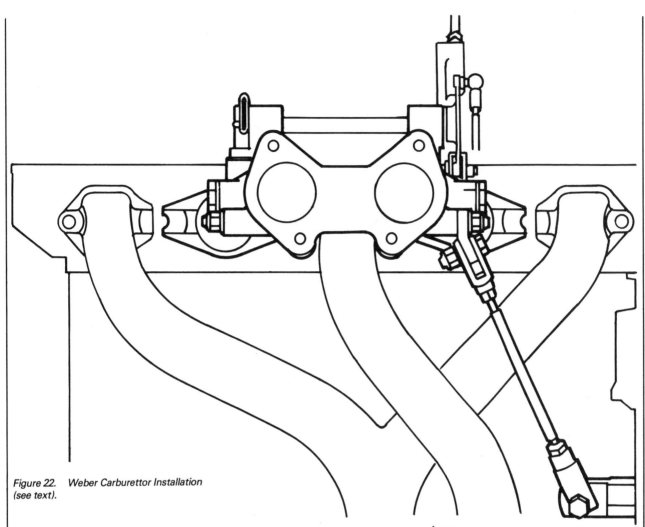

Figure 22.   Weber Carburettor Installation
(see text).

Better top-end power will be obtained at the expense of pick-up by fitting 38mm chokes and a 1.75mm main jet while a 3.5mm auxiliary venturi sometimes gives improved pick-up, but these are matters for trial and error. The type of manifolding used and the stage of tune of the rest of the engine will have an influence on the settings required.

Camshafts

A number of different camshafts are available giving, at the "hottest" end, an engine with greatly increased power over such a narrow rev range that everyday driving is all but impossible. The standard camshaft is fine for mild tuning, but some U.S. enthusiasts prefer a mild

Iskanderian cam and indeed, a noticeable power increase can be obtained with virtually no loss of flexibility but with an inevitable fuel penalty.

Distributor

ST3(A).   More advanced levels of tuning call for the Special Tuning distributor – which is still available.

To The Limit

It is possible to increase the power of the MGB beyond reasonable limits, indeed Abingdon themselves did just that with 8DBL: the car which Paddy Hopkirk drove at Sebring with an engine capacity of 2004cc. Larger valves (the inlets of a Nimonic alloy), 2 inch SU carburettors with flared intake trumpets and much other tuning work.

Power outputs increased to these levels put a great deal of strain on the clutch, and even the timing chain sprockets (Cooper "S" sprockets will fit, but give incorrect valve timing) so that the whole affair becomes complex, expensive, specialised and beyond the scope of this book.

Those readers who do wish to "take it to the limit" will find many specialist tuning guides available and a host of performance components still available for the MGB. The British M.G. Car Club is probably one of the best sources of tuning advice and offers the best opportunities to compete with an MGB in Britain.

ST4. John Hill's "reproduction" 1¾ inch SU inlet manifolds.

Running Gear & Suspension Uprating

Brake Discs

The author was impressed by an article which appeared in *Enjoying M.G.,* the M.G. Owners' Club magazine written by Peter Laidler on the subject of more efficient MGB disc brakes. The author is unable to verify the use or effectiveness of discs modified in the manner suggested by Peter but would like to convey grateful thanks to him for permission to quote from his article.

The article begins by explaining that the energy contained in the forward motion of the car is converted into heat by the effect of the friction within the braking system and so dissipated. The more efficiently the brakes can get rid of their heat, the more efficient they are. V8 brake discs, because they are thicker, are more efficient at dissipating heat and so provide a way of uprating the MGBs braking performance. But since V8 type

discs, callipers and backplates all need to be fitted together, the arrangement is rather expensive.

Peter Laidler's article continues, "Fitting the V8 system isn't as effective as what I am going to tell you now. What has not been discussed yet is ventilating the discs as per the high quality motorcycles.

RGS1. "Here are the mathematics of it all. The swept area of each disc is that area actually touched by the pad during one revolution of the wheel. In the case of the MGB/GT/V8 this swept area is approx. 12.2 in² per disc side or a total of 24 in² for both discs). Now, if there were 4 rows of holes, each hole 0.125 in (⅛ in) dia. and 10 degrees apart that would total 144 holes in each disc. The total area of those holes if added up would equal 19.2 in² on a GT and 24.9 in² on a V8 (the area of the V8 type is increased due to the disc being thicker) PER DISC. All this extra area is extra cooling area. Additionally, any water on the disc is swept into these holes by the pad. Therefore the pad does not have to shift the water before it starts stopping the car. Although this is not a serious problem with cast iron discs, it is worth while bearing in mind.

You might well say that because the discs are drilled, the area directly underneath the pad at any given moment is slightly decreased. That is true. But the difference is so slight that the extra cooling area and efficiency caused by the greater heat loss more than compensates for this.

Motor Cycle experience has shown that there is no greater wear on the disc pads with holes drilled in the discs. Just ask a motorcyclist yourself . . . The strength of the ventilated disc is such that I cannot with the facilities available to me, test one to destruction in a rotary plane. The first to go are the brake pipes, at a hydraulic pressure far greater than you could ever subject your braking system to.

So, how do you go about doing this modification? When the discs need grinding, take them to your local friendly machine shop operator and ask him if he has a milling machine with a boring facility and an indexed head. Before he skims the disc up, ask him to set the disc up in the index head and drill it as shown in Fig 23. Even if you don't understand it, he will. I appreciate that it is only cast iron he is drilling, but I would purchase and give him half a dozen DORMER high speed steel 0.125 in drills or drills of equal quality to ensure that all the holes are bright and sharp. All that is left to do now is to skim them up . . . magic.''

In a later letter to the author, he went on, ''The destruction testing of the 'B discs was quite thorough. I haven't kept any figures but with a side impact the ventilated discs cracked/broke at about half the rate for undrilled discs.

''The side impact destruction test is purely academic as once on the car it is of no value whatsoever as the disc is never subject to a side impact. But it does highlight the fact that ventilated discs should be handled with extra care in the workshop lest they are dropped and given a hairline crack which might only fail in use, with disastrous consequences.''

MGB brakes are perfectly efficient for normal use but some people find them heavy in use. A brake servo will help to make them feel lighter but it will not increase their efficiency because, as previously explained, their actual heat dissipation will not be any better.

Wheels & Tyres

Wire wheels are liable to run out of true and then patter at higher speeds. This fault cannot be rectified by balancing but has to be tackled at source. When wires which are true, or steel or aluminium wheels patter, they should be balanced both statically and dynamically with weights

ROW 1 STARTS 0·4 IN. FROM EDGE TO CENTRE OF HOLE
REMAINING ROWS 0·4 IN. APART FROM CENTRES
ROW 1+3 10° APART RADIALLY
ROW 1+2 5° APART RADIALLY
ROW 2+4 10° APART RADIALLY

NOT TO SCALE

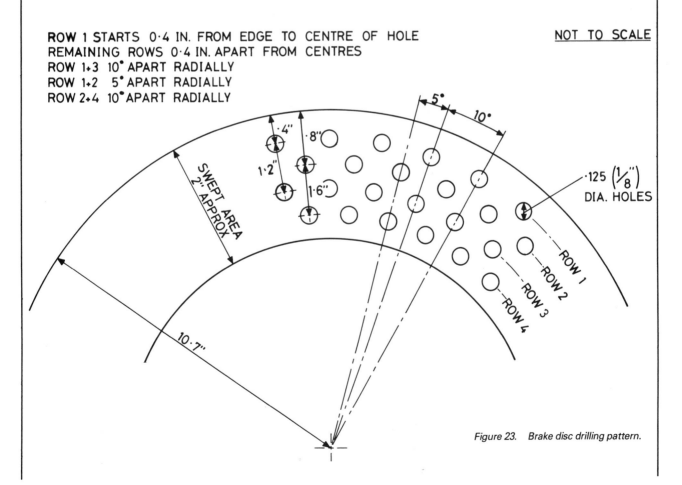

Figure 23. Brake disc drilling pattern.

placed on the inside and the outsides of the rims. Wheels which patter are in effect, losing adhesion, a fault which can be disastrous when cornering hard, particularly in the wet.

This leads on to a modification which should NOT be made to an MGB/GT or V8 — the fitting of over-large wheels or larger than 175 section tyres. Peter Laidler again supplies the technical background to the problem.

"It's not that there is insufficient room for bigger tyres, it is simply that with the geometry at the front of the car — long chassis legs supported by little else but the inner wing — over-large tyres cause a phenomena called 'scuttle shake' ".

Obviously, not every car is going to suffer badly from shake when fitted with oversize wheels and much must depend on the condition of front suspension bushes and general bodily soundness, but Peter's point is well worth bearing in mind if larger wheels and tyres are being contemplated. Also consider that where the latest MGBs used 185/70 × 14 tyres, they were fitted with weight saving all-alloy rims.

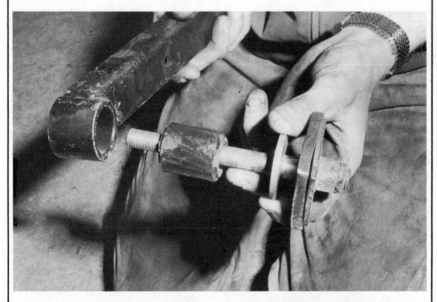

RGS2. The front suspension bushes themselves can be directly replaced by the far beefier — but rather more expensive — V8 bushes which are much longer lasting and less prone to "clonking".

Suspension

RGS3. It is at the rear of the car that the greatest improvement can be made to the suspension of any MGB, C or V8. Short of completely redesigning the rear end (as Gilbern did so successfully with their MGB-powered Gilbern GT 1800) which is hardly a practicable option, the best alternative is to fit a telescopic rear shock absorber conversion, using Spax shockers.

RGS4.   The spring mounting connections are less than elegant but the improvement in handling makes this no great burden, giving more neutral handling with less tendency for the rear wheels to break away too early.

Fitting stiffer front springs will not necessarily have an improved effect upon the car's handling. Their tendency will be to allow the car to corner "flatter" but, after a point, to suffer from increased understeer (the tendency of the front of the car to drift wide in a corner). Fitting a thicker front anti-roll bar will have the same effect.

"I think the shocks want replacing — tends to jump a bit on the corners . . ."

At the rear, thicker springs or anti-roll bar will tend to increase oversteer (the tendency of the rear end to drift causing tighter cornering and, ultimately, spinning). However, early raised ride-height cars benefit enormously from the fitting of an anti-roll bar to cut down the horrendous amount of body roll which they are capable of achieving.

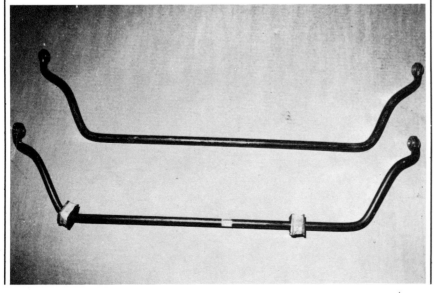

RGS5.   A GT anti-roll bar is thicker than that of the Roadster while a still thicker bar is also available.

RGS6. It is possible to lower the ride height of rubber-bumper cars but the work involved is fairly considerable. For instance, the crossmember shown here on the right has a raised chassis mounting point which raises the height at the front end. This has to be replaced by a complete crossmember from an earlier car, such as that shown on the left. Some owners have been known to fit shorter coil springs to achieve the effect of lowering the front end. This alters the suspension geometry and reduces suspension travel — not recommended.

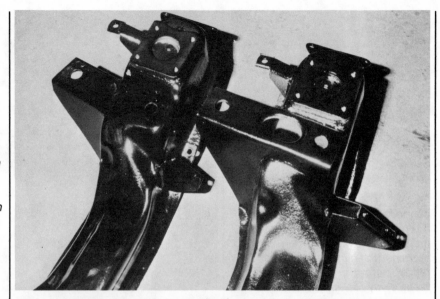

RGS7. An overdrive gearbox will not increase the top speed of the MGB since maximum revs. attainable in direct top are achieved at maximum bhp. However, fuel economy is improved along with quieter, calmer open-road motoring and an extra "gear" is obtained between third and fourth direct gears in the form of overdrive-third.

The overdrive gearbox bolts in as a direct replacement for the standard 'box and while overdrive and standard prop shafts have different part numbers, there is no perceptible difference in their length and the original can be retained. Power to the overdrive unit comes from a "spare" bullet connector found protruding from the wiring loom in the region of the fuse box (see wiring diagram in Workshop Manual) while the overdrive switch wires are taped to the loom behind the dash, ready to be connected to a switch. Simplicity itself!

Bolt on Performance & Costmetic Accessories

BP1. Front aprons are highly prone to corrosion on all the MGB variants but unbolt quite easily (provided that the nuts will move!)

BP2. A B.L. or accessory front spoiler can be bolted very simply in its place and may provide better high speed stability.

BP3. Many U.S. cars have been fitted with B.L.'s own striping kit which was often fitted, new, to 1973-75 cars. (Photo: Steve Glochowsky).

BP4. Although cars with effective synchromesh hardly need it, heel-&-toeing gives a sportier image. This is virtually impossible with the standard, earlier pedal arrangements, but John Hill's replacement throttle pedal makes it possible to impress . . .

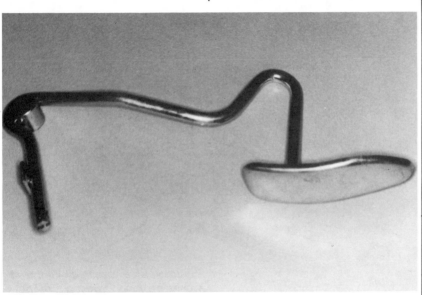

BP5. Rear quarter trim which fills the corner gaps between bumpers and rear light ''hulls'' are of aluminium and are corrosion-prone. They can easily be replaced by made-up alternatives in stainless steel sheet.

BP6. An aluminium rocker-box cover has more than cosmetic value. It also cuts down on MGBs infamous tappet noise.

BP7.   A stainless steel exhaust
and stainless steel fuel tank are two
items well worth fitting when
replacement time comes along.
Stainless exhausts are considerably
more expensive than their mild steel
counterparts (and are no less prone
to damage when driven over rough
ground) but make good long-term
economic sense. Stainless fuel
tanks, however, are no dearer than
the standard item and have an
indefinite life. They bolt on as a
direct replacement (though not for
the earlier strap-held tanks). Do
make sure one with internal baffling
is used. This prevents fuel slopping
around during cornering.

BP8.   Another John Hill
"reproduction" item are these
"Sebring" headlamp cowls which
can be fitted to all models of MGB.
Some clearance would have to be
made around the chrome strip on
road-going cars.

" – but you've got to admire the
way he's always fastest out of the
pits."

BP9.   MGC owners have
Downton Engineering's impressive
modification to emulate, but for a
straightforward engine transplant in
case of emergencies, there's
nothing like keeping an Austin
3-litre in the garden, as recognised
'C expert Derek McGlen will tell
you. With minor modifications, the
Austin 3-litre's engine will go
straight in.

Appendices

1 Workshop Procedures ~ Safety First

Professional motor mechanics are trained in safe working procedures. However enthusiastic you may be about getting on with the job in hand, do take the time to ensure that your safety is not put at risk. A moment's lack of attention can result in an accident, as can failure to observe certain elementary precautions.

There will always be new ways of having accidents, and the following points do not pretend to be a comprehensive list of all dangers; they are intended rather to make you aware of the risks and to encourage a safety-conscious approach to all work you carry out on your vehicle.

Essential DOs and DONT's

DON'T rely on a single jack when working underneath the vehicle. Always use reliable additional means of support, such as axle stands, securely placed under a part of the vehicle that you know will not give way.

DON'T attempt to loosen or tighten high-torque nuts (e.g. wheel hub nuts) while the vehicle is on a jack; it may be pulled off.

DON'T start the engine without first ascertaining that the transmission is in neutral (or 'Park' where applicable) and the parking brake applied.

DON'T suddenly remove the filler cap from a hot cooling system — cover it with a cloth and release the pressure gradually first, or you may get scalded by escaping coolant.

DON'T attempt to drain oil until you are sure it has cooled sufficiently to avoid scalding you.

DON'T grasp any part of the engine, exhaust or catalytic converter without first ascertaining that it is sufficiently cool to avoid burning you.

DON'T inhale brake lining dust — it is injurious to health.

DON'T allow any spilt oil or grease to remain on the floor — wipe it up straight away, before someone slips on it.

DON'T use ill-fitting spanners or other tools which may slip and cause injury.

DON'T attempt to lift a heavy component which may be beyond your capability — get assistance.

DON'T rush to finish a job, or take unverified short cuts.

DON'T allow children or animals in or around an unattended vehicle.

DO wear eye protection when using power tools such as drill, sander, bench grinder etc, and when working under the vehicle.

DO use a barrier cream on your hands prior to undertaking dirty jobs — it will protect your skin from infection as well as making the dirt easier to remove afterwards; but make sure your hands aren't left slippery.

DO keep loose clothing (cuffs, tie etc) and long hair well out of the way of moving mechanical parts.

DO remove rings, wristwatch etc, before working on the vehicle — especially the electrical system.

DO ensure that any lifting tackle used has a safe working load rating adequate for the job.

DO keep your work area tidy – it is only too easy to fall over articles left lying around.

DO get someone to check periodically that all is well, when working alone on the vehicle.

DO carry out work in a logical sequence and check that everything is correctly assembled and tightened afterwards.

DO remember that your vehicle's safety affects that of yourself and others. If in doubt on any point, get specialist advice.

IF, in spite of following these precautions, you are unfortunate enough to injure yourself, seek medical attention as soon as possible.

Fire

Remember at all times that petrol (gasoline) is highly flammable. Never smoke, or have any kind of naked flame around, when working on the vehicle. But the risk does not end there – a spark caused by an electrical short-circuit, by two metal surfaces contacting each other, or even by static electricity built up in your body under certain conditions can ignite petrol vapour, which in a confined space is highly explosive.

Always disconnect the battery earth (ground) terminal before working on any part of the fuel system, and never risk spilling fuel on to a hot engine or exhaust.

It is recommended that a fire extinguisher of a type suitable for fuel and electrical fires is kept handy in the garage or workplace at all times. Never try to extinguish a fuel or electrical fire with water.

Fumes

Certain fumes are highly toxic and can quickly cause unconsciousness and even death if inhaled to any extent. Petrol (gasoline) vapour comes into this category, as do the vapours from certain solvents such as trichloroethylene. Any draining or pouring of such volatile fluids should be done in a well ventilated area.

When using cleaning fluids and solvents, read the instructions carefully. Never use materials from unmarked containers – they may give off poisonous vapours.

Never run the engine of a motor vehicle in an enclosed space such as a garage. Exhaust fumes contain carbon monoxide which is extremely poisonous; if you need to run the engine, always do so in the open air or at least have the rear of the vehicle outside the workplace.

If you are fortunate enough to have the use of an inspection pit never drain or pour petrol, and never run the engine, while the vehicle is standing over it; the fumes, being heavier than air, will concentrate in the pit with possibly lethal results.

The battery

Never cause a spark, or allow a naked light, near the vehicle battery. It will normally be giving off a certain amount of hydrogen gas, which is highly explosive.

Always disconnect the battery earth (ground) terminal before working on the fuel or electrical systems.

If possible, loosen the filler plugs or cover when charging the battery from an external source. Do not charge at an excessive rate or the battery may burst.

Take care when topping up and when carrying the battery. The acid electrolyte, even when diluted, is very corrosive and should not be allowed to contact the eyes or skin.

If you ever need to prepare electrolyte yourself, always add the acid slowly to the water, and never the other way round. Protect against splashes by wearing rubber gloves and goggles.

Mains electricity

When using an electric power tool, inspection light etc which works from the mains, always ensure that the appliance is correctly connected to its plug and that, where necessary, it is properly earthed (grounded). Do not use such appliances in damp conditions and, again, beware of creating a spark or applying excessive heat in the vicinity of fuel or fuel vapour.

Ignition HT voltage

A severe electric shock can result from touching certain parts of the ignition system, such as the HT leads, when the engine is running or being cranked, particularly if components are damp or the insulation is defective. Where an electronic ignition system is fitted, the HT voltage is much higher and could prove fatal.

Compressed Gas Cylinders

There are serious hazards associated with the storage and handling of gas cylinders and fittings, and standard precautions should be strictly observed in dealing with them. Ensure that cylinders are stored in safe conditions, properly maintained and always handled with special care and make constant efforts to eliminate the possibilities of leakage, fire and explosion.

The cylinder gases that are commonly used are oxygen, acetylene and liquid petroleum gas (LPG). Safety requirements for all three gases are:
Cylinders must be stored in a fire resistant, dry and well ventilated space, away from any source of heat or ignition and protected from ice, snow or direct sunlight.

Valves of cylinders in store must always be kept uppermost and closed, even when the cylinder is empty.

Cylinders should be handled with care and only by personnel who are reliable, adequate informed and fully aware of all associated hazards. Damaged or leaking cylinders should be immediately taken outside into the open air, and the supplier should be notified.

No one should approach a gas cylinder store with a naked light or cigarette.

Care should be taken to avoid striking or dropping cylinders, or knocking them together.

Cylinders should never be used as rollers.

One cylinder should never be filled from another.

Every care must be taken to avoid accidental damage to cylinder valves.

Valves must be operated without haste, never fully opened hard back against the back stop (so that other users know the valve is open) and never wrenched shut but turned just securely enough to stop the gas.

Before removing or loosening any outlet connections, caps or plugs a check should be made that the valves are closed.

When changing cylinders, close all valves and appliance taps, and extinguish naked flames, including pilot jets, before disconnecting them.

When reconnecting ensure that all connections and washers are clean and in good condition and do not overtighten them.

Immediately a cylinder becomes empty, close its valve.

Safety requirements for acetylene:
Cylinders must always be stored and used in the upright position. If a cylinder becomes heated accidentally or becomes hot because of excessive backfiring, immediately shut the valve, detach the regulator, take the cylinder out

of doors well away from the building, immerse it in or continuously spray it with water, open the valve and allow the gas to escape until the cylinder is empty.

Safety requirements for oxygen:
No oil or grease should be used on valves or fittings.
Cylinders with convex bases should be used in a stand or held securely to a wall.

Safety requirements for LPG:
The store must be kept free of combustible material, corrosive material and cylinders of oxygen.

2 MGB's Specification

Please note that the specifications in this section relate to the MGB upon its introduction. Production modifications are listed separately.

Type designation	M.G. MGB Tourer M.G. MGB G.T.
Built	Abingdon, England, 1962-1980.
Engine	Cast iron block and head, pressed steel sump 4-cylinders in-line, overhead valve, camshaft in block. Capacity 1789cc. Bore & Stroke 80.26 × 88.9mm. Maximum power 92bhp (net) at 5,400rpm. Maximum torque 110lb.ft. at 3,000rpm. 2 SU HS4 1 ½ in. single jet with Cooper paper element air filters.
Transmission	Rear-wheel-drive from front mounted engine. Four-speed gearbox bolted to the rear engine plate. Synchromesh available on top three gears until October 1967, and on all forward gears thereafter. Overall gear ratios (1962) 1st 14.21, 2nd 8.66, 3rd 5.37, 4th 3.9 optional overdrive (from January 1963) 3.14. Rear axle of the three-quarter floating type, incorporating a hypoid final drive on early Tourers. Later Tourers and G.T.s, axle of the tubed semi-floating type.
Chassis	Main structural components: large section three-element side members (sills) and double bulkhead into which torsional loadings are fed via 18 gauge inner wing panels. Wheelbase: 7ft. 7ins.
Track	Front: 4ft. 1in. Rear: 4ft. 1.25in.

Suspension	Front: independent, coil springs. Rear: half-elliptic leaf springs.
Steering	Rack and pinion, 3 turns lock-to-lock.
Brakes	Front: Lockheed, discs, 10.75in. dia. Rear: Lockheed, drums, 10in. dia.
Wheels and Tyres	Ventilated pressed steel disc, 4 studs, 4in. width. (Optional wire wheels). 5.60 × 14in. tyres with tubes.
Bodywork	2-door, 2-seater convertible or fixed-head with *very* occasional rear seats. Unitary construction of pressed steel 20 gauge outer panels and aluminium bonnet. Pressed on British-made American-designed Hamilton, Toledo and Danby presses at British Motor Holding Group's Pressed Steel Fisher Company's factory at Swindon, Wiltshire, England. GT body assembled at Swindon but Tourer assembled at Pressed Steel Fisher, Coventry. Body panels joined by spot welding. Dimensions: overall length 12ft. 9.2in., overall width 4ft. 11.9in., overall height 4ft. 1.4in., ground clearance 5in., turning circle 31ft, kerb weight 18.1 cwt. weight distribution (dry) 54% front/46% rear.
Electrical System	12 volt 58 amp.hr. (twin × 6 batteries mounted under rear "scuttle"). Positive earth Lucas dynamo with Lucas RB340-type voltage regulator. Lucas coil ignition and wiring harness made up to standard Lucas colour coding scheme. Headlamp, Lucas sealed-filament 50-40 watts.

Performance	Maximum speed, 106mph.
	 Speed in gears, (approx):
	     3rd gear 90mph.
	     2nd gear 55mph.
	     1st gear 30mph.
	 Acceleration, 0-60: 12.2 sec.
	 Standing ¼ mile: 18.7 sec.
	 Acceleration in gears:
	     Top: 20-40mph, 9.0 sec. 50-70mph, 10.0 sec.
	     Third: 20-40mph, 5.6 sec. 50-70mph, 7.7 sec.
	 Fuel consumption: 21 to 29mpg.

③ Production Modifications

The Chassis Number (or Car Number) is stamped on a plate which is held on the left-hand wing balance just ahead of the radiator. The engine Number is stamped on a plate found on the right-hand side of the cylinder block.

The Chassis, or Car Number, consists of a code which presents the following information:

1st Numeral indicates make (G = MG)
2nd Numeral indicates engine type (H = "B"-series engine)
3rd Numeral indicates body type (N = 2 seater tourer; D = GT)
4th Numeral indicates series (1 and 2 = MGA; 3 = 1st series MGB; 4 = 2nd series, 5 = 3rd series. No series changes made after October 1979)
5th Numeral indicates market destination (L = LHD; U = USA)
6th Numeral indicates model year from 1970 (A = 1970; B = 1971; C = 1972 and so on).

Thus: G-HN3 = MG; fitted with "B"-series engine; Tourer; 1st Series MGB. (Also, UK market

because no L or U after number). And: G-HD5UE = MG; fitted with "B"-series engine; GT; 3rd Series MGB; USA; 1974.

There is some confusion over the generic terms "MkI", "MkII", "MkIII" and so on. No cars were ever originally referred to as MkI — first cars were desigated "3rd-Series" as successors to 1st and 2nd Series MGAs and in any case this designation only came into colloquial use when there was a MkII (officially, 4th-Series) to replace it. All cars after October 1969 were known as 5th-Series and are known colloquially as "MkIII". However, subsequent production changes have prompted unofficial "MkIV" and "MkV" labels to be applied, but the usage of these designations is less than unanimous and so cannot sensibly be applied here. 1975-on cars are generally known as "rubber bumper" or "black bumper" models.

Production modifications

Note: G-HN3, 4 and 5 are Roadsters; G-HD3, 4 and 5 are GTs.

Chassis numbers quoted here are what manufacturers know as "pure" chassis numbers (ie *all* cars after the number shown are fitted with those parts which relate to the chassis number change point). However, it may well be that, because of production line supply techniques, some cars which appear before the given change point will be fitted with later parts. On the other hand, no cars *after* a chassis number change point will have been fitted with earlier parts — a point worth bearing in mind when buying or judging Concours cars.

June 1962: MGB Roadster Chassis No. G-HN3 101 Production begins.
September 1962: Cars first released with 3-main bearing "B" series engine of 1798cc. (18G designation, known as 18GA from

early 1964). Front suspension descended from YA, TD, TF, MGA but softer sprung. MGA-type "banjo" rear axle. Options included: heater, wire wheels, oil cooler (standard for export), front anti-roll bar, folding hood (from G-HN3 19259) tonneau cover (standard for North America).

Early 1963: Laycock overdrive (D-type) available as option.

June 1963: "Works" glassfibre hardtop available.

February 1964: Closed-circuit crankcase breathing on engine, now known as 18GA. Chassis No. G-HN3 31021.

October 1964. Chassis No. G-HN3 48766. 5-main bearing engine fitted, with fully-floating gudgeon pins replacing circlips in pistons. Oil-cooler fitted as standard. Electronic rev-counter replaced mechanical type. Gearbox fitted with larger first motion shaft spigot end and bush in engine crank enlarged accordingly.

March 1965: Chassis No. G-HN3 56743. Fuel tank capacity increased from 10 Imp. gallons to 12 Imp. gallons. Held by 9 bolts instead of 2 steel straps as previously. Chassis No. G-HN3 57986. Door handles changed from pull-out to pushbutton type externally. Mechanism, locks and door shape also modified.

October 1965: GT launched, Chassis No. G-HD3 71933. Fixed head Coupe with large rear door, more luggage space than Roadster and taller windscreen and window glasses. Presented as "2 + 2" but rear seats adequate only for small children. Styled at Abingdon, "detailed" by Pininfarina. Salisbury (or "tube-type") rear axle (not commonised with Roadster).

November 1966: Chassis No. G-HN3 108039. Anti-roll bar standard.

April 1967: G-HN3 132923 (wire-wheeled cars); G-HN3 139215 (disc-wheeled cars). Salisbury (or "tube-type") rear axle previously fitted to GT commonised with Roadster. However, it should be noted that from G-HN3 123716 to 132922 either a banjo or tube axle is fitted.

October 1967: G-HN4 138401; "MkII" models (4th-Series) G-HD4

139472. Engine numbers 18GD, later 18GG (U.K.) and 18GF, later 18GH (U.S.A.). Engines fitted with emission control equipment (air pumps, check valve, gulp valve, modified cylinder head, modified carburettors and inlet manifolding). Modified engine backplate fitted to all engines from now on. Pre-engaged starter motor replaces "bendix" type. All-synchro gearbox with optional automatic, as developed for MGC. Gearbox tunnel/toeboard area modified to accept new automatic transmission. Reversing lights fitted as standard. Negative earth alternator (Lucas 16AC type) replaces dynamo. U.S. cars fitted with completely different heavily-padded fascia and dash with glove compartment. Also fitted with energy-absorbing steering column and dual circuit brakes (for which servo not available).

October 1969: G-HN5 187211; G-HD5 187841 "Mk III" models (5th-Series); 18GH engines (Federal) now with exhaust emission controls. New recessed radiator grille in black with chrome surround. New smaller steering wheel with 3 drilled aluminium spokes. B.L. emblems on front wings (except Arab countries where B.L. then blacklisted!) Rubber inserts on over-riders. Rostyle wheels (wires still optional). Reclining seats as standard, upholstered in Vinyl, with longitudinal strips forming ventilated centre panel. Minor fascia re-arrangement. U.S.-style padded-fascia standard for Sweden. Dipping interior rear-view mirror. Optional headrests (from G-HN5 209784 to 258000 and G-HD5 207650 to 25800).

September 1970: G-HN5 219001. Telescopic boot and bonnet stays. Improved ventilation and revised heater. Interior courtesy light. New folding hood (designed by Michelotti) standardised. Interior boot light. More emission control equipment for U.S. market including engine-driven air pump. Automatic seatbelts standardised on North American tourers from G-HN5 268080.

October 1971: G-HN5/G-HD5

258001. Final engine change to 18V ("V" for vertical) and 18GK (U.S.) types. New fascia with face-level air-vents situated in space where radio previously fitted. New rocker switches and controls. New centre console with ashtray, lift-up armrest with storage space beneath. U.S. fascias still of heavily-padded type but with glove compartment. Brushed nylon seat facings. Door-mounted mirror fitted. Collapsible energy-absorbing steering column optional (non-U.S. markets).

May 1972: G-HN5/G-HD5 282420. One-hand seatbelts fitted.

October 1972: G-HN5 294251; G-HD5 296001. New grille with vertical centre bar and black mesh. New padded-steering wheel with slotted spokes. Matching "upholstered" gear knob. Padded door armrests/pulls. Matt black windscreen wipers. Cigar lighter fitted as standard. Tonneau standard (U.K.). Heated rear screen fitted as standard on G.T. Automatic seatbelts optional, radial-ply tyres standard (U.K.). Black-spoked steering wheel available on G.T. (U.K. only) from G-HD5 320197.

September 1973: G-HN5/G-HD5 328101. Radial-ply tyres standard (all markets). Automatic gearbox option withdrawn. Engine bay/flitch panels commonised with V8. Vertically rectangular rubber over-riders fitted to U.S. cars (G-HN5 339095 to 368081 and G-HD5 339472 to 367803).

September/December 1974: G-HN5 360301/G-HD5 361001, except U.S.A., where G-HN5 363082. G.T. no longer available in U.S.A. "Federal bumper" models with large black bumpers front and rear, faired into bodyline at front with heavy steel reinforcement covered by impact resistant urethane padding. Raised ride height. Single Zenith/Stromberg carburettor and further reduced performance (U.S.A.). Revised switch layout with B.L. corporate column controls for wash/wipe and lights. U.S.-style padded fascia commonised to all L.H.D. cars (G-HN5 360301 — on). Hazard warning lights, door mirrors, servo brake assistance all

standard. Modified Laycock overdrive (LH-type) with slightly lower (0.82 to 1) step-up ratio. Single 12-volt battery replacing 2 × 6 volt batteries. Catalytic converter added for California cars.

May 1975: Jubilee special to commemorate B.L.'s version of MG's 50th Anniversary. 750 cars built, mechanically standard but in British Racing Green with gold striping, head-restraints, tinted-glass, overdrive, V8-type wheels and 175-section tyres. (MGB GT "Jubilee" chassis numbers interspersed with standard MGBs).

June 1975: G-HN5 380278/G-HD5 379495. Overdrive fitted as standard.

August 1976: G-HN5 410001. Thicker anti-roll bar at front and anti-roll bar at rear as standard. Electric radiator cooling fan (2 for U.S.A.). New fascia/console with electric clock. Lower geared steering (3½ turns lock-to-lock, replacing 3 turn) and smaller 4-spoke steering wheel. Striped fabric seat trim. Gearlever-mounted overdrive switch. Halogen headlights (U.K.). Tinted-glass on GT. Carpet on floor, 2-speed heater fan, lockable glovebox, sealed cooling system with separate radiator catch tank. Pedal pad positions altered to allow, for first time, "heel-and-toeing".

April 1977: Inertia reel seatbelt as standard.

January 1978: Twin door-mounted speakers and aerial as standard.

June 1980: Rear foglamps fitted as standard (U.K.).

October 1980: MGB Roadster and GT-Limited Edition. G-HN5 522581/G-HD5 522422. Last 1,000 cars made (420 Tourers) known as "Limited Edition". GTs finished in Pewter Silver. Tourers in Bronze, both with body stripe. Integral front spoilers, alloy or wire wheels (on Tourer), distinctive badges.

October 22, 1980: Last MGB Roadster, G-HN5 523001, last MGB GT G-HD5 523002 produced at Abingdon, Oxford, England.

MGC: Chassis Number sequences:

July 1967 to August 1969 (Total Built 8,999)

G/CN 101-9099 Roadsters

G/CD 110-9102 GTs

The above comprised:
4,542 Roadsters
4,457 GTs
of which:
1,403 Roadsters
2,034 GTs

3,437 were for the UK market.

Engine No. Prefix is 29G

(Austin 3-Litre engine no. prefix is 29A)

MGB GT V8: Chassis Number sequences:

Early 1973 to late 1976 (Total Built 2,591)

G/D2D1-101-2903 GTs only.

Virtually all were sold in U.K.

USA Cars

1962-67 cars: Almost identical to U.K. specification cars. Only differences are left hand drive, and the tail lamp lenses having both top and bottom pieces coloured red. Oil cooler was standard equipment in the U.S.A.

1968 cars: The beginning of the "Federalization Era," and regulations from the U.S. Government on all cars sold in the U.S. Emission controls were introduced, as was a padded dashboard, which no longer had a glovebox. Instrument layout was also revised. Oil and temperature gauges were now separate units, with the oil pressure gauge being a unique rectangular shape. Negative ground electricals with alternator

were introduced. U.K. automatic transmission option was never available in the U.S.A. on MGBs, but all synchro manual gearbox was now standard in the U.S.A., as well.

1969 cars: New solid coloured leather seats (no piping), with headrests were used this year only. Stick on reflectors were mounted on all four wings, front wings had amber reflectors, and rear wings had red reflectors.

1970 cars: New features included "blacked out" grille, fold down top, and one piece red and amber tail lamp lenses. Unlike the U.K. style tail lamp lenses, the amber portion is in the centre of the lens, rather than at the top of the U.K. style lens. Side marker lamps with built in hazard flashers replaced the previous reflectors, again with lamps on front wings being amber, and red lamps on the rear wings. New steering wheel and vinyl seats were added. British Leyland badge is mounted on both front wings. Split rear bumper is featured this year only. Rostyle wheels replaced disc wheels as the standard wheels, with wire wheels still being optional. New badging for the tailgate, and vinyl inserts in the seats were changes exclusive to the MGB GT.

1971 cars: British Leyland badge on right (passenger) front wing only.

1972 cars: Face level air vents and lockable glove box added to dash. Centre of M.G. Octagon on steering wheel hub is now coloured red.

1973 cars: New grille introduced, incorporating basic shape of old grille, without vertical bars, but rather black honeycomb centre, to left and right of chrome centre of grille. M.G. badge is red and chrome rather than black, red and chrome as in old grille. SU HIF 4 carburettors replace the SU HS 4 carburettors. Armrests are added to inside of doors. Steering wheel has one long cutout in each of the three spokes, rather than the previous series of small round holes. New MGB GT tailgate badge. Pattern of vinyl seats is revised.

1974 cars: Oversized black rubber overriders are used this year only. Steering wheel spoke cutouts are

replaced by filled in recessed area.

1974-½ cars: The last of the MGB GTs are imported to the U.S.A. Full rubber bumpers are now fitted, along with single 12 volt battery.

1975 cars: Single Zenith Stromberg carburettor replaces twin SU carbs. This new carburettor also incorporated automatic choke. "MGB" badge removed from boot lid. M.G. badging on front bumper and boot lid are gold and black in colour, as well as centre of M.G. Octagon on steering wheel hub being coloured gold, in honour of M.G.'s 50th anniversary.

1976 cars: M.G. badging on front bumper and boot lid changed to chrome and black. Catalytic

converter now fitted, and unleaded fuel is required.

1977 cars: Dashboard is revised with larger, modern-style instruments, new four spoke steering wheel, clock and interior fan now has two speeds. New soft top is featured with zip-out rear window. Pattern of vinyl seats is revised. Front and rear sway (anti-roll) bars are added.

1978 cars: Crankshaft is strengthened.

1979 cars: The "Limited Edition" package is offered as an option.

Included was special black paint and silver striping, Triumph Stag wheels with M.G. hubcaps, special steering wheel, and dash plaque. Front air dam is also incorporated into "Limited Edition" package.

1980 cars: 80 Miles Per Hour speedometer is fitted, along with six digit odometer.

Colour Schemes

Where colours apply to Roadster or GT only, this is indicated in brackets

1962-69* (MGB)

Colour of: Body Exterior and B.L. Paint Code	Colour of: Seats, Door liners and Seals	Colour of: A Hood B Tonneau C Hard Top D Headlining	Colour of: Carpets/Mats
Tartan Red (RD 9)	Black Red	A. Red or Black B. Black or Red C. Red, Black, Old English White or Grey D. Grey	Black Red
Iris Blue (BU 12) (Tourer only)	Blue	A. Blue or Black B. Black or Blue C. Blue, Black or Old English White	Blue
Chelsea Grey (GR 15) (Tourer only)	Red	A. Grey or Black B. Red C. Red, Black, Old English White or Grey	Red
Old English White (WT 3)	Black Red	A. Grey or Black B. Black or Red C. Red, Black, Old English White or Grey D. Grey	Red Black

Colour of: Body Exterior and B.L. Paint Code	Colour of: Seats, Door liners and Seals	Colour of: A Hood B Tonneau C Hard Top D Headlining	Colour of: Carpets/Mats
Black* (BK 1; BLVC 122)	Black Red Autumn Leaf	A. Grey or Black B. Black or Red C. Red, Black Old English White or Grey D. Grey	Black Red Autumn Leaf
British Racing Green* GN 25 or GN 29	Black Red	A. Black or Grey B. Black C. Black or Old English White D. Grey	Black Red
Mineral Blue (BU 19)	Black Blue	A. Black B. Black or Blue C. Black, Blue Old English White D. Grey	Black Blue
Pale Primrose* (YL 12)	Black	A. Grey or Black B. Black or Red C. Red, Black, Old English White or Grey D. Grey	Black Red
Sandy Beige (BG 15) (GT only)	Black Red Mushroom	D. Beige D. Grey	Black Red
Grampian Grey (GR 12) (GT only)	Black Red	D. Grey	Black Red
Snowberry White (WT 4)	Black	A. Grey or Black B. Black or Red C. Red, Black, Old English White or Grey D. Grey	Black Red
Midnight Blue*	Black	A. Black B. Black C. Black D. Grey	Black
Blue Royale* (BU 38)	Black	A. Blue or Black B. Black or Blue C. Blue, Black or Old English White D. Grey	Blue

Colour of: Body Exterior and B.L. Paint Code	Colour of: Seats, Door liners and Seals	Colour of: A Hood B Tonneau C Hard Top D Headlining	Colour of: Carpets/Mats
Bermuda Blue* (BU 40)	Black	A. Blue or Black B. Black or Blue C. Blue, Black or Old English White D. Grey	Black
Golden Beige (BG 19) (GT only)	Black Mushroom	D. Grey	Black Brown
Riviera Blue (BU 47)	Black	A. Blue or Black B. Black or Blue C. Blue, Black or Old English White D. Grey	Black

These colours were also used after 1969

1970-76* (MGB)

Colour of: Body Exterior and B.L. Paint Code	Colour of: Seats, Door liners and Seals	Colour of: A Hood B Tonneau C Hard Top D Headlining	Colour of: Carpets/Mats
Limeflower (BLVC 20)	Navy	A. Black B. Black C. Black D. Grey	Navy
Black Tulip (BLVC 23)	Ochre	A. Black B. Black C. Black D. Grey	Ochre
Damask Red* (RDS; BLVC 99)	Navy Black	A. Black B. Black C. Black D. Grey	Navy
Bedouin (BLVC 4)	Black Autumn Leaf	A. Black B. Black C. Black D. Grey	Black Autumn Leaf
Antelope (BLVC 7)	Black	A. Black B. Black C. Black D. Grey	Black
Bronze Yellow (BLVC 15)	Black Navy	A. Black B. Black C. Black	Black Navy D. Grey
Green Mallard (BLVC 22)	Autumn Leaf Ochre	A. Black B. Black C. Black	Autumn Leaf Ochre D. Grey

Colour of: Body Exterior and B.L. Paint Code	Colour of: Seats, Door liners and Seals	Colour of: A Hood B Tonneau C Hard Top D Headlining	Colour of: Carpets/Mats
Blaze (BLVC 16)	Black Navy	A. Black B. Black C. Black D. Grey	Black Navy
Teal Blue (BLVC 18)	Black Autumn Leaf Ochre	A. Black B. Black C. Black D. Grey	Black Autumn Leaf Ochre
Racing Green (BLVC 25)	Black Autumn Leaf	A. Black B. Black C. Black D. Grey	Black Autumn Leaf
Glacier White* (BLVC 59)	Black Navy Autumn Leaf	A. Black B. Black C. Black D. Grey	Black Navy Autumn Leaf
Aqua (BLVC 60)	Black Navy	A. Black B. Black C. Black D. Grey	Black Navy
Citron (BLVC 73)	Black	A. Black B. Black C. Black D. Grey	Black
Tundra (BLVC 94)	Autumn Leaf	A. Black B. Black C. Black D. Grey	Autumn Leaf
Aconite (BLVC 95)	Autumn Leaf	A. Black B. Black C. Black D. Grey	Autumn Leaf
Bracken (BLVC 93)	Autumn Leaf Black	A. Black B. Black C. Black D. Grey	Autumn Leaf Black
Flame Red (BLVC 61)	Black Navy	A. Black B. Black C. Black D. Grey	Black Navy
Harvest Gold (BLVC 19)	Navy Black	A. Black B. Black C. Black D. Grey	Navy Black

Colour of: Body Exterior and B.L. Paint Code	Colour of: Seats, Door liners and Seals	Colour of: A Hood B Tonneau C Hard Top D Headlining	Colour of: Carpets/Mats
Tahiti Blue* **(BLVC 65)**	Black Autumn Leaf	A. Black B. Black C. Black D. Grey	Black Black Autumn Leaf
Flamenco* **(BLVC 133)**	Black	A. Black B. Black C. Black D. Grey	Black Black
Mirage **(BLVC 11)**	Black	A. Black B. Black C. Black D. Grey	Black

These colours were used until 1977.

1976 onwards (MGB)

Latest MGBs have their paint code (VIN paint code) shown on their chassis number plate

Body Exterior and B.L. Paint Code	VIN paint code	Model T-Roadster GT-GT	VIN Trim Code	Carpets Mats	Liners	Door Seals	A. Hood B. Tonneau C. Hard Top D. Headlining
Triumph White **(BLVC 206)**	NAB	T. Black T. Orange/ Brown GT. Orange/ Brown	PMA AMH AMH	Black	Black	Black	A. Black B. Black C. Black D. Grey
Chartreuse **(BLVC 167)**	FMJ	T. Black T. Silver Grey GT. Silver Grey	PMA LMH LMH	Black	Black	Black	A. Black B. Black C. Black D. Grey
Brooklands Green **(BLVC 169)**	HMM	T. Autumn Leaf T. Orange/ Brown GT. Orange/ Brown	AMA AMH AMH	Black Chestnut Chestnut	Black A. Leaf Black	Black A. Leaf Black	A. Black B. Black C. Black D. Grey
Sandglow **(BLVC 63)**	AMF	T. A. Leaf T. Orange/ Brown GT. Orange/ Brown	AMA AMH AMH	Black Chestnut Chestnut	Black A. Leaf Black	Black A. Leaf Black	A. Black B. Black C. Black D. Grey

Body Exterior and B.L. Paint Code	VIN paint code	Model: T-Roadster GT-GT	VIN Trim Code	Carpets Mats	Liners	Door Seals	A. Hood B. Tonneau C. Hard Top D. Headlining
Tahiti Blue	JMP	T. A. Leaf	AMA	Black	Black	Black	A. Black
		T. Silver Grey	LMH	Chestnut	A. Leaf	A. Leaf	B. Black
							C. Black
		GT. Silver Grey	LMH	Chestnut	Black	Black	D. Grey
Carmine (BLVC 209)	CAA	T. Black	AMA	Black	Black	Black	A. Black
		T. Silver Grey	LMH	Black	Black	Black	B. Black
							C. Black
		GT. Silver Grey	LMH	Black	Black	Black	D. Grey
Flamenco (BLVC 133)	EMG	T. Black	PMA	Black	Black	Black	A. Black
		T. Silver Grey	LMH	Black	Black	Black	B. Black
							C. Black
		GT. Silver Grey	LMH	Black	Black	Black	D. Grey
Inca Yellow (BLVC 207)	FAB	T. Silver Grey	PMA	Black	Black	Black	A. Black
							B. Black
		T. Black	LMH	Chestnut	Black	Black	C. Black
		GT. Silver Grey	LMH	Chestnut	Black	Black	D. Grey
Russet Brown (BLVC 205)	AAE	T. Orange/ Brown	AMH	Black	Beige	Beige	A. Black
							B. Black
		T. Beige	AAA	Chestnut	Black	Black	C. Black
		GT. Orange/ Brown	AMH	Chestnut	Black	Black	D. Grey
Vermillion (BLVC 118)	CML	T. Silver Grey	LMH	Black	Black	Black	A. Black
							B. Black
		T. Beige	AAA	Chestnut	Black	Black	C. Black
		GT. Orange/ Grey	AMH	Chestnut	Black	Black	D. Grey
Pageant Blue (BLVC 224)	JNA	T. Silver Grey	LMH	Black	Black	Black	A. Black
							B. Black
		T. Beige	AAA	Black	Black	Black	C. Black
		GT. Silver Grey	LMH	Black	Black	Black	D. Grey
Ermine (ex-Leyland White) (BLVC 243)	NME	T. Orange/ Brown	AMH	Black	Black	Black	A. Black
							B. Black
		T. Black	PMA	Black	Black	Black	C. Black
		GT. Black	PMA	Black	Black	Black	D. Grey
Snapdragon (BLVC 235)	FMN	T. Black	PMA	Black	Black	Black	A. Black
		T. Silver Grey	LMH				B. Black
							C. Black
		GT. Silver Grey	LMH	Black	Black	Black	D. Grey

MGC – All Years

Body Exterior and B.L. Paint Code	Model N – Roadster D – GT	Seats	Seat Piping	Liners	A. Hood, Tonneau Cover, and Hard Top B. Headlining	Door Seals	Carpet/Mats
Sandy Beige (BG.15) (GT only)	D	Black Red Black	White White Black	Black Red Black	B. Beige B. Beige B. Grey	Black Red Black	Black Red Black
Metallic Golden Beige (BG. 19)	N D	Black Red	White White	Black Red	A. Black B. Beige A. Black B. Beige	Black Red	Black Red
Black (BK. 1)	N D	Black Red Black Black	White Black Blue Black	Black Red Black Black	A. Black B. Grey Grey Grey Grey	Black Red Black Black	Black Red Black Black
Mineral Blue (BU. 9)	D N D	Black Blue Black	BLue Blue Black	Black Blue Black	Grey B. Grey A. Black B. Grey	Black Blue Black	Black Blue Black
Metallic Riviera Silver Blue	N D	Black Blue	Black Blue	Black Blue	Grey Grey	Black Blue	Black Blue
British Racing Green (GN. 29)	N D D	Black Black Red	White Black Black	Black Black Red	Grey Grey B. Grey	Black Black Red	Black Black Red
Grampian Grey (GR. 12) (GT only)	D	Red Black Black	Black White Black	Red Black Black	B. Grey Grey Grey	Red Black Black	Red Black Black
Tartan Red (RD. 9)	N D D	Black Black Red	Red Black Black	Black Black Red	A. Black B. Grey Grey B. Grey	Black Black Red	Black Black Red
Old English White (WT. 3)	N D	Black Red Red Black	White White Black Red	Black Red Red Black	A. Black Black B. Grey B. Grey	Black Red Red Black	Black Red Red Black
Snowberry White (WT. 4)	N D	Black Black	White Black	Black Black	A. Black B. Grey Grey	Black Black	Black Black
Pale Primrose (YL. 12)	N D	Black Black	Black Black	Black Black	A. Black B. Grey Grey	Black Black	Black Black

5 Clubs & Specialists

The following list of Clubs and Suppliers is by no means a complete one. It is restricted to those with whom the author has had some personal contact or experience but there are undoubtedly others on both sides of the Atlantic who are equally useful. The best way to widen one's knowledge of suppliers is through the appropriate club.

Clubs

American MGB Association (AMGBA): "It's so far spread, it's a bit like running a club to cater for all the peoples of Europe" says Steve Glochowsky, President. First rate quarterly magazine with excellent technical service. National Annual Convention. Area co-ordinators. Discounts on key products and publications.

AMGBA, P.O. Box 11401, Chicago, Illinois, 606011, U.S.A.

U.K. Chapter — Ken Smith, Broomhill Villa, 185, Broomhill Road, Old Whitington, Chesterfield, England.

M.G. Owners' Club: Generally accepted as *the* British club for MGB owners. Social activities throughout semi-autonomous Area Centres. Special offers on spares and tools. "Recommended Suppliers" system. National and "Mini-National" meetings. Monthly magazine plus, annual Year Book. Trade discounts for members at every B.L. dealer. Now goes MGB racing, too.

Address — M.G. Owners' Club, Secretary — Roche Bentley, 13 Church End, Over, Cambridgeshire, England.

M.G. Car Club: Direct descendant from original, factory-supported club. Excellent for racing connections. Polished monthly magazine with good historical, technical content. Secretaries for areas and also for most models of M.G. Not commercially minded. M.G. Car Club, Assistant Secretary — Sheila Lawrence, 67 Wide Bargate, Boston, Lincolnshire PE21 6LE, England.

Specialists

University Motors (USA): John H. Twist, the proprietor was trained by the old University Motors concern in the U.K. before returning to set up his own busienss in the U.S.A. John is Technical Secretary to the American MGB Association and has a technical knowledge of MGBs which is second to none. John is always ready to advise owners and he and his team are ready for on the spot service in Grand Rapids. There is also a popular mail order service for enthusiasts in other parts of the 'States.

University Motors Ltd., 614, Eastern Avenue S.E., Grand Rapids, Michigan, 49503, U.S.A.

John Hill's MGB Centre (U.K.): John Hill and his stores manager,

Jon Miller, are Spares Secretaries to the M.G. Owners' Club. John stocks two whole warehouses of MGB parts and The MGB Centre has B.L. Heritage approval for the reproduction of obsolete MGB parts — a concession becoming increasingly valuable. As well as stocking all the available B.L. Parts, John's replacement parts are as good as the originals, being made to the same specifications. John Hill and Jon Miller know MGBs inside out, and are able to supply advice as detailed as their parts — right down to the last screw and clip. The range of stock carried by The MGB Centre makes it nothing short of a restorer's paradise!

John Hill's MGB Centre, Arthur Street, Redditch, Worcs. BP8 8JY, England. Tel: Redditch 20880.

Autotech Ltd (U.K.): Props. — Graeme Barson, Chris Reynolds. Bodywork specialists of the highest repute. Proprietors both ex-B.L. Styling employees who carried out work on MGB ''variants''.

Autotech Ltd., Nash Works, Belbroughton, West Midlands DY9 9TD.

Waxoyl: Rust inhibiting fluid from, Finnigan's Speciality Paints Ltd., Eltringham Works, Prudhoe, Northumberland, England.

Lifesure Ltd., Insurance and Mortgage Brokers, 34, New Street, St. Neots, Huntingdon, Cambs. PE19 1NQ.

Windscreen Services (Birmingham) Ltd., Safety Glass Stockists, Unit 16, Shrub Hill Industrial Estate, Worcester.

Abingdon Classic Car Co., B.L. Heritage approved restorers, Unit 2, Wootton, Abingdon-on-Thames, Oxfordshire. OX13 6LO.

The V8 Conversion Company, Oak Farm, Green Street Green, Orpington, Kent.

⑥ Sales Performance & Historical Value Patterns

It's easy to see that both the MGB's major model types rose steadily in price throughout their production runs ending up, in the case of the Roadster, at a level seven times higher than it started at. But is it a true picture of what happened? At the same time as the price of the 'B rose, the value of the money buying it was falling due to inflation. What it means is simply this. The number of pounds Sterling needed to buy the car went up, but so did the number of pounds earned through wages, so that the rise was not really in the order of seven times.

The chart shows the actual selling prices across the top while the graphs show the effective prices AFTER the effects of inflation have been allowed for. The thick line is at the level of the cars' original selling price (*i.e.* 100% of the original price). When the cost of the Tourer reached £3,024 in 1977 it was only 4% higher than its original selling price in *real* terms, after allowing for inflation. Thus its position on the graph is only just higher than the thick black line.

Quite apart from their general interest, these charts make one very important point regarding the viability of the MGB. B.L. claimed that it was dropped because there was no demand (see Roy Brocklehurst's comments in Chapter One). But look at the MGB's sales figures and note that the key falls in sales in the 'Seventies were in 1975 and, at the end, in 1979 and 1980.

Then, remembering that price rises were usually brought in during the autumn and would therefore have their greatest effect in the following year, look at the MGB's price in real terms on the graph. In 1974, the MGB's cost rose to 130-135% of its original price and sales slumped in '75 while by 1979 just before the end, the cost was 144-152% of its original price. On the other hand, the years of the MGB's highest sales were those of the dips in the graph, when it was nearest to its original value.

Did the MGB die because no one wanted it? Or did the post-1977 leap in the car's real-term's value kill it? Management and accountants just don't make the mistake of lifting the price way above the rate of inflation by accident. So who murdered the 'B . . .?

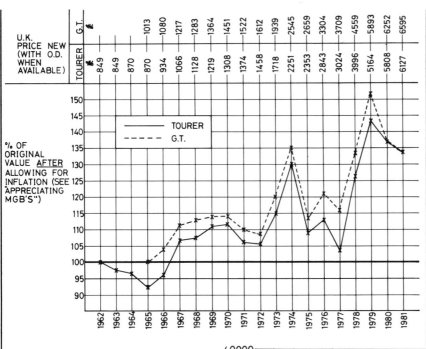

| U.K. PRICE NEW (WITH O.D. WHEN AVAILABLE) | G.T. | | | 1013 | 1080 | 1217 | 1283 | 1364 | 1451 | 1522 | 1612 | 1939 | 2545 | 2659 | 3304 | 3709 | 4559 | 5893 | 6252 | 6595 |
| | TOURER | 849 | 849 | 870 | 870 | 934 | 1066 | 1128 | 1219 | 1308 | 1374 | 1458 | 1718 | 2251 | 2353 | 2843 | 3024 | 3996 | 5164 | 5808 | 6127 |

% OF ORIGINAL VALUE AFTER ALLOWING FOR INFLATION (SEE "APPRECIATING MGB'S")

— TOURER
---- G.T.

Figure 24. MGB Historcal value pattern (UK).

Figure 25. MGB Unit sales from 1962.

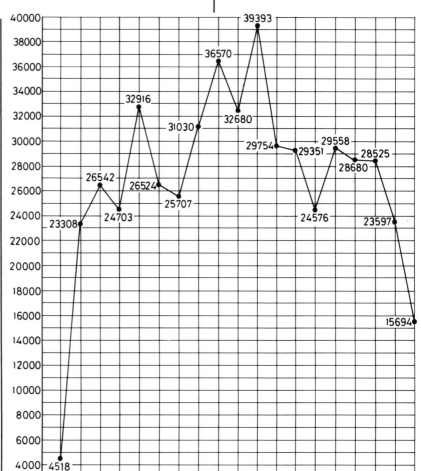

M.G.B. UNIT SALES

7 British & American Thread Systems

The MGB from 1963-1980 uses Unified National Fine (UNF) in almost all applications, which is completely compatible with American Fine (AF) or SAE threads. A few applications use a Unified National Coarse (UNC) compatible with American coarse threads (some studs into the block and gearcase). There are only a few applications of BSF (British Standard Fine) or BSW (British Standard Whitworth — coarse). The dampers (shock absorbers) use a BSF thread for their filler screws. All Lucas electrics use Whitworth until around 1969 when the change was made to metric.

	BSW	UNC	BSF	UNF
		Threads per Inch		
⅛ (.125)	40	(US) No. 5-40		
³/₁₆ (.1875)	24	(US) No. 10-24	32	(US) No. 10-32 (.190 dia)
¼ (.250)	20	20 (190 dia)	26	28
⁵/₁₆ (.3125)	18	18	22	24
⅜ (.375)	16	16	20	24
⁷/₁₆ (.4375)	14	14	18	20
½ (.500)	12	13	16	20

Note: Although the BSW and UNC threads per inch are the same in popular sizes, the angle of the thread differs, and they are incompatible. The BSF and UNF are not compatible either, as the tpi are different for each dia.

Screws used in the MGB are almost all crosshead. Slotted-head screws are simply not acceptable for a good restoration. A popular screw size in the MGB is 2BA (British Association), but that size is fully compatible with the American No. 10-32 screw.

	Diameter	Threads/inch	
2BA	.185	31.358	(the BA screws use a metric pitch)
No. 10-32	.190	32	
4BA	.1417	38.5	These screws are not as compatible as the 2BA or 10-32, but
No. 6-40	.1372	40	are infrequently used.

Except for the interior panels and a very few applications in other places, all the screws are "machine thread" NOT self tapping.

British Standard Pipe

In the applications listed below, BSP threads are used. These ARE NOT compatible with any American threading system, and the proper BSP screws and fittings MUST be used.

Size	Diameter	Threads/inch
⅛	.3830	28
¼	.5180	19
⅜	.6560	19
½	.8250	14

Uses of B.S.P. on MGB

Radiator drain hole (if fitted)		¼ BSP
Oil Cooler and fittings		½ BSP
Engine Block:	Sump drain plug	¼ BSP
	Water drain plug	¼ BSP
	Oil hole plug (left side)	⅜ BSP
	Oil pressure relief valve	½ BSP
	Oil outlet (right rear)	½ BSP
Fuel tank:	drain (if fitted)	¼ or ⅛
	fuel line	¼ BSP
Fuel pump:	banjo bolts	⅜ BSP
Fuel line:	at bulkhead	¼ BSP

Most of these BSP applications require the use of BSF/BSW wrenches.

⑧ British & American Technical Terms

As this book has been written in England, it uses the appropriate English component names, phrases, and spelling. Some of these differ from those used in America. Normally, these cause no difficulty, but to make sure, a glossary is printed below. In ordering spare parts remember the parts list will probably use these words:

English	American	English	American
Aerial	Antenna	Layshaft (of gearbox)	Countershaft
Accelerator	Gas pedal	Leading shoe (of brake)	Primary shoe
Alternator	Generator (AC)	Locks	Latches
Anti-roll bar	Stabiliser or sway bar	Motorway	Freeway, turnpike etc
Battery	Energizer	Number plate	License plate
Bodywork	Sheet metal	Paraffin	Kerosene
Bonnet (engine cover)	Hood	Petrol	Gasoline
Boot lid	Trunk lid	Petrol tank	Gas tank
Boot (luggage compartment)	Trunk	'Pinking'	'Pinging'
Bottom gear	1st gear	Propeller shaft	Driveshaft
Bulkhead	Firewall	Quarter light	Quarter window
Cam follower or tappet	Valve lifter or tappet	Retread	Recap
Carburettor	Carburetor	Reverse	Back-up
Catch	Latch	Rocker cover	Valve cover
Choke/venturi	Barrel	Roof rack	Car-top carrier
Circlip	Snap-ring	Saloon	Sedan
Clearance	Lash	Seized	Frozen
Crownwheel	Ring gear (of differential)	Side indicator lights	Side marker lights
Disc (brake)	Rotor/disk	Side light	Parking light
Drop arm	Pitman arm	Silencer	Muffler
Drop head coupe	Convertible	Spanner	Wrench
Dynamo	Generator (DC)	Sill panel (beneath doors)	Rocker panel
Earth (electrical)	Ground	Split cotter (for valve spring cap)	Lock (for valve spring retainer)
Engineer's blue	Prussian blue	Split pin	Cotter pin
Estate car	Station wagon	Steering arm	Spindle arm
Exhaust manifold	Header	Sump	Oil pan
Fast back (Coupe)	Hard top	Tab washer	Tang; lock
Fault finding/diagnosis	Trouble shooting	Tailgate	Liftgate
Float chamber	Float bowl	Tappet	Valve lifter
Free-play	Lash	Thrust bearing	Throw-out bearing
Freewheel	Coast	Top gear	High
Gudgeon pin	Piston pin or wrist pin	Trackrod (of steering)	Tie-rod (or connecting rod)
Gearchange	Shift	Trailing shoe (of brake)	Secondary shoe
Gearbox	Transmission	Transmission	Whole drive line
Halfshaft	Axleshaft	Tyre	Tire
Handbrake	Parking brake	Van	Panel wagon/van
Hood	Soft top	Vice	Vise
Hot spot	Heat riser	Wheel nut	Lug nut
Indicator	Turn signal	Windscreen	Windshield
Interior light	Dome lamp	Wing/mudguard	Fender

Miscellaneous points

An 'oil seal' is fitted to components lubricated by grease!

A 'damper' is a 'shock absorber', it damps out bouncing, and absorbs shocks of bump impact. Both names are correct, and both are used haphazardly.

Note that British drum brakes are different from the Bendix type that is common in America, so different descriptive names result. The shoe end furthest from the hydraulic wheel cylinder is on a pivot; interconnection between the shoes as on Bendix brakes is most uncommon. Therefore the phrase 'Primary' or 'Secondary' shoe does not apply. A shoe is said to be 'Leading' or 'Trailing'. A 'Leading' shoe is one on which a point on the drum, as it rotates forward, reaches the shoe at the end worked by the hydraulic cylinder before the anchor end. The opposite is a 'Trailing' shoe, and this one has no self servo from the wrapping effect of the rotating drum.